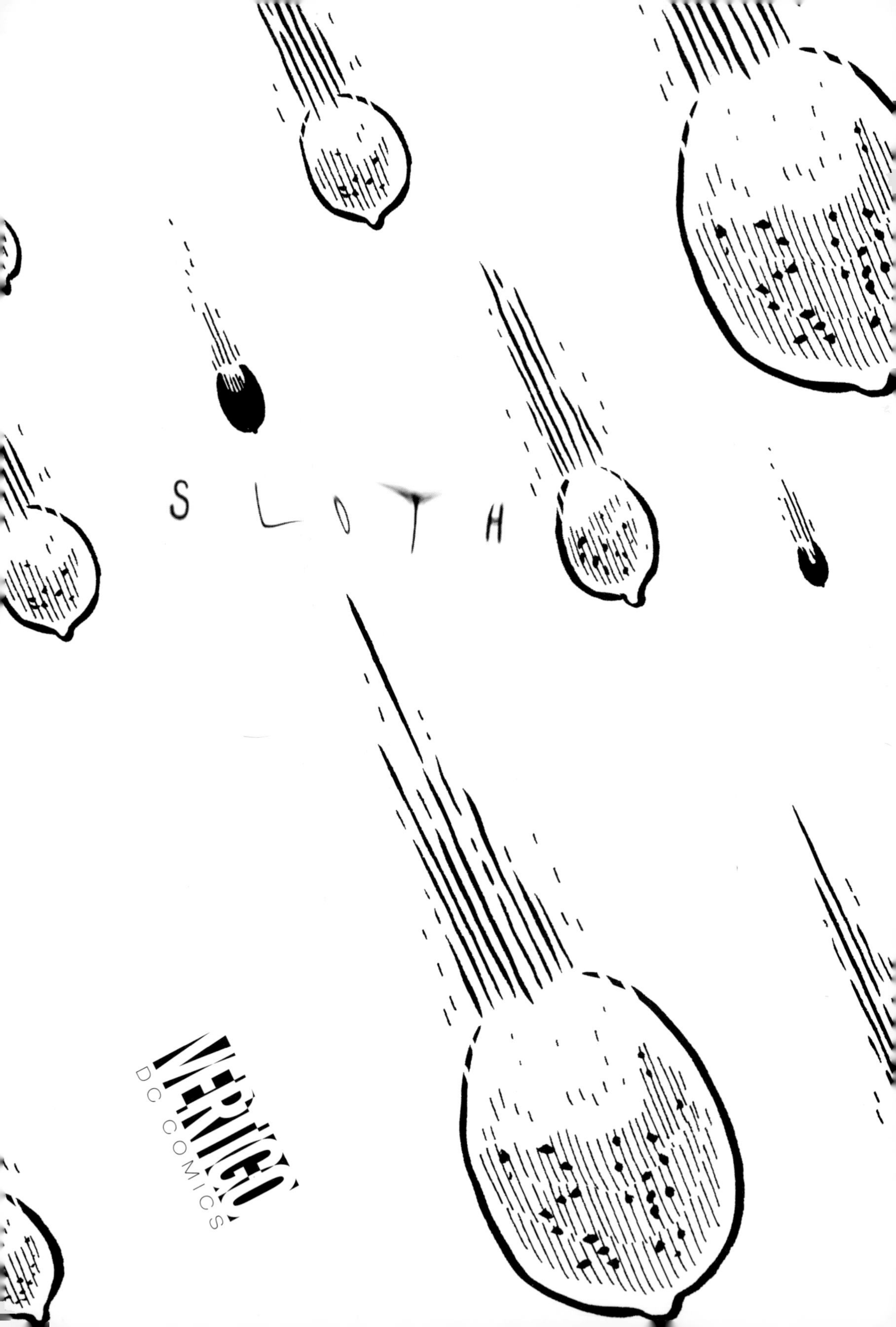
SLOTH
VERTIGO
DC COMICS

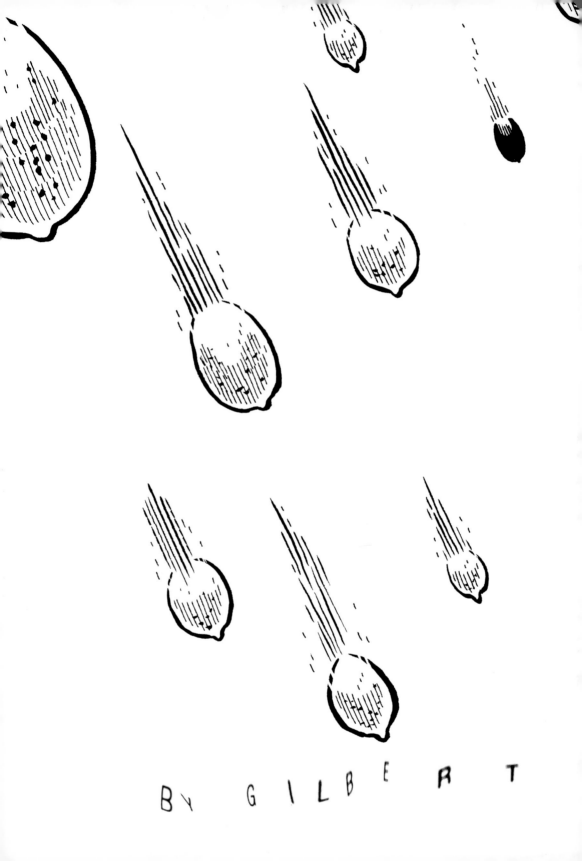

BY GILBERT

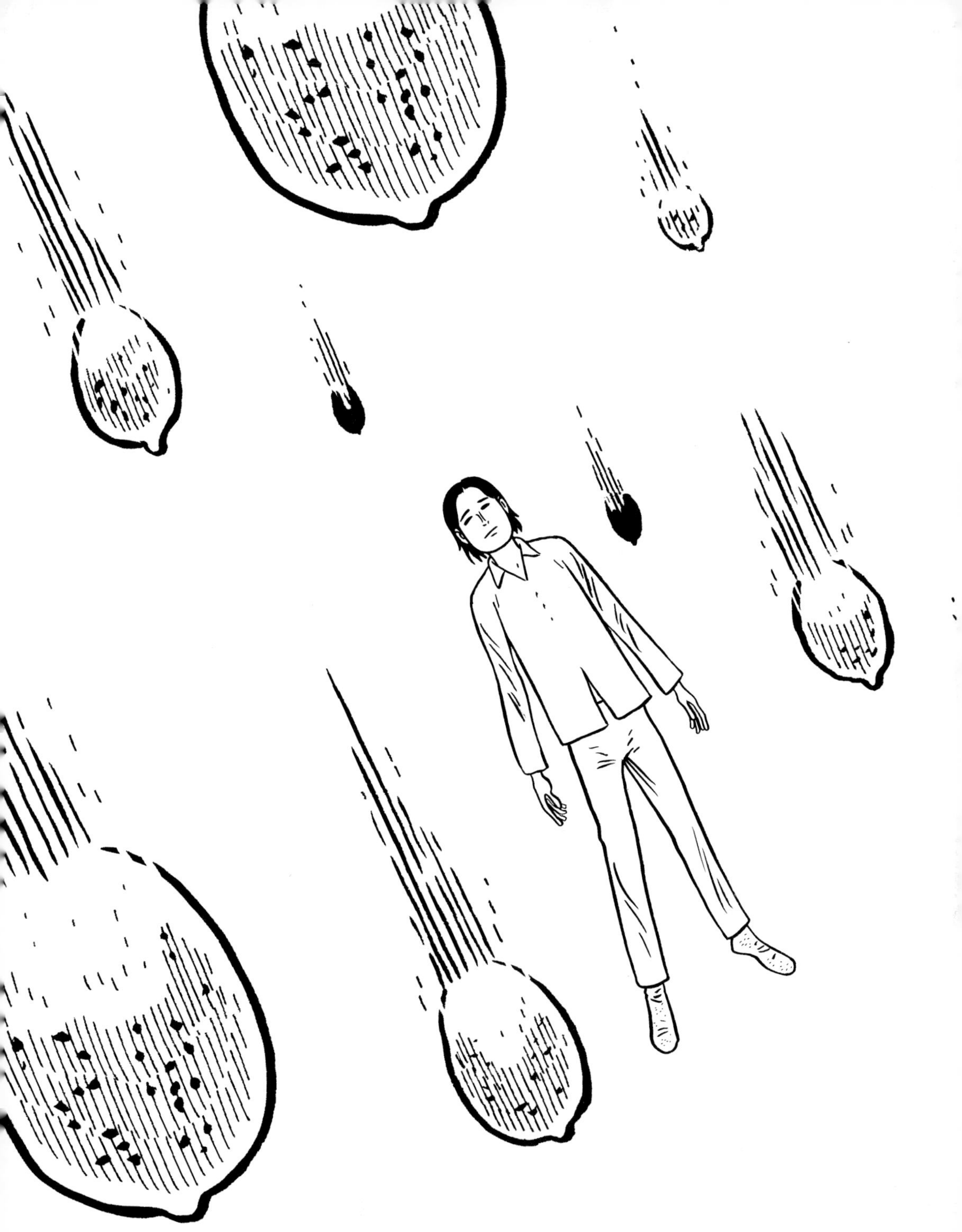

HERNANDEZ

LETTERING BY JARED K. FLETCHER

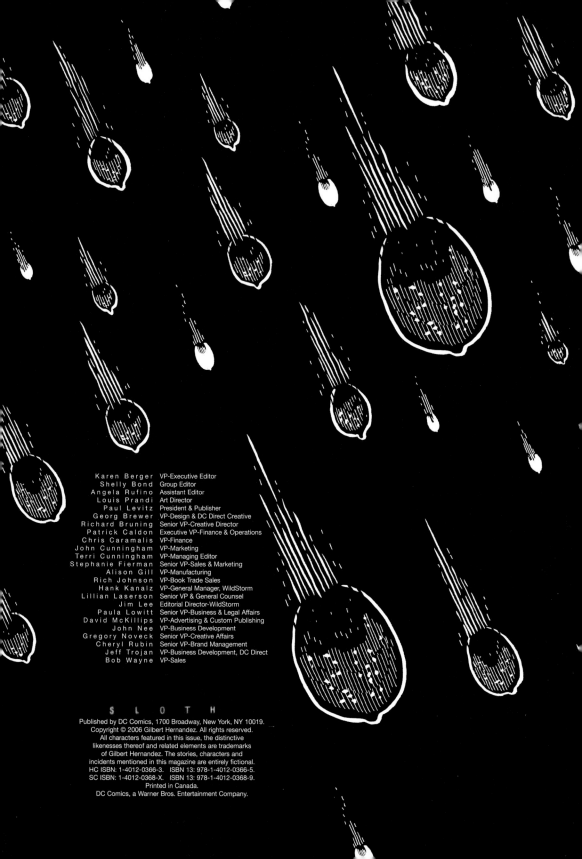

SLOTH

Published by DC Comics, 1700 Broadway, New York, NY 10019.
Copyright © 2006 Gilbert Hernandez. All rights reserved.
All characters featured in this issue, the distinctive
likenesses thereof and related elements are trademarks
of Gilbert Hernandez. The stories, characters and
incidents mentioned in this magazine are entirely fictional.
HC ISBN: 1-4012-0366-3. ISBN 13: 978-1-4012-0366-5.
SC ISBN: 1-4012-0368-X. ISBN 13: 978-1-4012-0368-9.
Printed in Canada.
DC Comics, a Warner Bros. Entertainment Company.

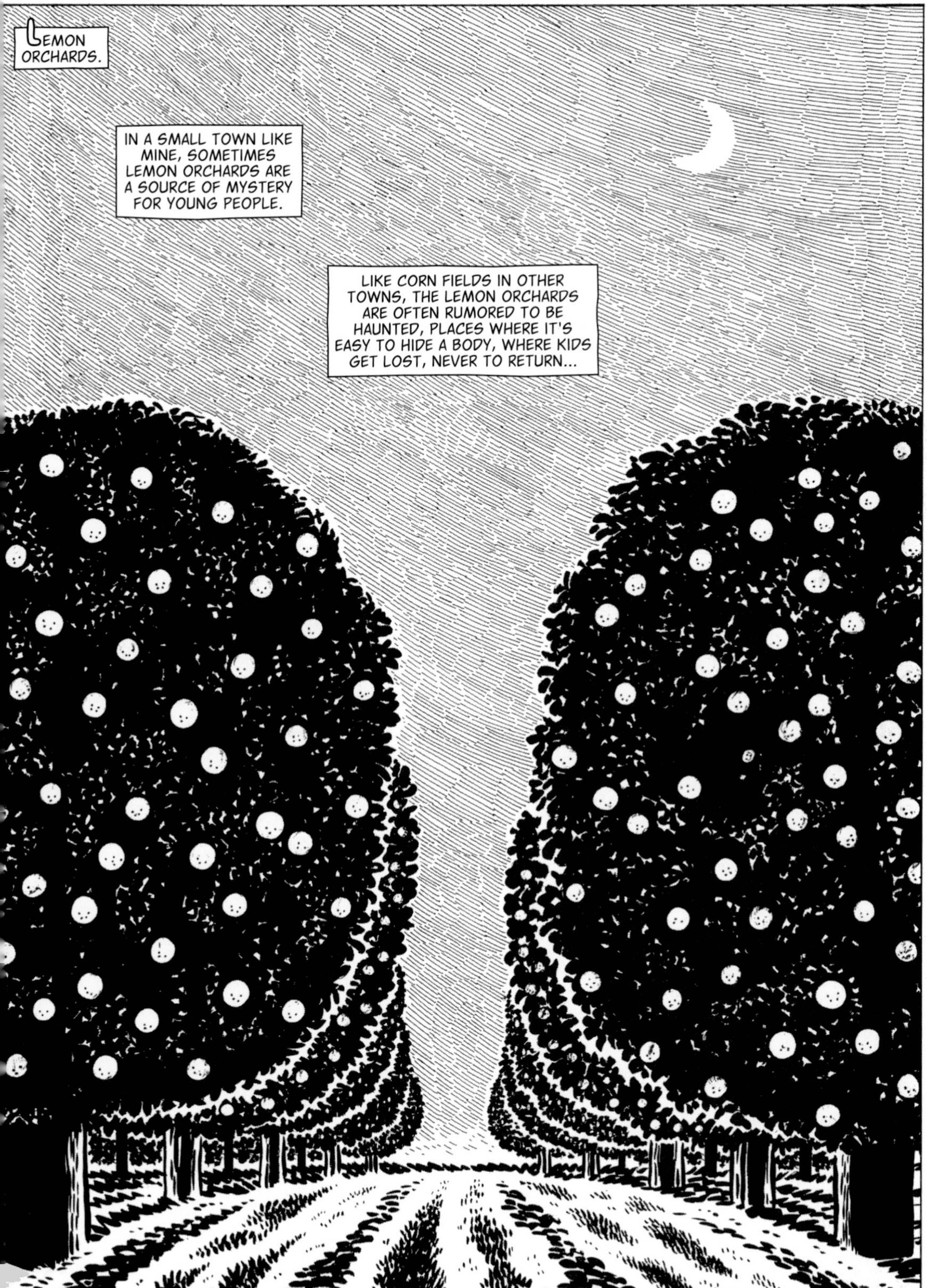
LEMON ORCHARDS.
IN A SMALL TOWN LIKE MINE, SOMETIMES LEMON ORCHARDS ARE A SOURCE OF MYSTERY FOR YOUNG PEOPLE.
LIKE CORN FIELDS IN OTHER TOWNS, THE LEMON ORCHARDS ARE OFTEN RUMORED TO BE HAUNTED, PLACES WHERE IT'S EASY TO HIDE A BODY, WHERE KIDS GET LOST, NEVER TO RETURN...

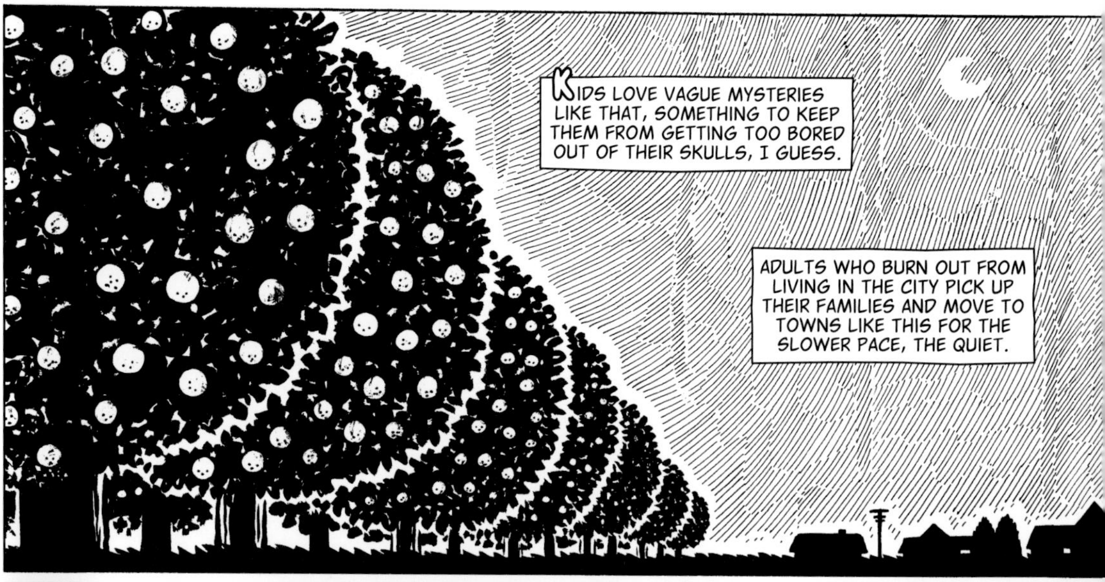
KIDS LOVE VAGUE MYSTERIES LIKE THAT, SOMETHING TO KEEP THEM FROM GETTING TOO BORED OUT OF THEIR SKULLS, I GUESS.
ADULTS WHO BURN OUT FROM LIVING IN THE CITY PICK UP THEIR FAMILIES AND MOVE TO TOWNS LIKE THIS FOR THE SLOWER PACE, THE QUIET.

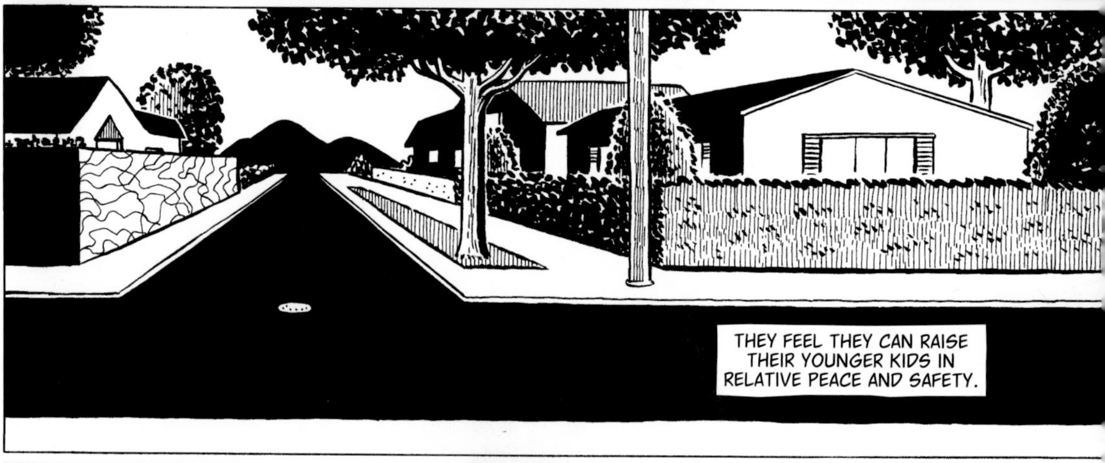
THEY FEEL THEY CAN RAISE THEIR YOUNGER KIDS IN RELATIVE PEACE AND SAFETY.

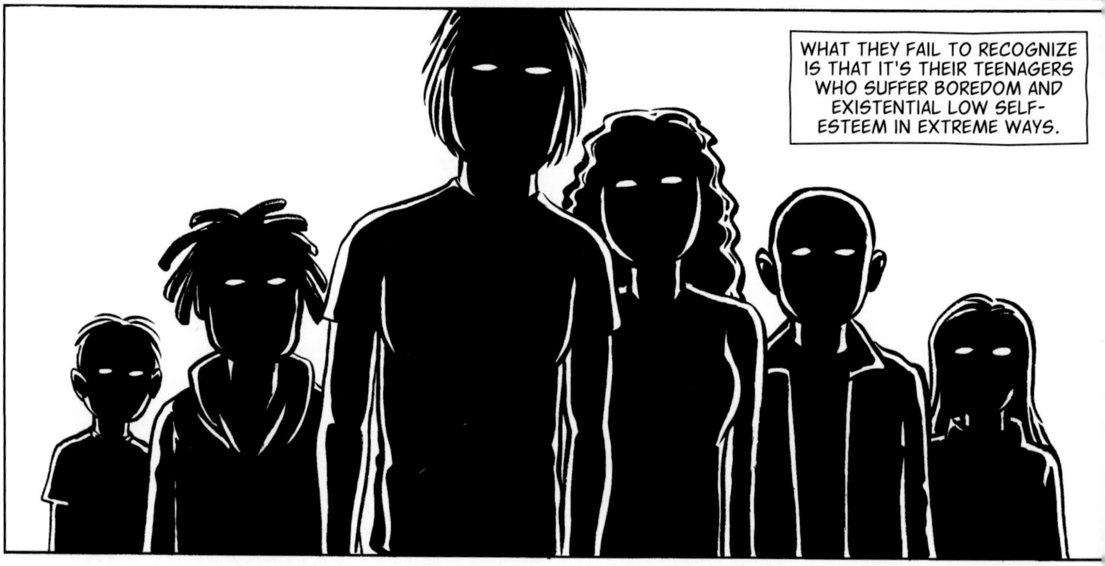
WHAT THEY FAIL TO RECOGNIZE IS THAT IT'S THEIR TEENAGERS WHO SUFFER BOREDOM AND EXISTENTIAL LOW SELF-ESTEEM IN EXTREME WAYS.

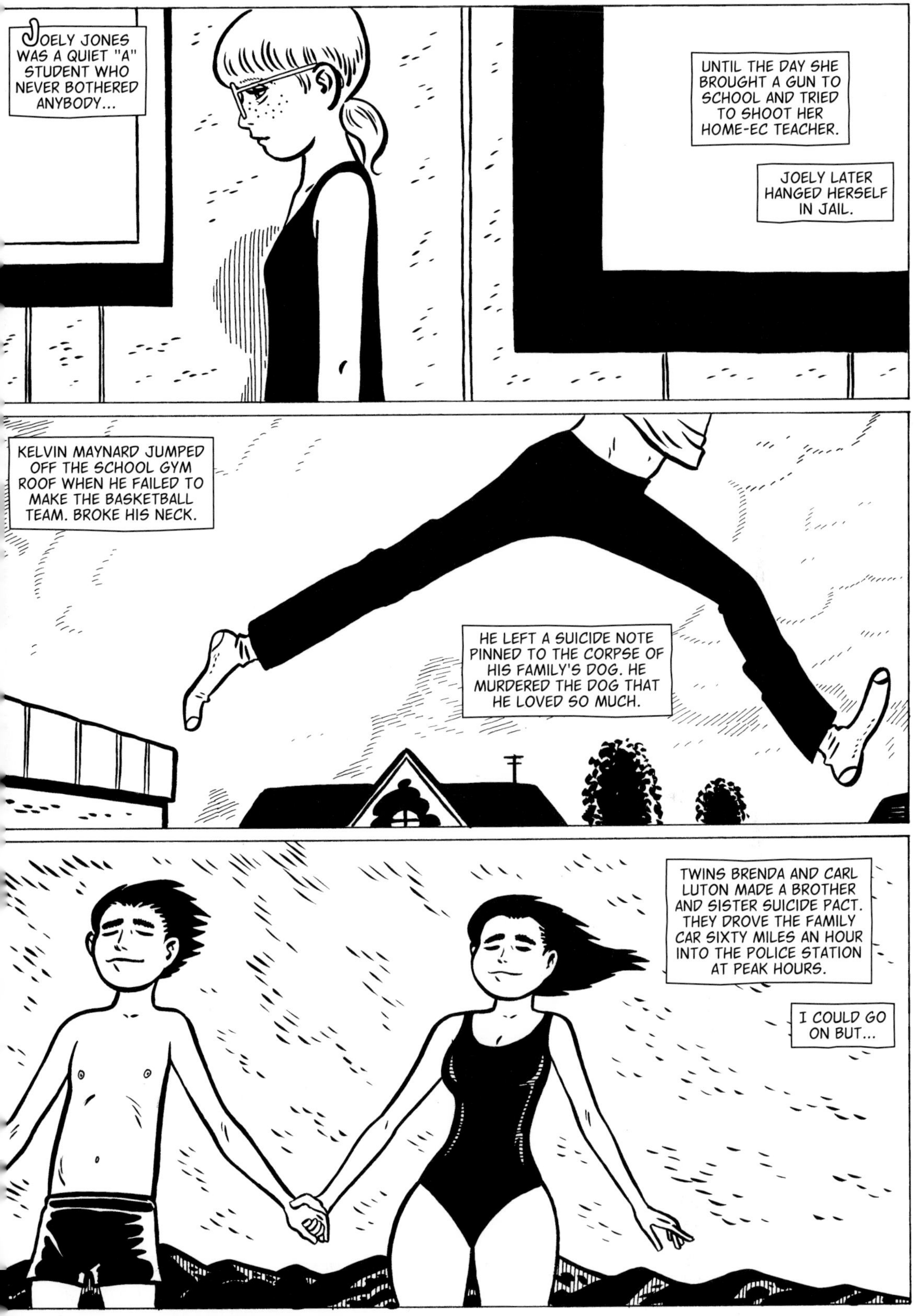
JOELY JONES WAS A QUIET "A" STUDENT WHO NEVER BOTHERED ANYBODY...
UNTIL THE DAY SHE BROUGHT A GUN TO SCHOOL AND TRIED TO SHOOT HER HOME-EC TEACHER.
JOELY LATER HANGED HERSELF IN JAIL.
KELVIN MAYNARD JUMPED OFF THE SCHOOL GYM ROOF WHEN HE FAILED TO MAKE THE BASKETBALL TEAM. BROKE HIS NECK.
HE LEFT A SUICIDE NOTE PINNED TO THE CORPSE OF HIS FAMILY'S DOG. HE MURDERED THE DOG THAT HE LOVED SO MUCH.
TWINS BRENDA AND CARL LUTON MADE A BROTHER AND SISTER SUICIDE PACT. THEY DROVE THE FAMILY CAR SIXTY MILES AN HOUR INTO THE POLICE STATION AT PEAK HOURS.
I COULD GO ON BUT...

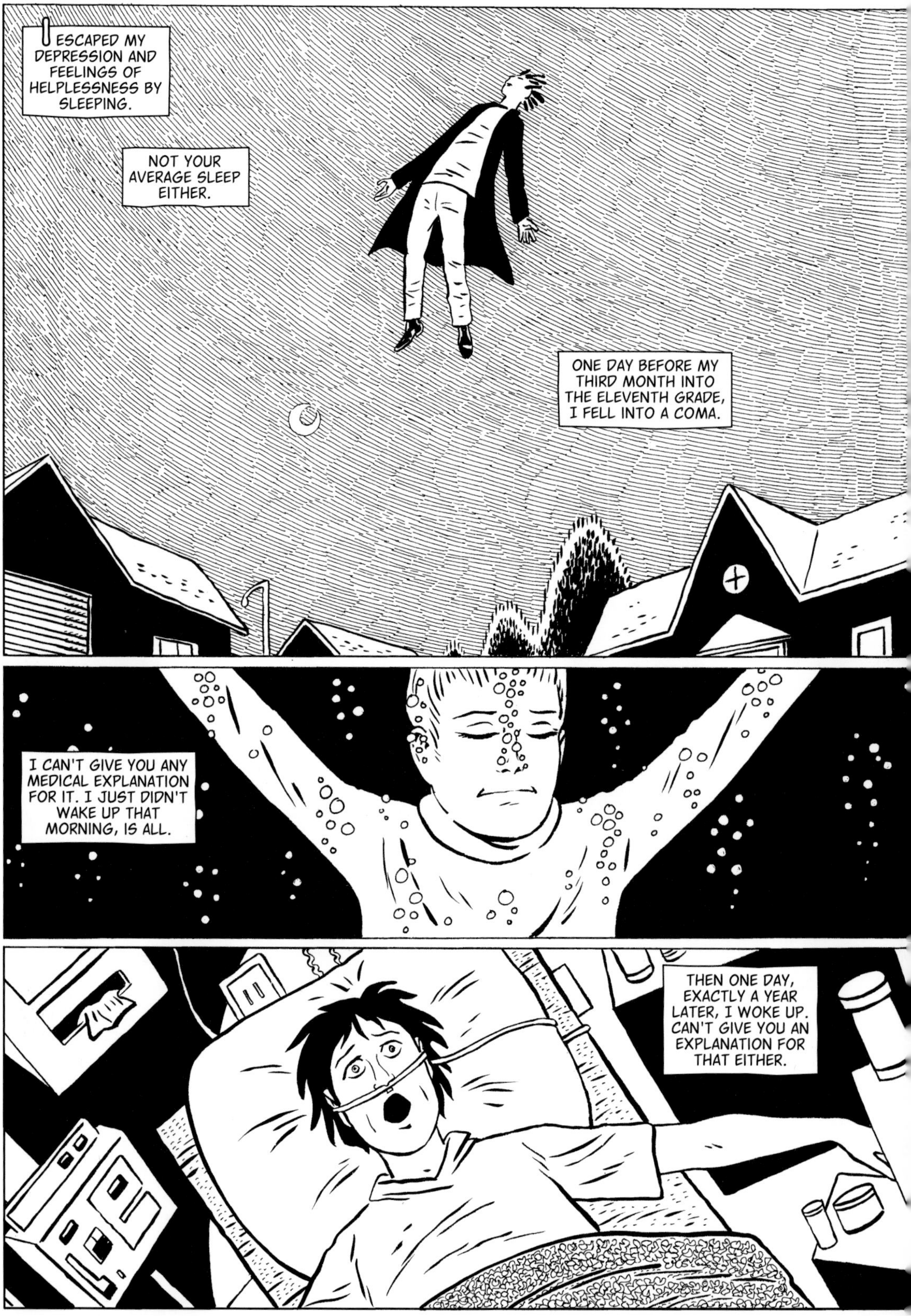
I ESCAPED MY DEPRESSION AND FEELINGS OF HELPLESSNESS BY SLEEPING.
NOT YOUR AVERAGE SLEEP EITHER.
ONE DAY BEFORE MY THIRD MONTH INTO THE ELEVENTH GRADE, I FELL INTO A COMA.
I CAN'T GIVE YOU ANY MEDICAL EXPLANATION FOR IT. I JUST DIDN'T WAKE UP THAT MORNING, IS ALL.
THEN ONE DAY, EXACTLY A YEAR LATER, I WOKE UP. CAN'T GIVE YOU AN EXPLANATION FOR THAT EITHER.

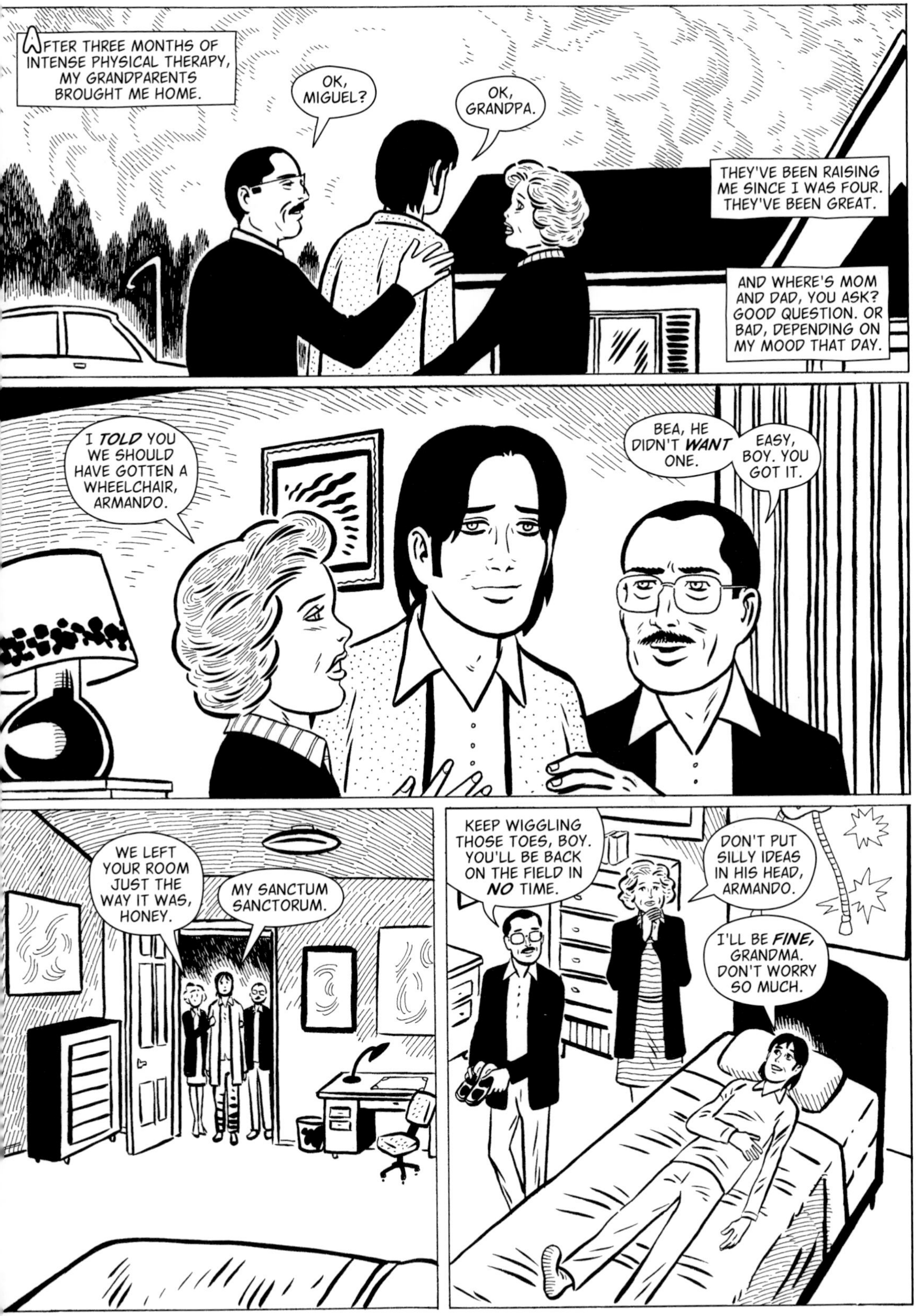
AFTER THREE MONTHS OF INTENSE PHYSICAL THERAPY, MY GRANDPARENTS BROUGHT ME HOME.
OK, MIGUEL?
OK, GRANDPA.
THEY'VE BEEN RAISING ME SINCE I WAS FOUR. THEY'VE BEEN GREAT.
AND WHERE'S MOM AND DAD, YOU ASK? GOOD QUESTION. OR BAD, DEPENDING ON MY MOOD THAT DAY.
I *TOLD* YOU WE SHOULD HAVE GOTTEN A WHEELCHAIR, ARMANDO.
BEA, HE DIDN'T *WANT* ONE.
EASY, BOY. YOU GOT IT.
WE LEFT YOUR ROOM JUST THE WAY IT WAS, HONEY.
MY SANCTUM SANCTORUM.
KEEP WIGGLING THOSE TOES, BOY. YOU'LL BE BACK ON THE FIELD IN *NO* TIME.
DON'T PUT SILLY IDEAS IN HIS HEAD, ARMANDO.
I'LL BE *FINE,* GRANDMA. DON'T WORRY SO MUCH.

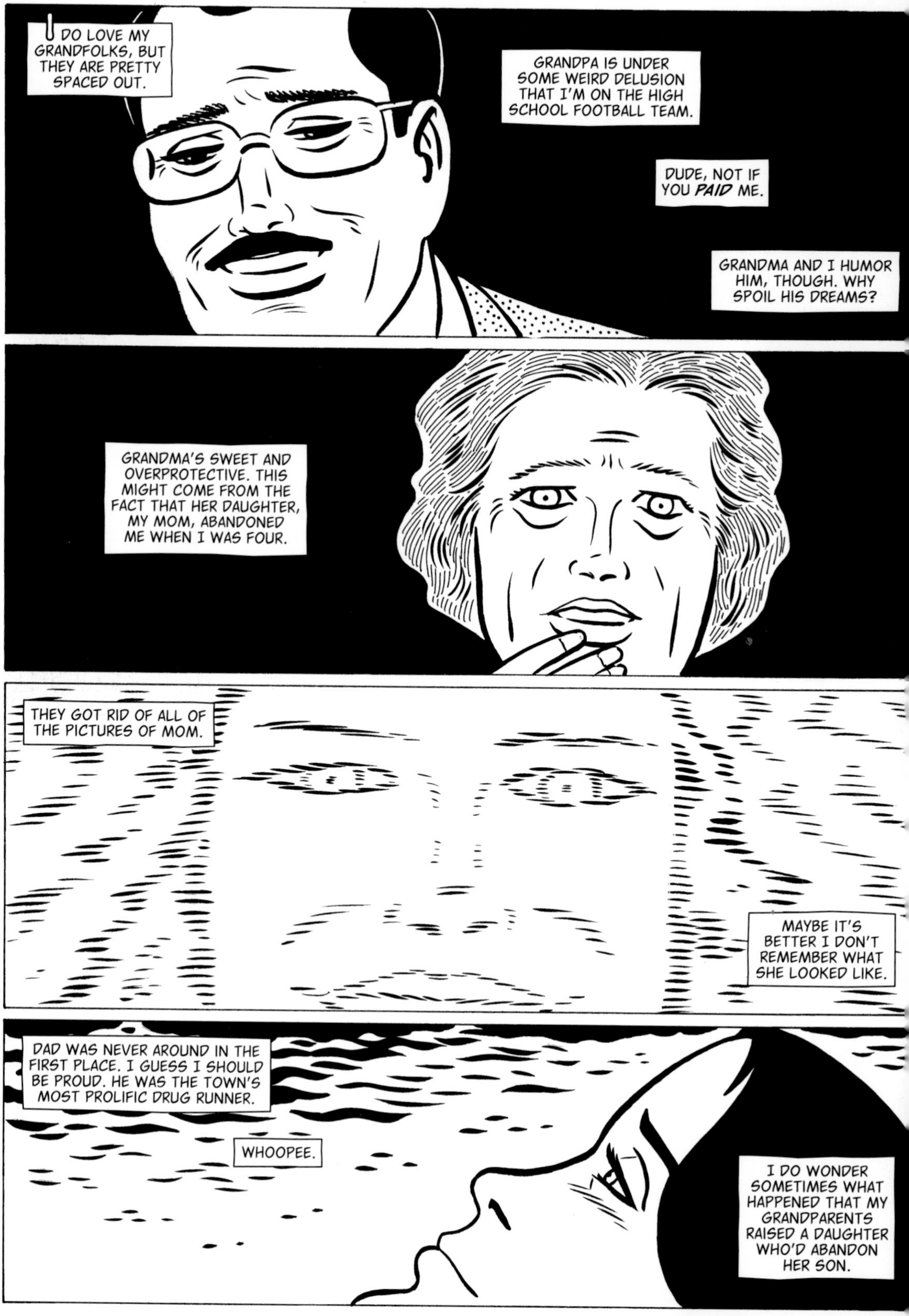
I DO LOVE MY GRANDFOLKS, BUT THEY ARE PRETTY SPACED OUT.
GRANDPA IS UNDER SOME WEIRD DELUSION THAT I'M ON THE HIGH SCHOOL FOOTBALL TEAM.
DUDE, NOT IF YOU *PAID* ME.
GRANDMA AND I HUMOR HIM, THOUGH. WHY SPOIL HIS DREAMS?
GRANDMA'S SWEET AND OVERPROTECTIVE. THIS MIGHT COME FROM THE FACT THAT HER DAUGHTER, MY MOM, ABANDONED ME WHEN I WAS FOUR.
THEY GOT RID OF ALL OF THE PICTURES OF MOM.
MAYBE IT'S BETTER I DON'T REMEMBER WHAT SHE LOOKED LIKE.
DAD WAS NEVER AROUND IN THE FIRST PLACE. I GUESS I SHOULD BE PROUD. HE WAS THE TOWN'S MOST PROLIFIC DRUG RUNNER.
WHOOPEE.
I DO WONDER SOMETIMES WHAT HAPPENED THAT MY GRANDPARENTS RAISED A DAUGHTER WHO'D ABANDON HER SON.

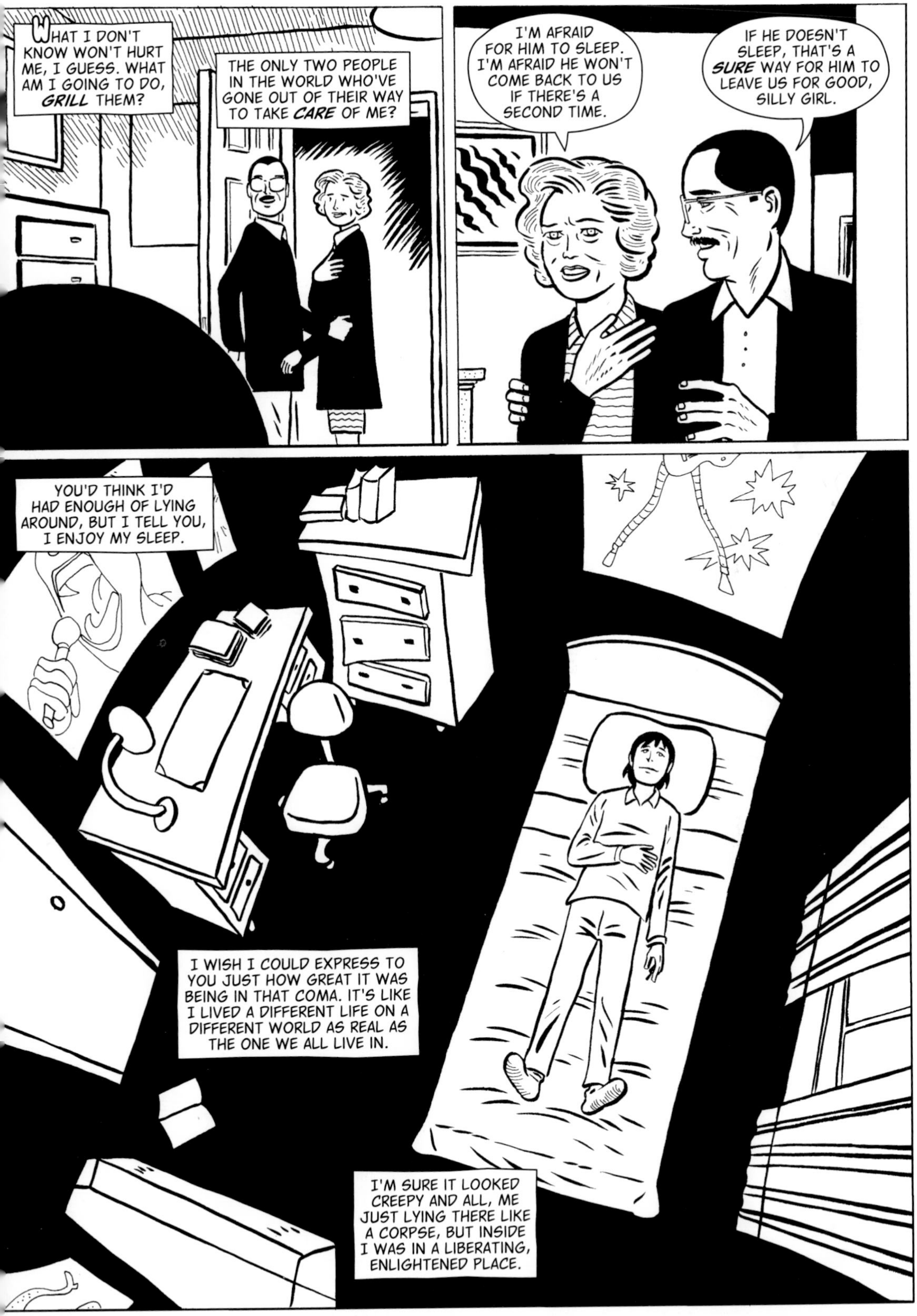
WHAT I DON'T KNOW WON'T HURT ME, I GUESS. WHAT AM I GOING TO DO, GRILL THEM?
THE ONLY TWO PEOPLE IN THE WORLD WHO'VE GONE OUT OF THEIR WAY TO TAKE CARE OF ME?
I'M AFRAID FOR HIM TO SLEEP. I'M AFRAID HE WON'T COME BACK TO US IF THERE'S A SECOND TIME.
IF HE DOESN'T SLEEP, THAT'S A SURE WAY FOR HIM TO LEAVE US FOR GOOD, SILLY GIRL.
YOU'D THINK I'D HAD ENOUGH OF LYING AROUND, BUT I TELL YOU, I ENJOY MY SLEEP.
I WISH I COULD EXPRESS TO YOU JUST HOW GREAT IT WAS BEING IN THAT COMA. IT'S LIKE I LIVED A DIFFERENT LIFE ON A DIFFERENT WORLD AS REAL AS THE ONE WE ALL LIVE IN.
I'M SURE IT LOOKED CREEPY AND ALL, ME JUST LYING THERE LIKE A CORPSE, BUT INSIDE I WAS IN A LIBERATING, ENLIGHTENED PLACE.

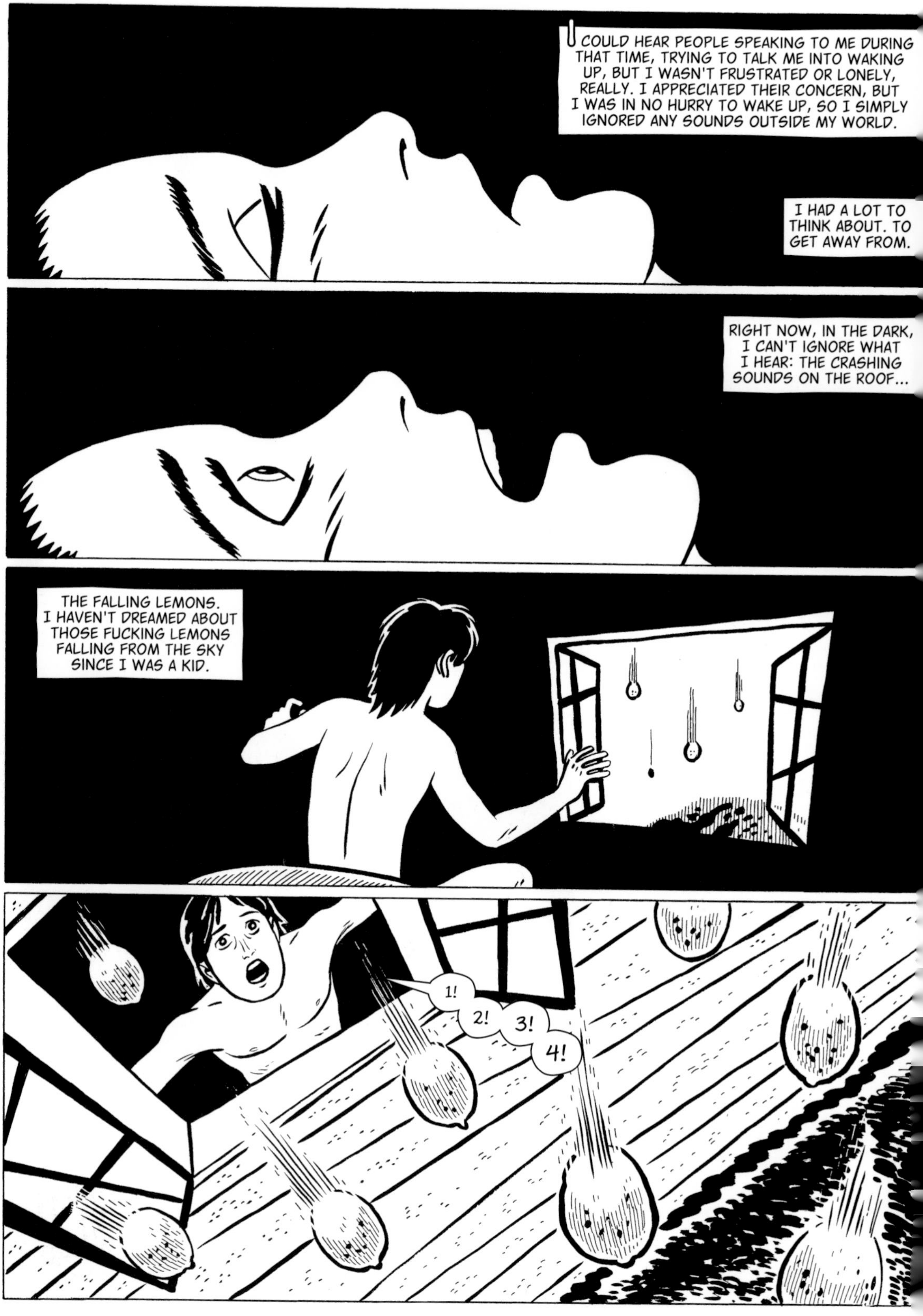
I COULD HEAR PEOPLE SPEAKING TO ME DURING THAT TIME, TRYING TO TALK ME INTO WAKING UP, BUT I WASN'T FRUSTRATED OR LONELY, REALLY. I APPRECIATED THEIR CONCERN, BUT I WAS IN NO HURRY TO WAKE UP, SO I SIMPLY IGNORED ANY SOUNDS OUTSIDE MY WORLD.
I HAD A LOT TO THINK ABOUT. TO GET AWAY FROM.
RIGHT NOW, IN THE DARK, I CAN'T IGNORE WHAT I HEAR: THE CRASHING SOUNDS ON THE ROOF...
THE FALLING LEMONS. I HAVEN'T DREAMED ABOUT THOSE FUCKING LEMONS FALLING FROM THE SKY SINCE I WAS A KID.
1!
2!
3!
4!

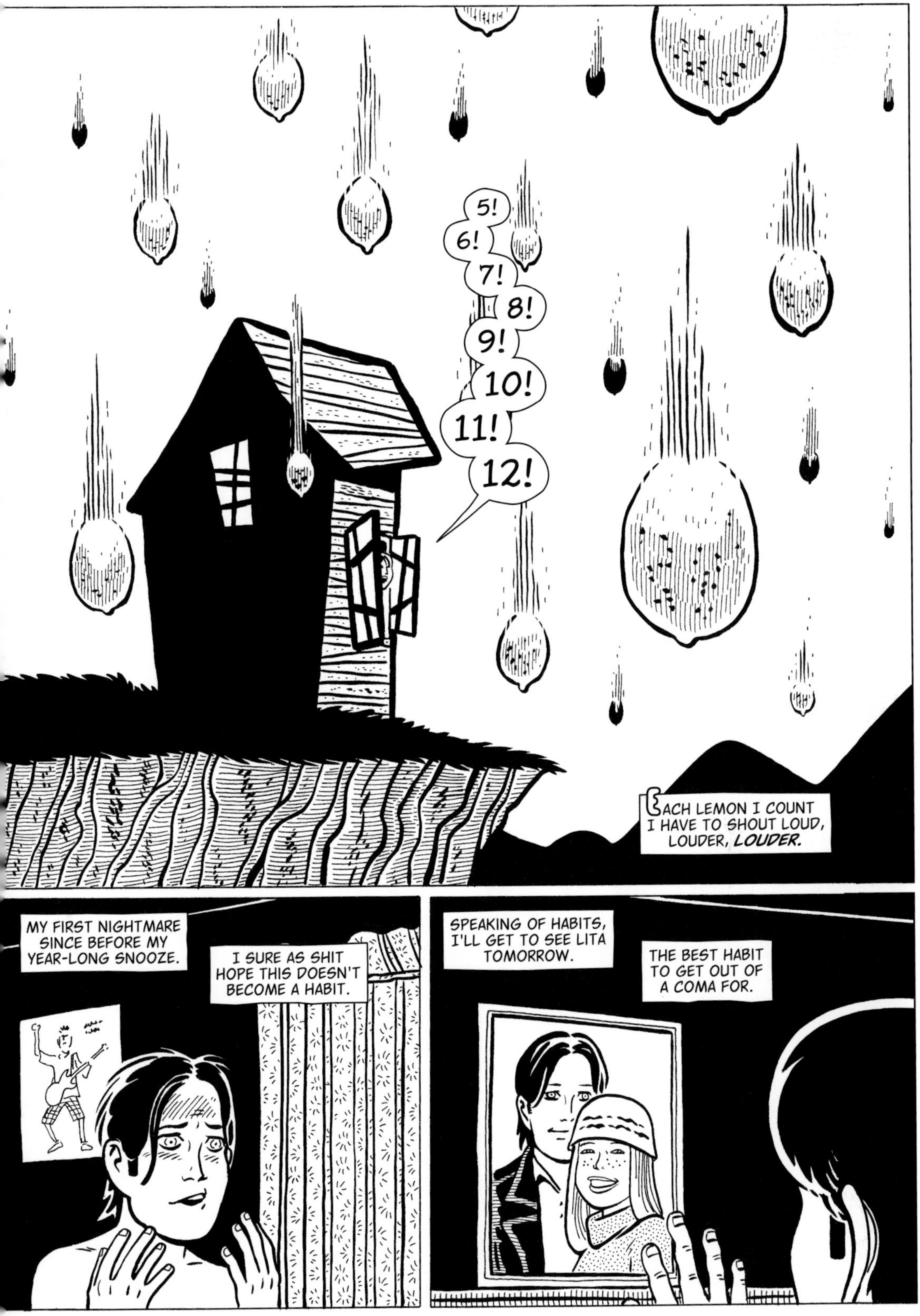
5!
6!
7!
8!
9!
10!
11!
12!
EACH LEMON I COUNT I HAVE TO SHOUT LOUD, LOUDER, *LOUDER.*
MY FIRST NIGHTMARE SINCE BEFORE MY YEAR-LONG SNOOZE.
I SURE AS SHIT HOPE THIS DOESN'T BECOME A HABIT.
SPEAKING OF HABITS, I'LL GET TO SEE LITA TOMORROW.
THE BEST HABIT TO GET OUT OF A COMA FOR.

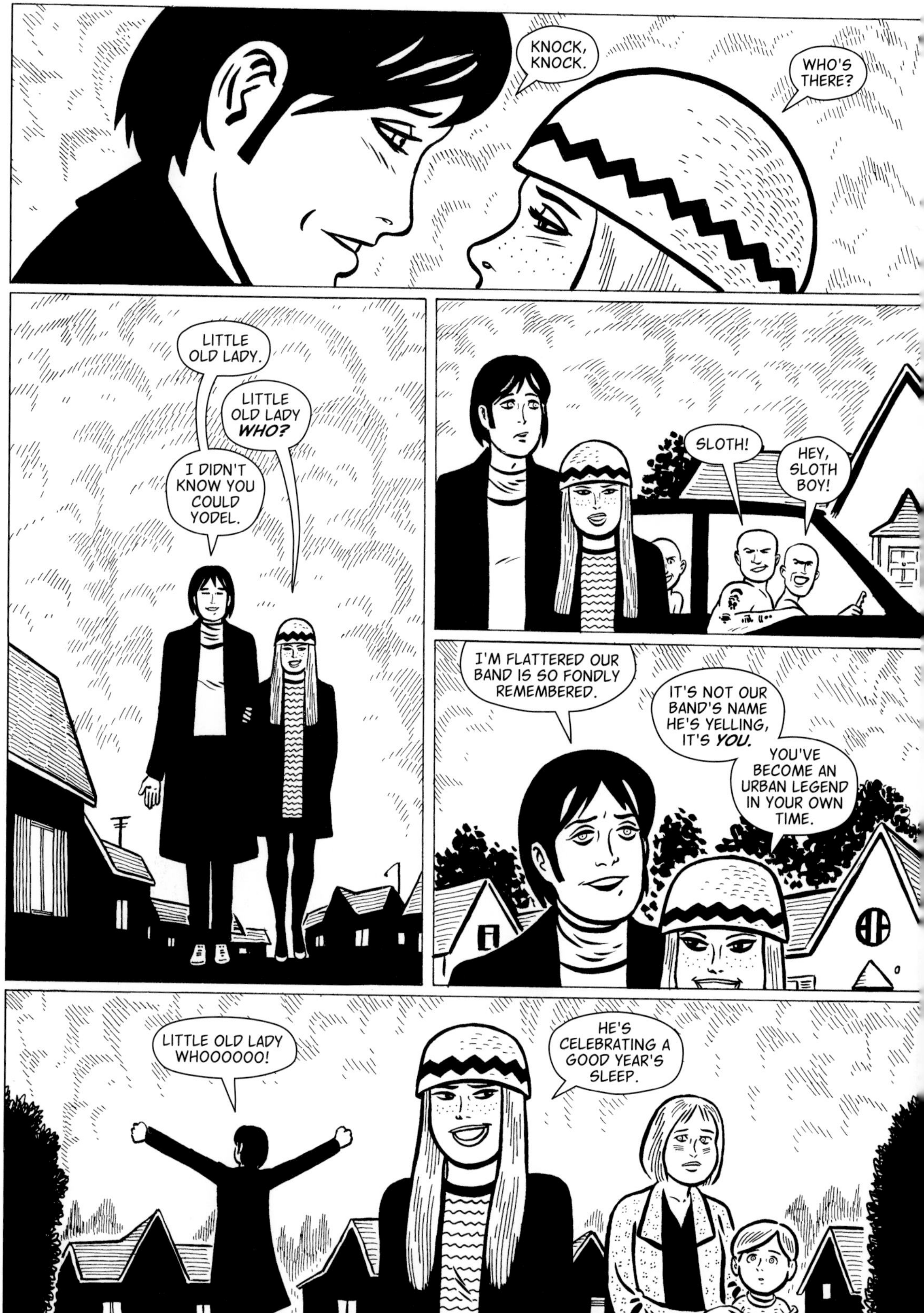
KNOCK, KNOCK.
WHO'S THERE?
LITTLE OLD LADY.
LITTLE OLD LADY *WHO?*
I DIDN'T KNOW YOU COULD YODEL.
SLOTH!
HEY, SLOTH BOY!
I'M FLATTERED OUR BAND IS SO FONDLY REMEMBERED.
IT'S NOT OUR BAND'S NAME HE'S YELLING, IT'S *YOU.*
YOU'VE BECOME AN URBAN LEGEND IN YOUR OWN TIME.
LITTLE OLD LADY WHOOOOOO!
HE'S CELEBRATING A GOOD YEAR'S SLEEP.

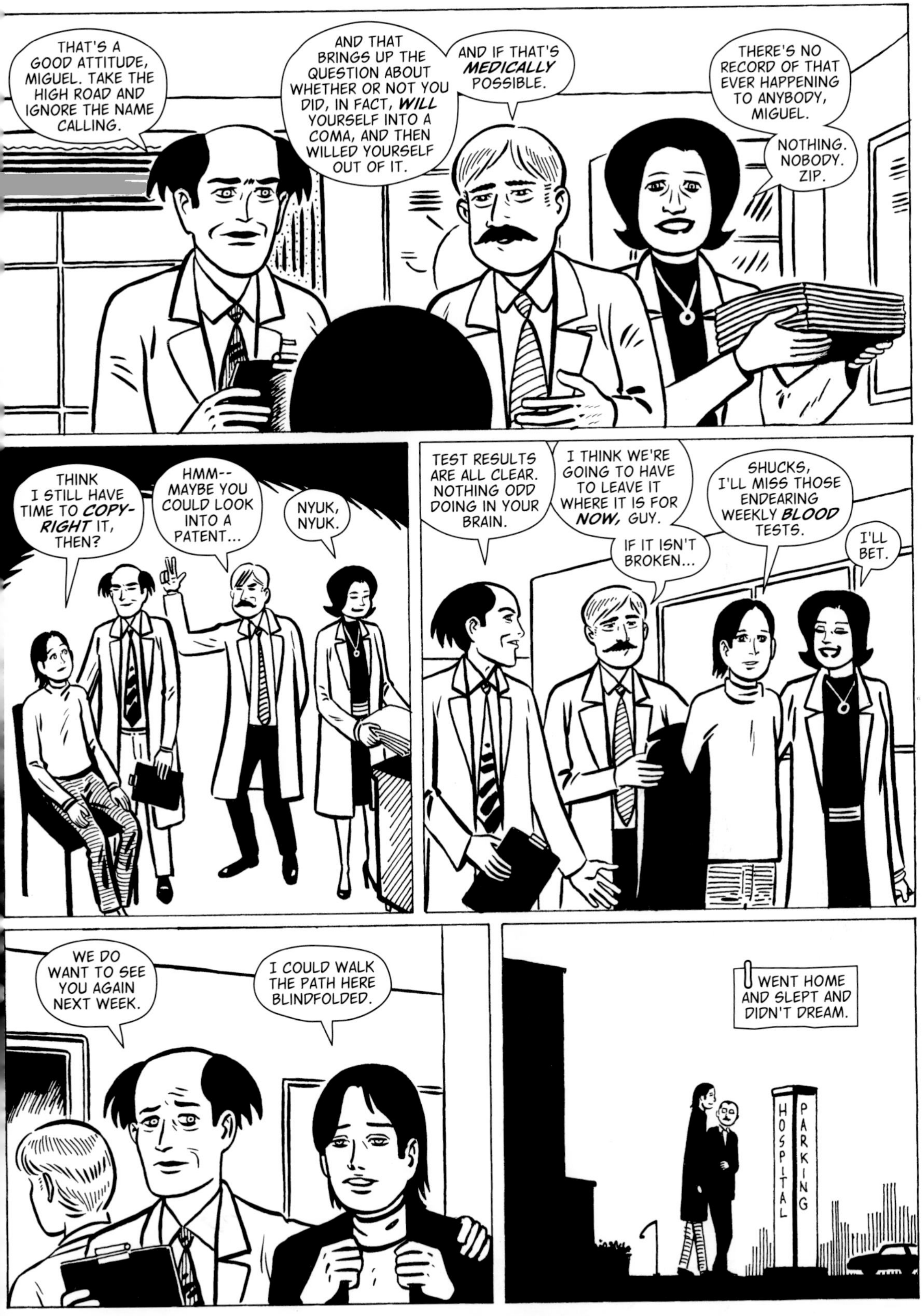
THAT'S A GOOD ATTITUDE, MIGUEL. TAKE THE HIGH ROAD AND IGNORE THE NAME CALLING.
AND THAT BRINGS UP THE QUESTION ABOUT WHETHER OR NOT YOU DID, IN FACT, WILL YOURSELF INTO A COMA, AND THEN WILLED YOURSELF OUT OF IT.
AND IF THAT'S MEDICALLY POSSIBLE.
THERE'S NO RECORD OF THAT EVER HAPPENING TO ANYBODY, MIGUEL.
NOTHING. NOBODY. ZIP.
THINK I STILL HAVE TIME TO COPYRIGHT IT, THEN?
HMM-- MAYBE YOU COULD LOOK INTO A PATENT...
NYUK, NYUK.
TEST RESULTS ARE ALL CLEAR. NOTHING ODD DOING IN YOUR BRAIN.
I THINK WE'RE GOING TO HAVE TO LEAVE IT WHERE IT IS FOR NOW, GUY.
IF IT ISN'T BROKEN...
SHUCKS, I'LL MISS THOSE ENDEARING WEEKLY BLOOD TESTS.
I'LL BET.
WE DO WANT TO SEE YOU AGAIN NEXT WEEK.
I COULD WALK THE PATH HERE BLINDFOLDED.
I WENT HOME AND SLEPT AND DIDN'T DREAM.
HOSPITAL
PARKING

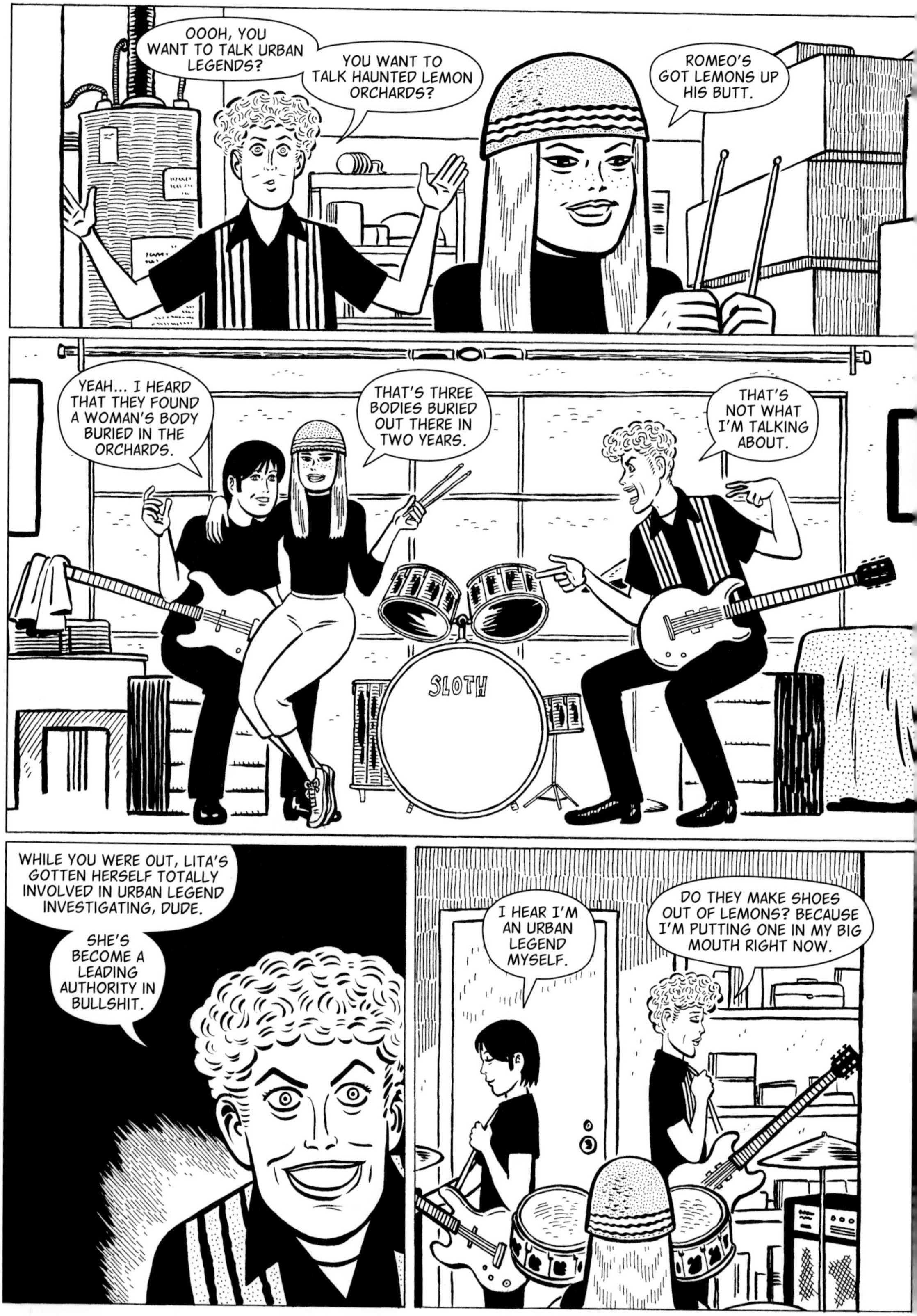
OOOH, YOU WANT TO TALK URBAN LEGENDS?
YOU WANT TO TALK HAUNTED LEMON ORCHARDS?
ROMEO'S GOT LEMONS UP HIS BUTT.
YEAH... I HEARD THAT THEY FOUND A WOMAN'S BODY BURIED IN THE ORCHARDS.
THAT'S THREE BODIES BURIED OUT THERE IN TWO YEARS.
THAT'S NOT WHAT I'M TALKING ABOUT.
SLOTH
WHILE YOU WERE OUT, LITA'S GOTTEN HERSELF TOTALLY INVOLVED IN URBAN LEGEND INVESTIGATING, DUDE.
SHE'S BECOME A LEADING AUTHORITY IN BULLSHIT.
I HEAR I'M AN URBAN LEGEND MYSELF.
DO THEY MAKE SHOES OUT OF LEMONS? BECAUSE I'M PUTTING ONE IN MY BIG MOUTH RIGHT NOW.

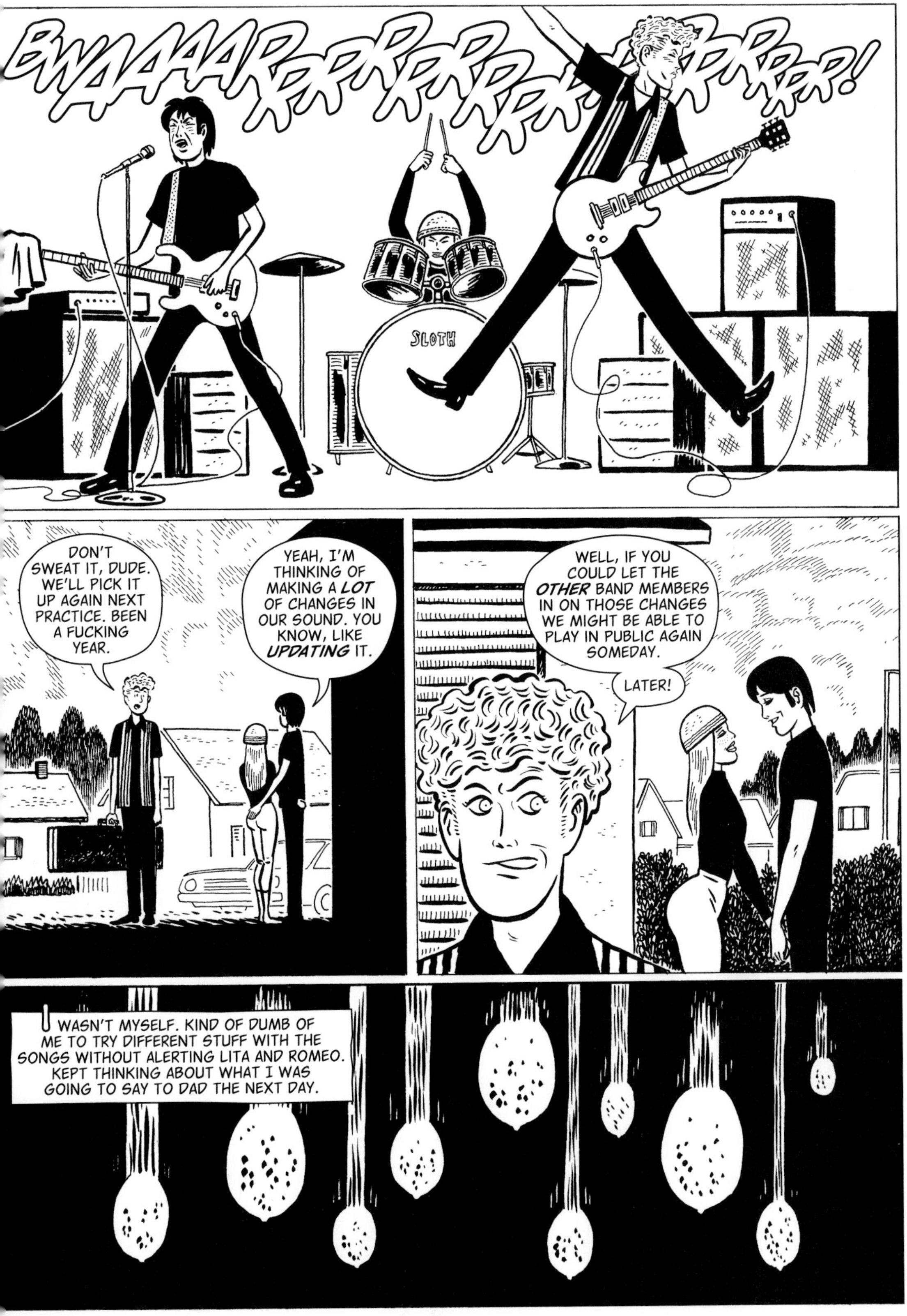
BWAAAARRRRRRRRRRRRRRRRRRRRR!
SLOTH
DON'T SWEAT IT, DUDE. WE'LL PICK IT UP AGAIN NEXT PRACTICE. BEEN A FUCKING YEAR.
YEAH, I'M THINKING OF MAKING A LOT OF CHANGES IN OUR SOUND. YOU KNOW, LIKE UPDATING IT.
WELL, IF YOU COULD LET THE OTHER BAND MEMBERS IN ON THOSE CHANGES WE MIGHT BE ABLE TO PLAY IN PUBLIC AGAIN SOMEDAY.
LATER!
I WASN'T MYSELF. KIND OF DUMB OF ME TO TRY DIFFERENT STUFF WITH THE SONGS WITHOUT ALERTING LITA AND ROMEO. KEPT THINKING ABOUT WHAT I WAS GOING TO SAY TO DAD THE NEXT DAY.

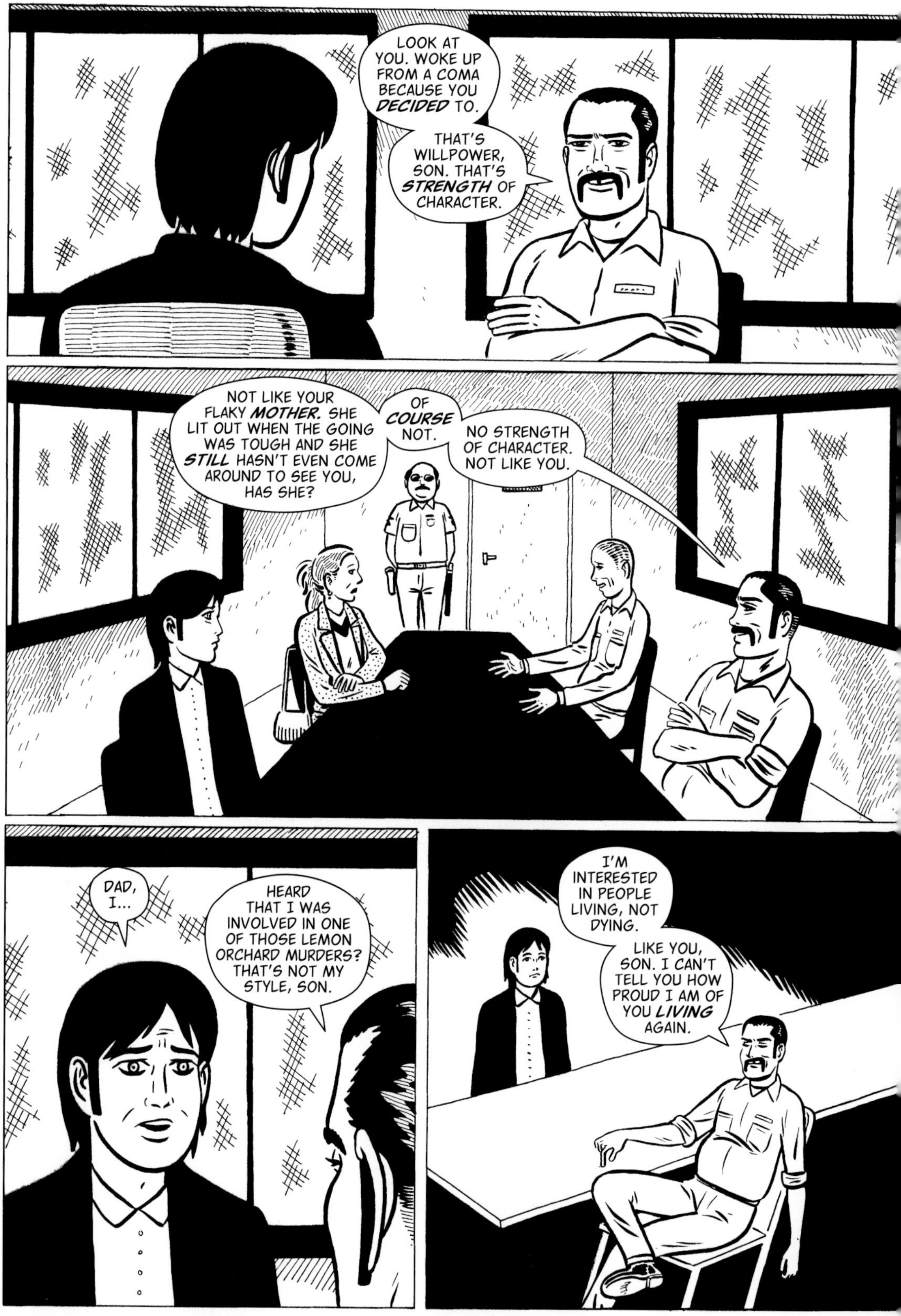
LOOK AT YOU. WOKE UP FROM A COMA BECAUSE YOU *DECIDED* TO.
THAT'S WILLPOWER, SON. THAT'S *STRENGTH* OF CHARACTER.
NOT LIKE YOUR FLAKY *MOTHER.* SHE LIT OUT WHEN THE GOING WAS TOUGH AND SHE *STILL* HASN'T EVEN COME AROUND TO SEE YOU, HAS SHE?
OF *COURSE* NOT.
NO STRENGTH OF CHARACTER. NOT LIKE YOU.
DAD, I...
HEARD THAT I WAS INVOLVED IN ONE OF THOSE LEMON ORCHARD MURDERS? THAT'S NOT MY STYLE, SON.
I'M INTERESTED IN PEOPLE LIVING, NOT DYING.
LIKE YOU, SON. I CAN'T TELL YOU HOW PROUD I AM OF YOU *LIVING* AGAIN.

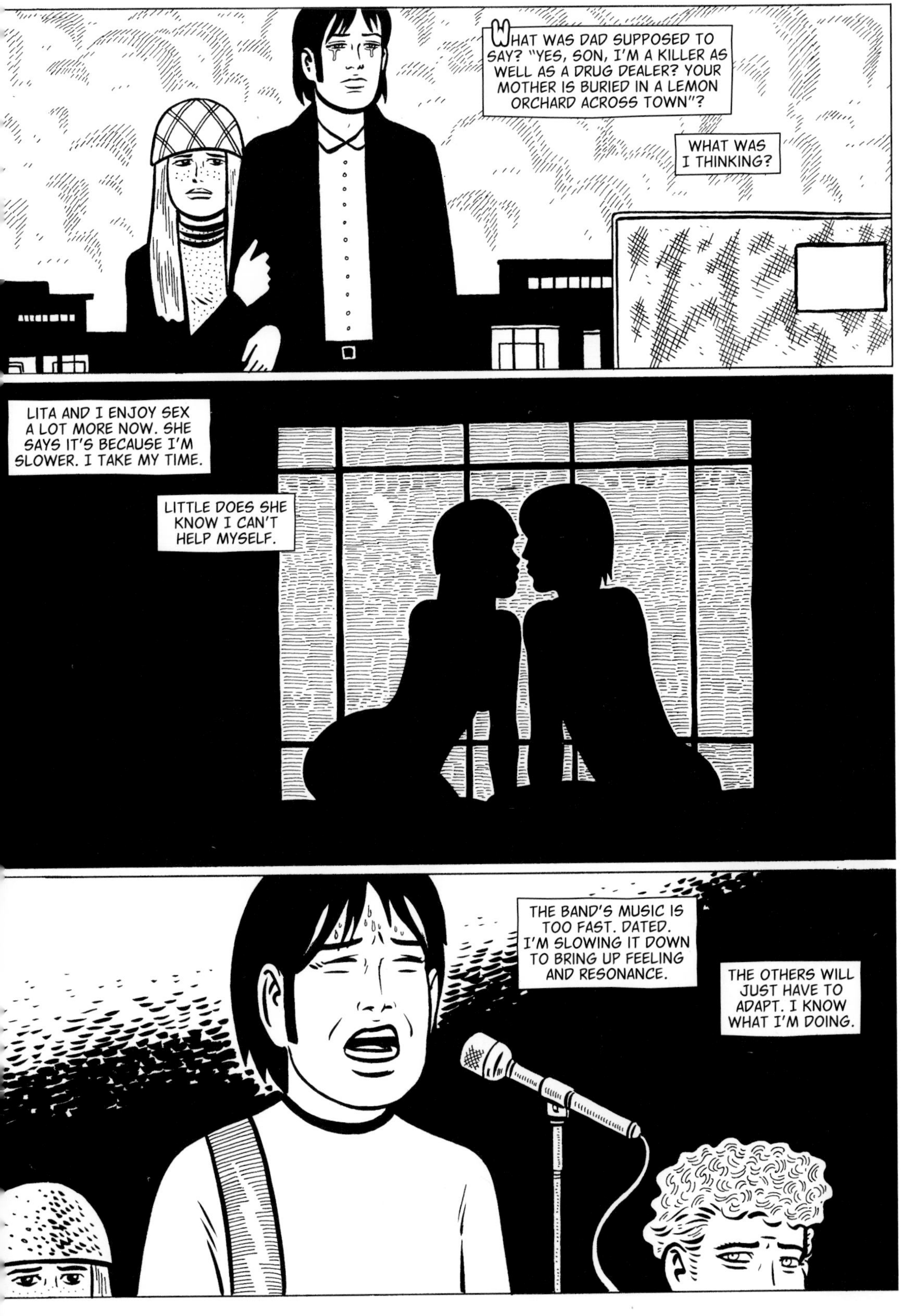
WHAT WAS DAD SUPPOSED TO SAY? "YES, SON, I'M A KILLER AS WELL AS A DRUG DEALER? YOUR MOTHER IS BURIED IN A LEMON ORCHARD ACROSS TOWN"?
WHAT WAS I THINKING?
LITA AND I ENJOY SEX A LOT MORE NOW. SHE SAYS IT'S BECAUSE I'M SLOWER. I TAKE MY TIME.
LITTLE DOES SHE KNOW I CAN'T HELP MYSELF.
THE BAND'S MUSIC IS TOO FAST. DATED. I'M SLOWING IT DOWN TO BRING UP FEELING AND RESONANCE.
THE OTHERS WILL JUST HAVE TO ADAPT. I KNOW WHAT I'M DOING.

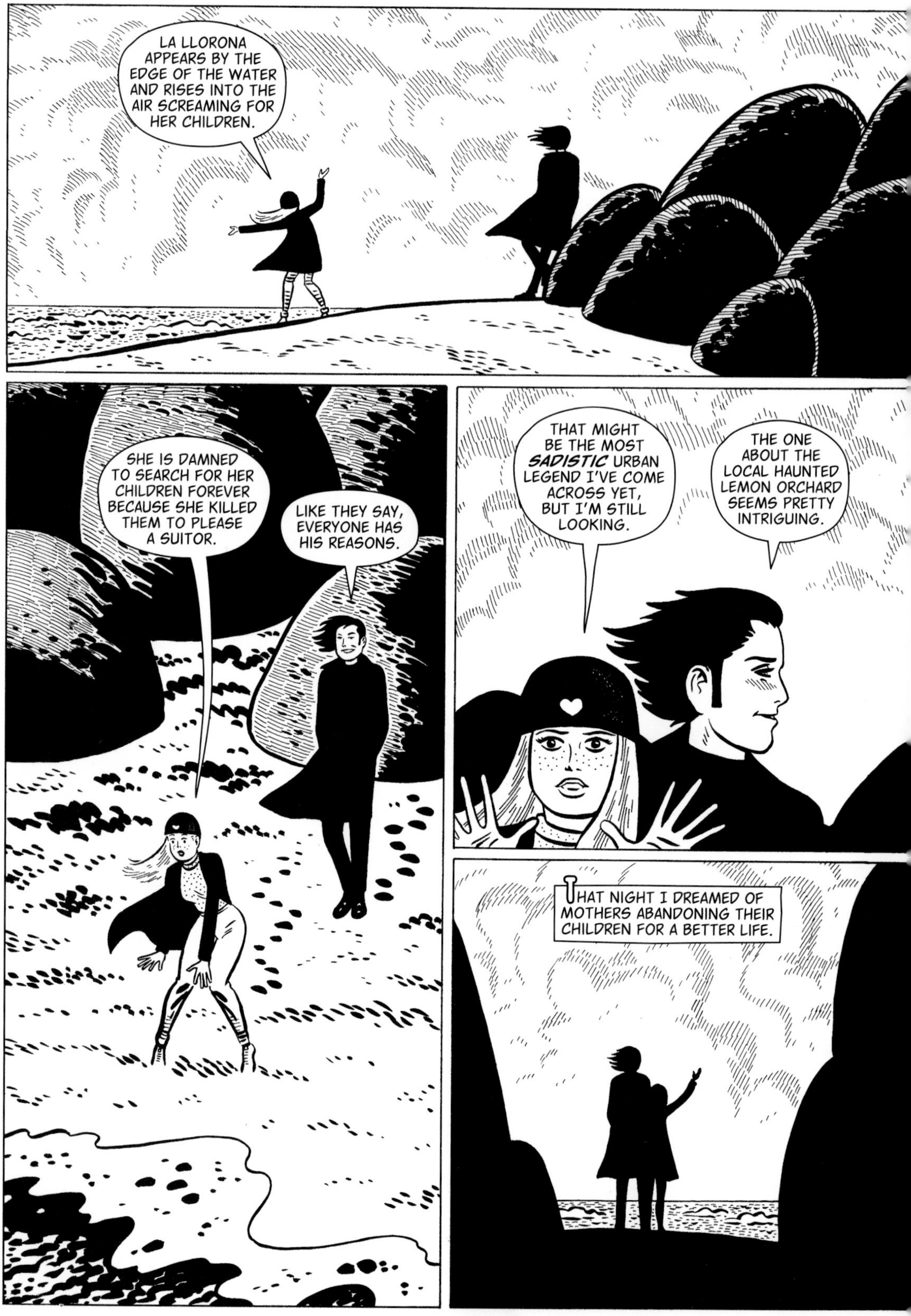
LA LLORONA APPEARS BY THE EDGE OF THE WATER AND RISES INTO THE AIR SCREAMING FOR HER CHILDREN.
SHE IS DAMNED TO SEARCH FOR HER CHILDREN FOREVER BECAUSE SHE KILLED THEM TO PLEASE A SUITOR.
LIKE THEY SAY, EVERYONE HAS HIS REASONS.
THAT MIGHT BE THE MOST SADISTIC URBAN LEGEND I'VE COME ACROSS YET, BUT I'M STILL LOOKING.
THE ONE ABOUT THE LOCAL HAUNTED LEMON ORCHARD SEEMS PRETTY INTRIGUING.
THAT NIGHT I DREAMED OF MOTHERS ABANDONING THEIR CHILDREN FOR A BETTER LIFE.

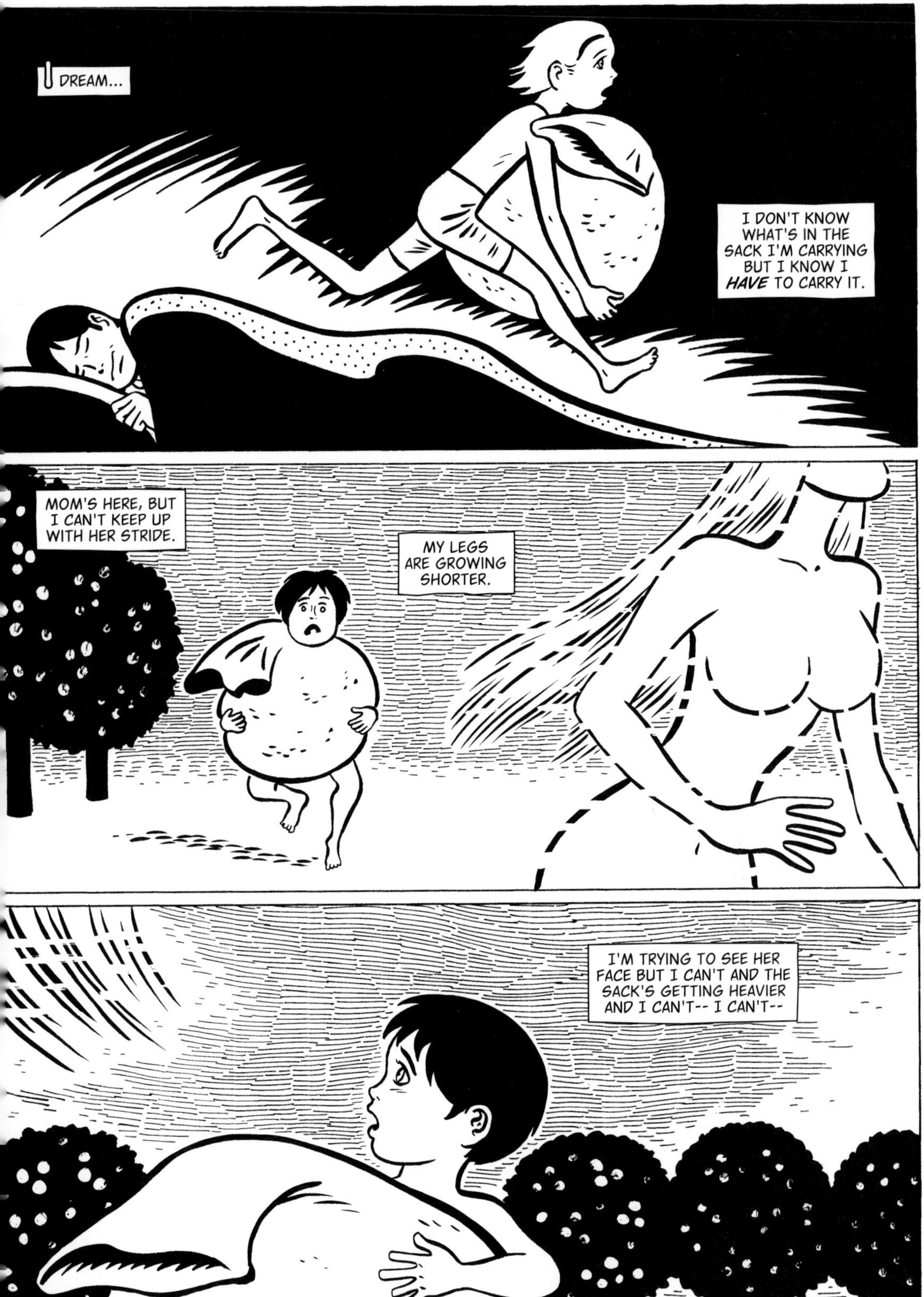
I DREAM...
I DON'T KNOW WHAT'S IN THE SACK I'M CARRYING BUT I KNOW I *HAVE* TO CARRY IT.
MOM'S HERE, BUT I CAN'T KEEP UP WITH HER STRIDE.
MY LEGS ARE GROWING SHORTER.
I'M TRYING TO SEE HER FACE BUT I CAN'T AND THE SACK'S GETTING HEAVIER AND I CAN'T-- I CAN'T--

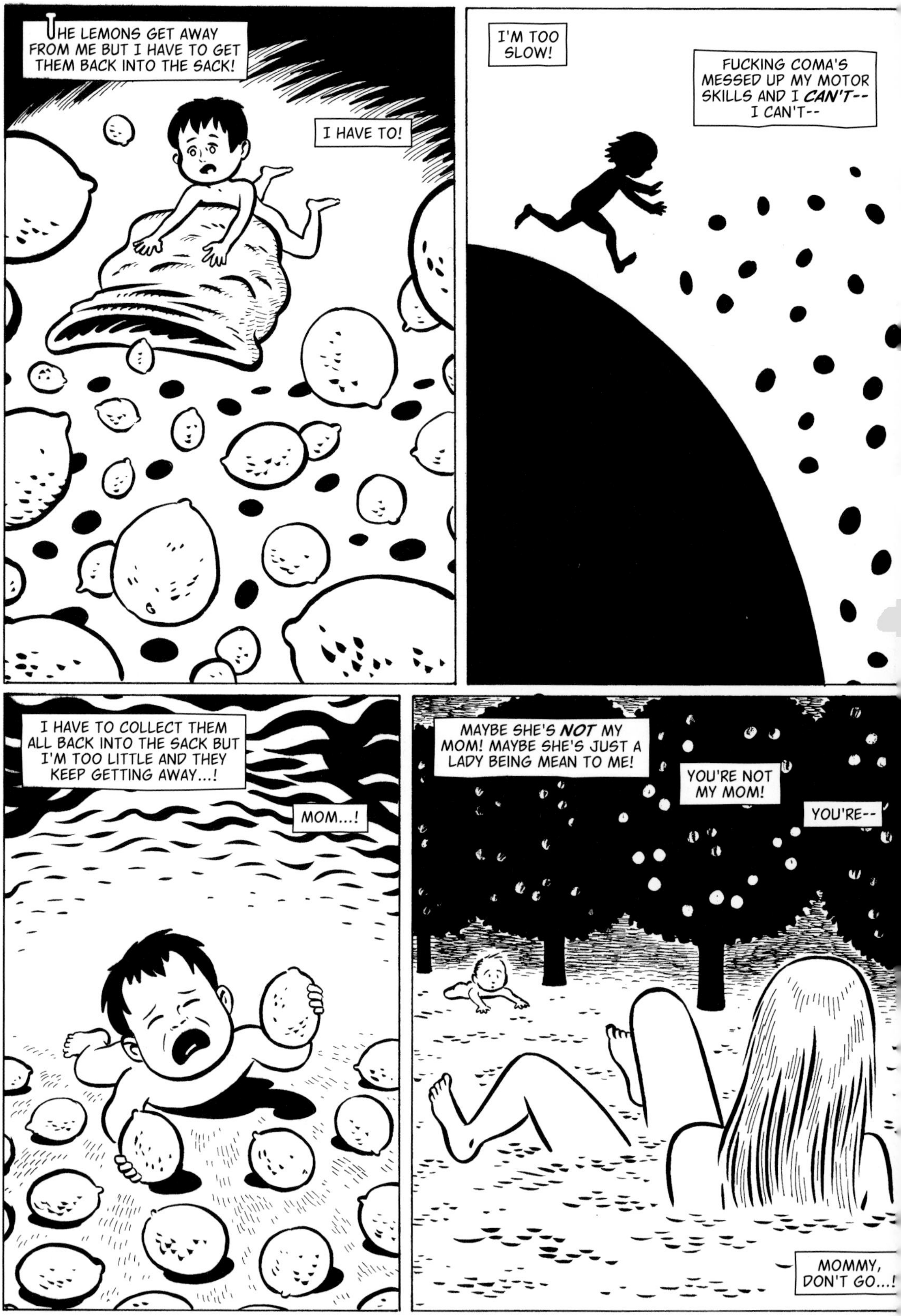
THE LEMONS GET AWAY FROM ME BUT I HAVE TO GET THEM BACK INTO THE SACK!
I HAVE TO!
I'M TOO SLOW!
FUCKING COMA'S MESSED UP MY MOTOR SKILLS AND I CAN'T-- I CAN'T--
I HAVE TO COLLECT THEM ALL BACK INTO THE SACK BUT I'M TOO LITTLE AND THEY KEEP GETTING AWAY...!
MOM...!
MAYBE SHE'S NOT MY MOM! MAYBE SHE'S JUST A LADY BEING MEAN TO ME!
YOU'RE NOT MY MOM!
YOU'RE--
MOMMY, DON'T GO...!

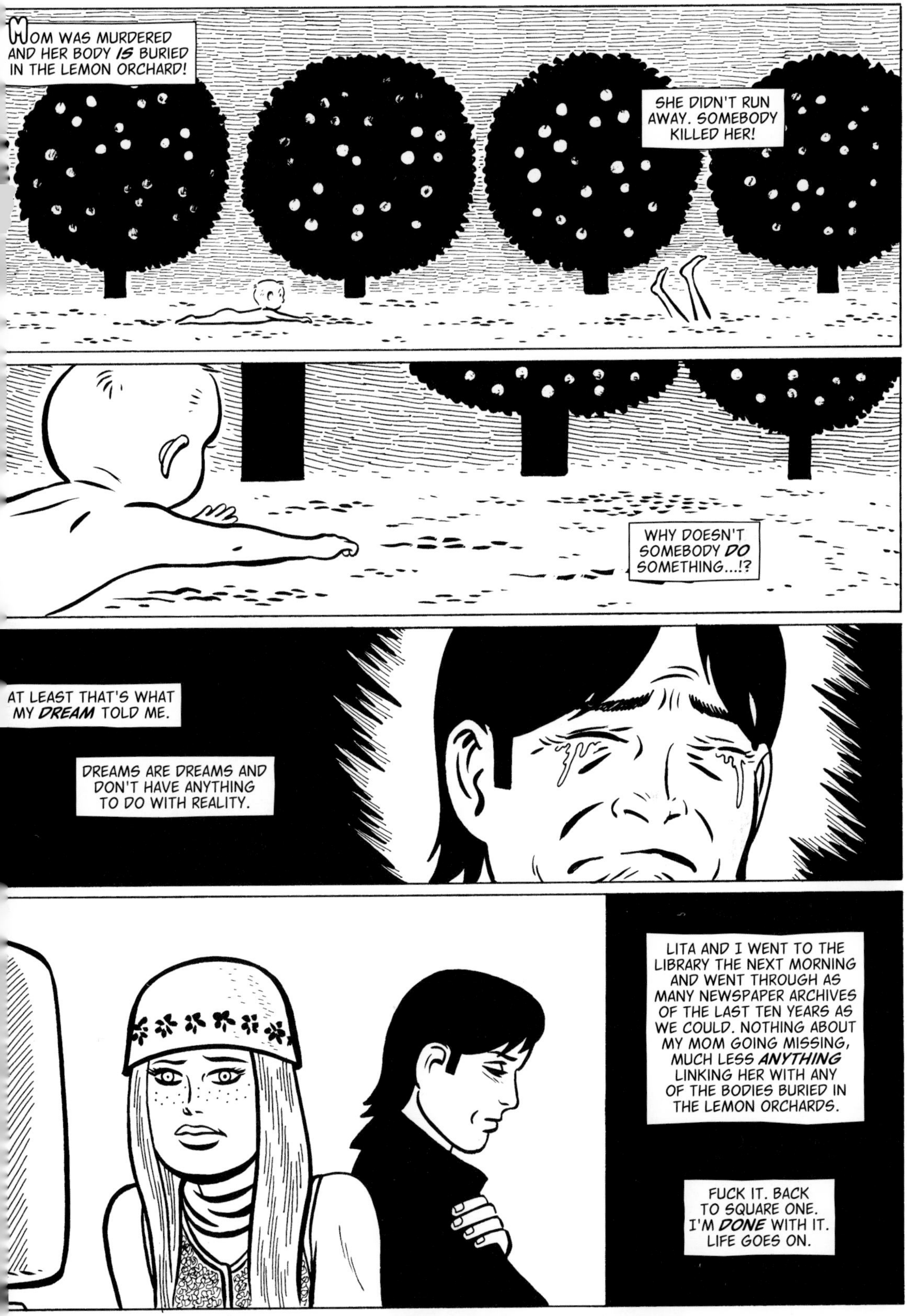
MOM WAS MURDERED AND HER BODY *IS* BURIED IN THE LEMON ORCHARD!
SHE DIDN'T RUN AWAY. SOMEBODY KILLED HER!
WHY DOESN'T SOMEBODY *DO* SOMETHING...!?
AT LEAST THAT'S WHAT MY *DREAM* TOLD ME.
DREAMS ARE DREAMS AND DON'T HAVE ANYTHING TO DO WITH REALITY.
LITA AND I WENT TO THE LIBRARY THE NEXT MORNING AND WENT THROUGH AS MANY NEWSPAPER ARCHIVES OF THE LAST TEN YEARS AS WE COULD. NOTHING ABOUT MY MOM GOING MISSING, MUCH LESS *ANYTHING* LINKING HER WITH ANY OF THE BODIES BURIED IN THE LEMON ORCHARDS.
FUCK IT. BACK TO SQUARE ONE. I'M *DONE* WITH IT. LIFE GOES ON.

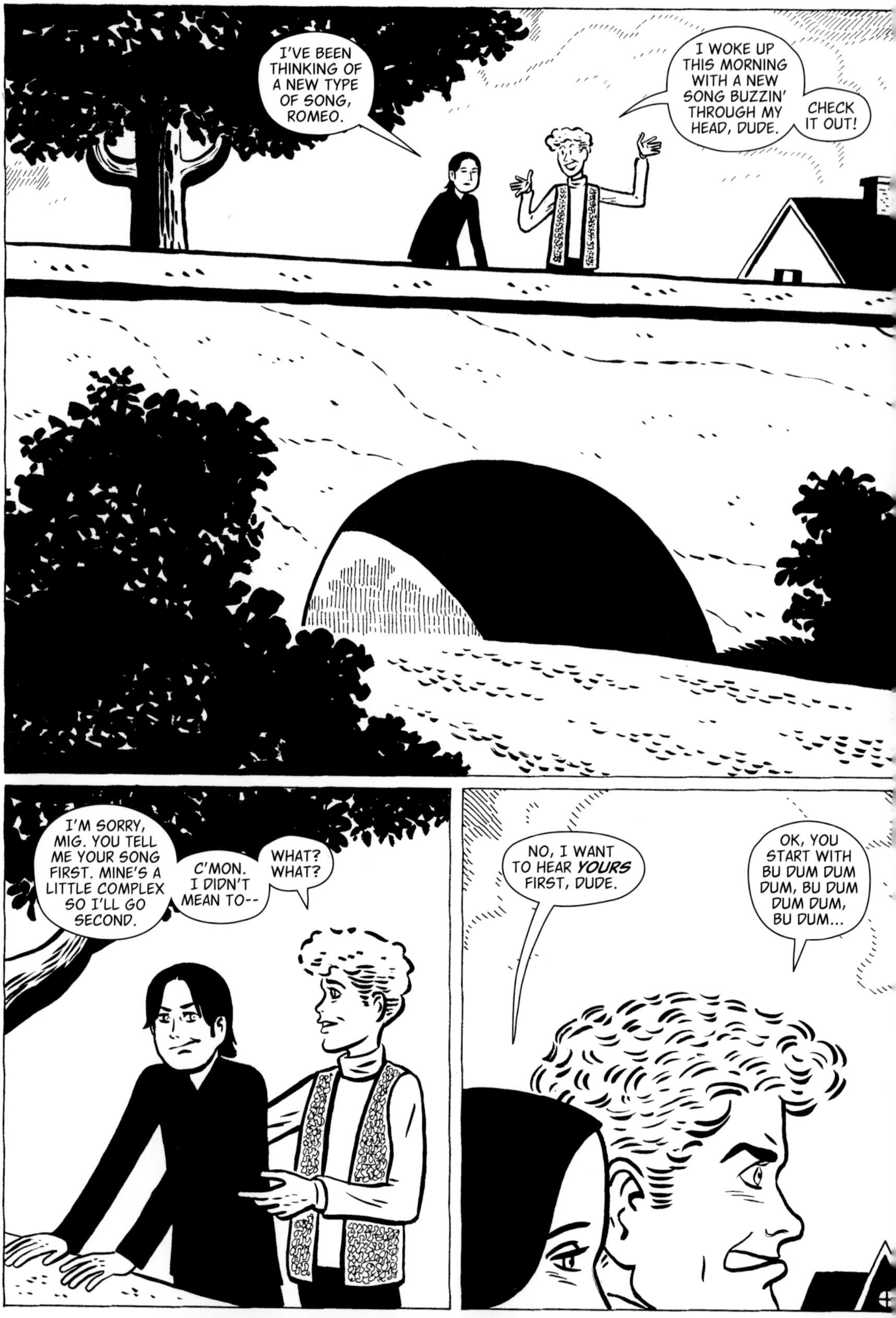
I'VE BEEN THINKING OF A NEW TYPE OF SONG, ROMEO.
I WOKE UP THIS MORNING WITH A NEW SONG BUZZIN' THROUGH MY HEAD, DUDE.
CHECK IT OUT!
I'M SORRY, MIG. YOU TELL ME YOUR SONG FIRST. MINE'S A LITTLE COMPLEX SO I'LL GO SECOND.
C'MON. I DIDN'T MEAN TO--
WHAT? WHAT?
NO, I WANT TO HEAR *YOURS* FIRST, DUDE.
OK, YOU START WITH BU DUM DUM DUM, BU DUM DUM DUM, BU DUM...

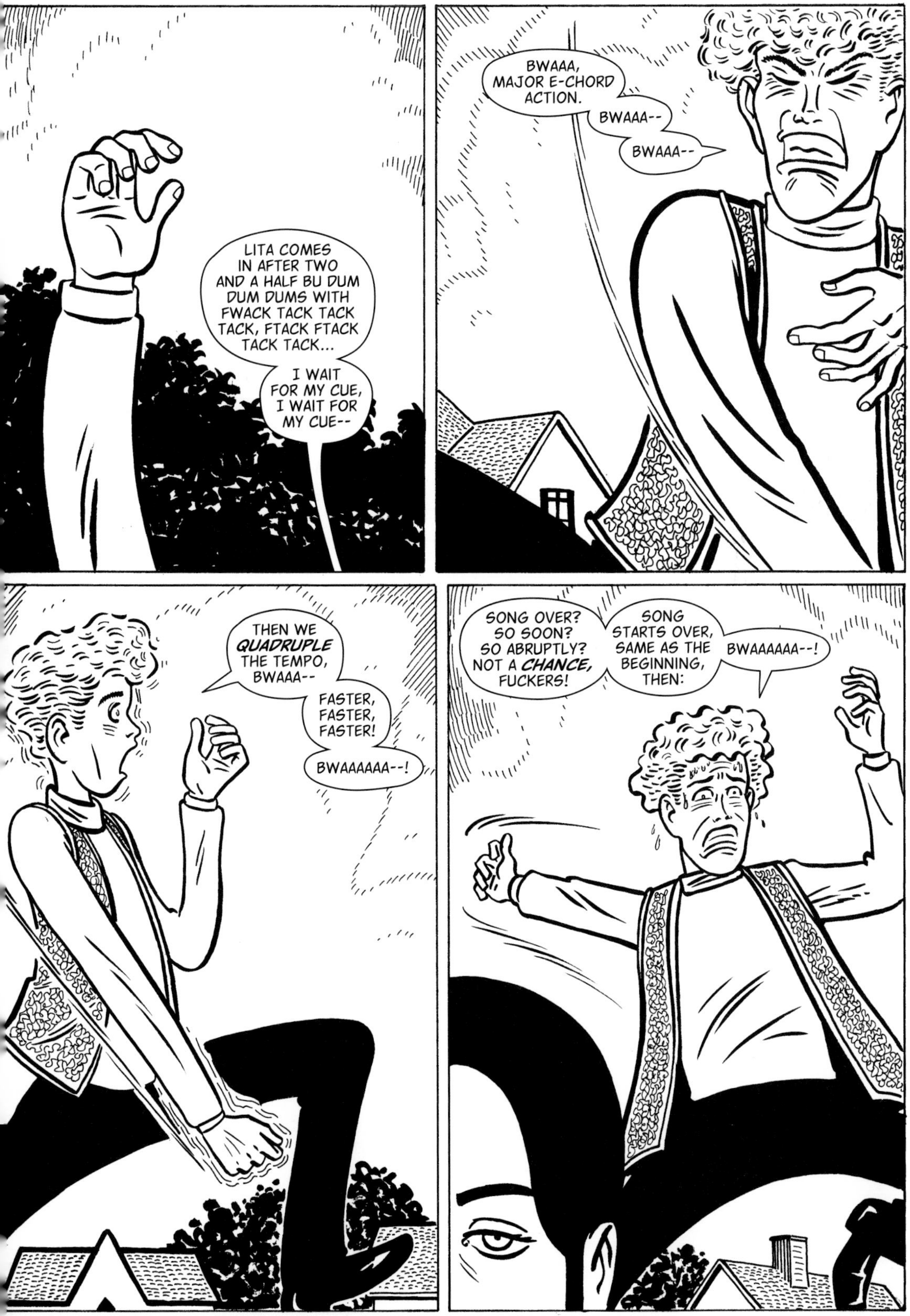
LITA COMES IN AFTER TWO AND A HALF BU DUM DUM DUMS WITH FWACK TACK TACK TACK, FTACK FTACK TACK TACK...
I WAIT FOR MY CUE, I WAIT FOR MY CUE--
BWAAA, MAJOR E-CHORD ACTION.
BWAAA--
BWAAA--
THEN WE *QUADRUPLE* THE TEMPO, BWAAA--
FASTER, FASTER, FASTER!
BWAAAAAA--!
SONG OVER? SO SOON? SO ABRUPTLY? NOT A *CHANCE,* FUCKERS!
SONG STARTS OVER, SAME AS THE BEGINNING, THEN:
BWAAAAAA--!

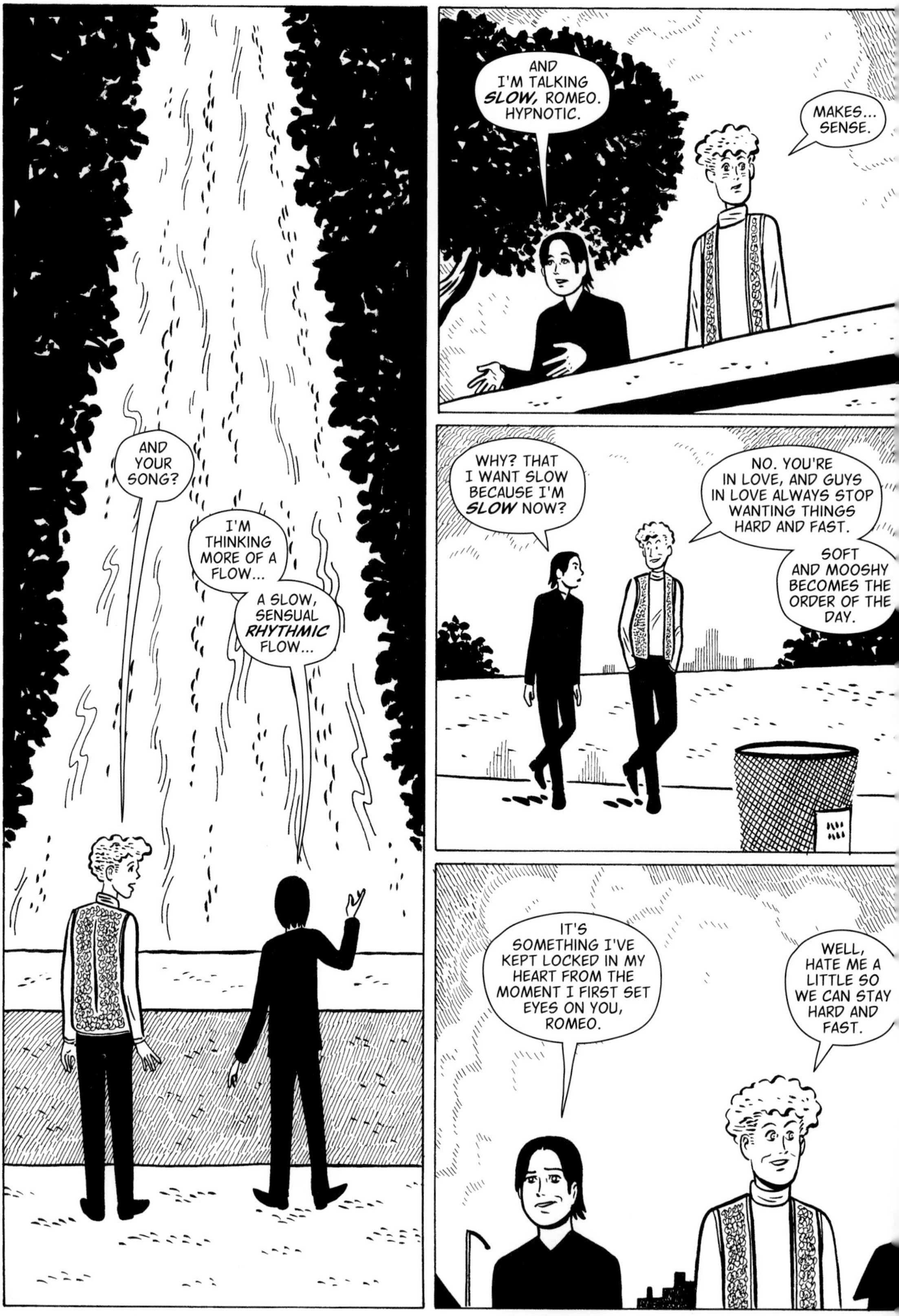
AND YOUR SONG?
I'M THINKING MORE OF A FLOW...
A SLOW, SENSUAL *RHYTHMIC* FLOW...
AND I'M TALKING *SLOW,* ROMEO. HYPNOTIC.
MAKES... SENSE.
WHY? THAT I WANT SLOW BECAUSE I'M *SLOW* NOW?
NO. YOU'RE IN LOVE, AND GUYS IN LOVE ALWAYS STOP WANTING THINGS HARD AND FAST.
SOFT AND MOOSHY BECOMES THE ORDER OF THE DAY.
IT'S SOMETHING I'VE KEPT LOCKED IN MY HEART FROM THE MOMENT I FIRST SET EYES ON YOU, ROMEO.
WELL, HATE ME A LITTLE SO WE CAN STAY HARD AND FAST.

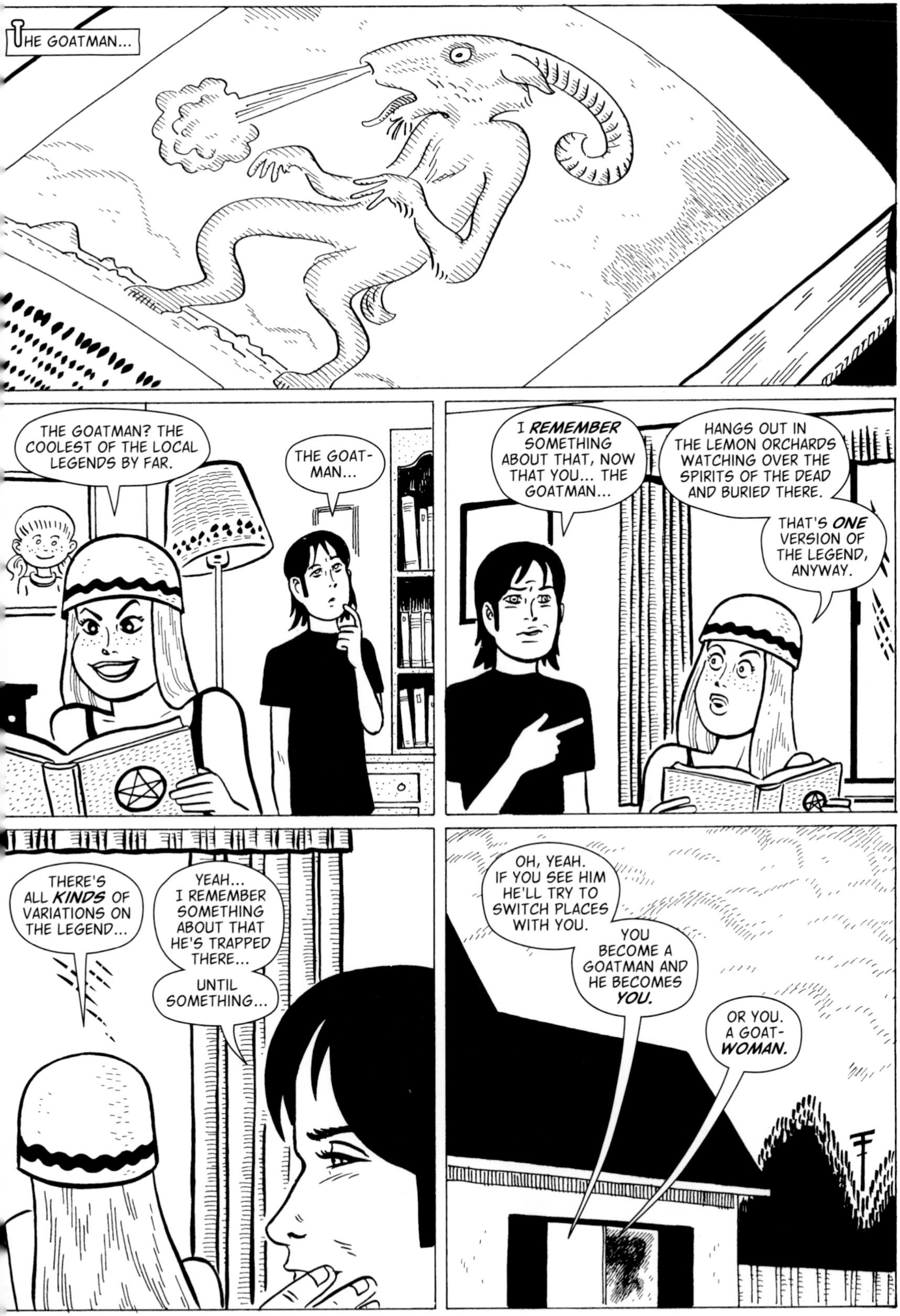
THE GOATMAN...
THE GOATMAN? THE COOLEST OF THE LOCAL LEGENDS BY FAR.
THE GOAT-MAN...
I REMEMBER SOMETHING ABOUT THAT, NOW THAT YOU... THE GOATMAN...
HANGS OUT IN THE LEMON ORCHARDS WATCHING OVER THE SPIRITS OF THE DEAD AND BURIED THERE.
THAT'S ONE VERSION OF THE LEGEND, ANYWAY.
THERE'S ALL KINDS OF VARIATIONS ON THE LEGEND...
YEAH... I REMEMBER SOMETHING ABOUT THAT HE'S TRAPPED THERE...
UNTIL SOMETHING...
OH, YEAH. IF YOU SEE HIM HE'LL TRY TO SWITCH PLACES WITH YOU.
YOU BECOME A GOATMAN AND HE BECOMES YOU.
OR YOU. A GOAT-WOMAN.

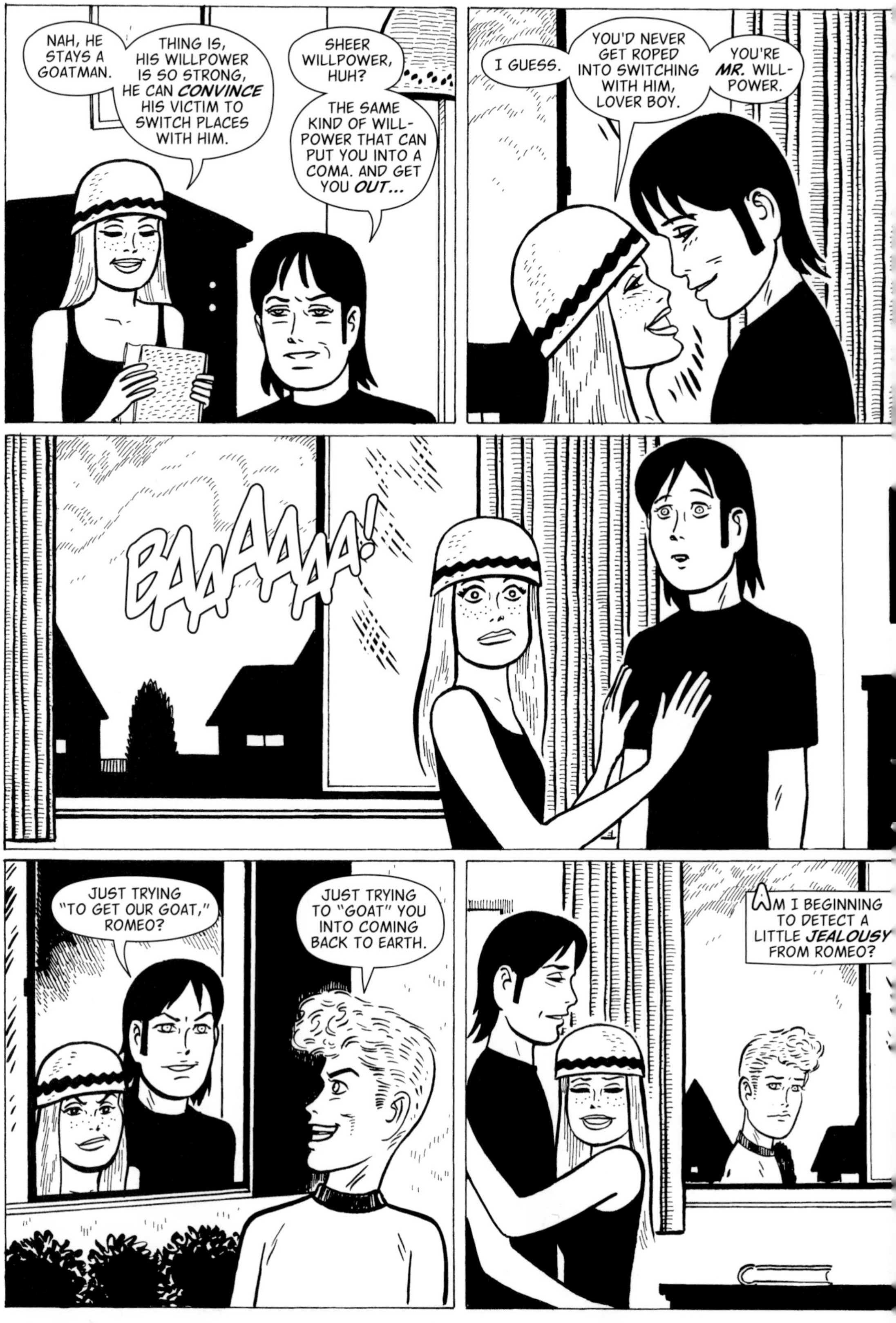
NAH, HE STAYS A GOATMAN.
THING IS, HIS WILLPOWER IS SO STRONG, HE CAN CONVINCE HIS VICTIM TO SWITCH PLACES WITH HIM.
SHEER WILLPOWER, HUH?
THE SAME KIND OF WILL-POWER THAT CAN PUT YOU INTO A COMA. AND GET YOU OUT...
I GUESS.
YOU'D NEVER GET ROPED INTO SWITCHING WITH HIM, LOVER BOY.
YOU'RE MR. WILL-POWER.
BAAAAAA!
JUST TRYING "TO GET OUR GOAT," ROMEO?
JUST TRYING TO "GOAT" YOU INTO COMING BACK TO EARTH.
AM I BEGINNING TO DETECT A LITTLE JEALOUSY FROM ROMEO?

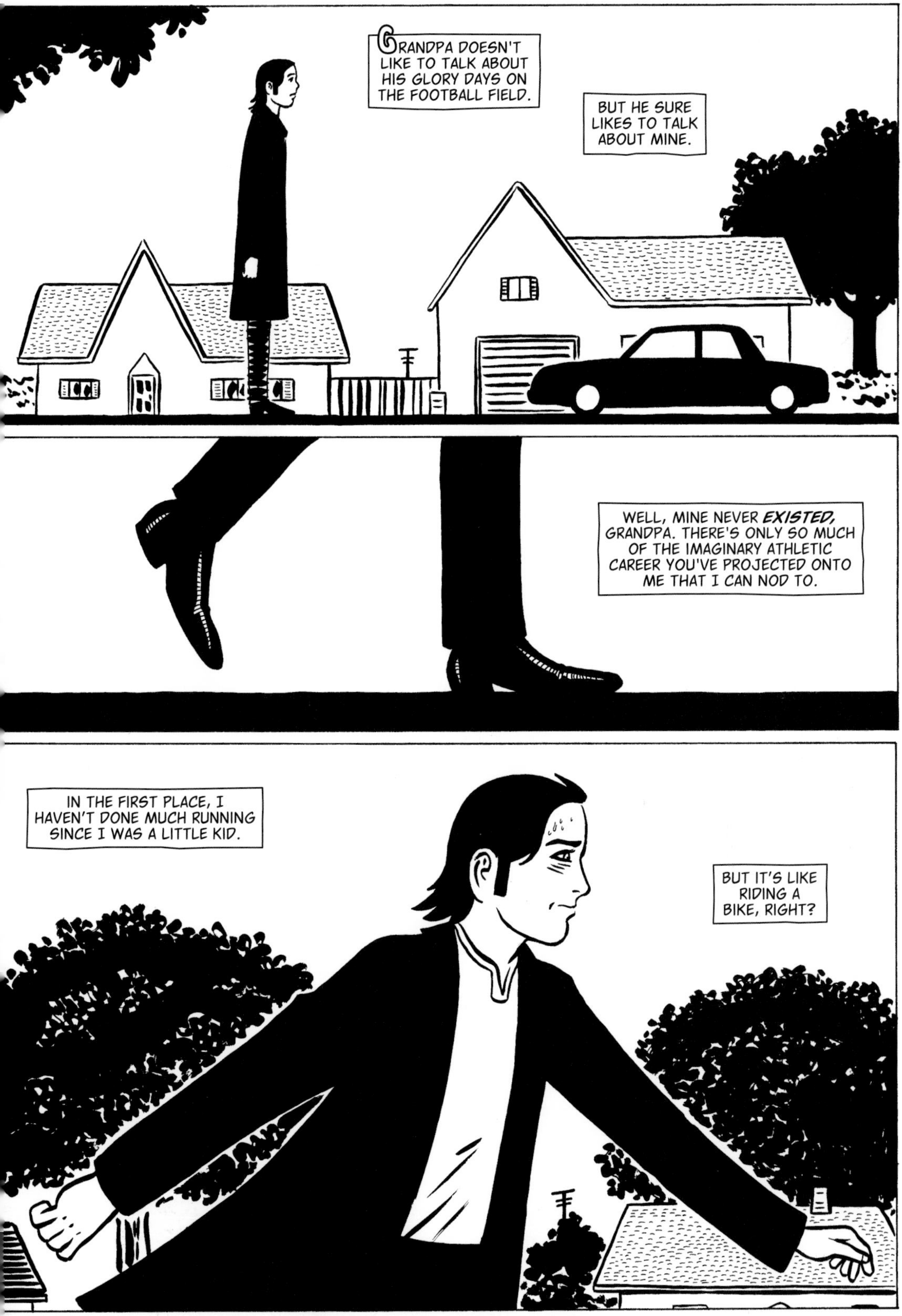

GRANDPA DOESN'T LIKE TO TALK ABOUT HIS GLORY DAYS ON THE FOOTBALL FIELD.
BUT HE SURE LIKES TO TALK ABOUT MINE.
WELL, MINE NEVER *EXISTED,* GRANDPA. THERE'S ONLY SO MUCH OF THE IMAGINARY ATHLETIC CAREER YOU'VE PROJECTED ONTO ME THAT I CAN NOD TO.
IN THE FIRST PLACE, I HAVEN'T DONE MUCH RUNNING SINCE I WAS A LITTLE KID.
BUT IT'S LIKE RIDING A BIKE, RIGHT?

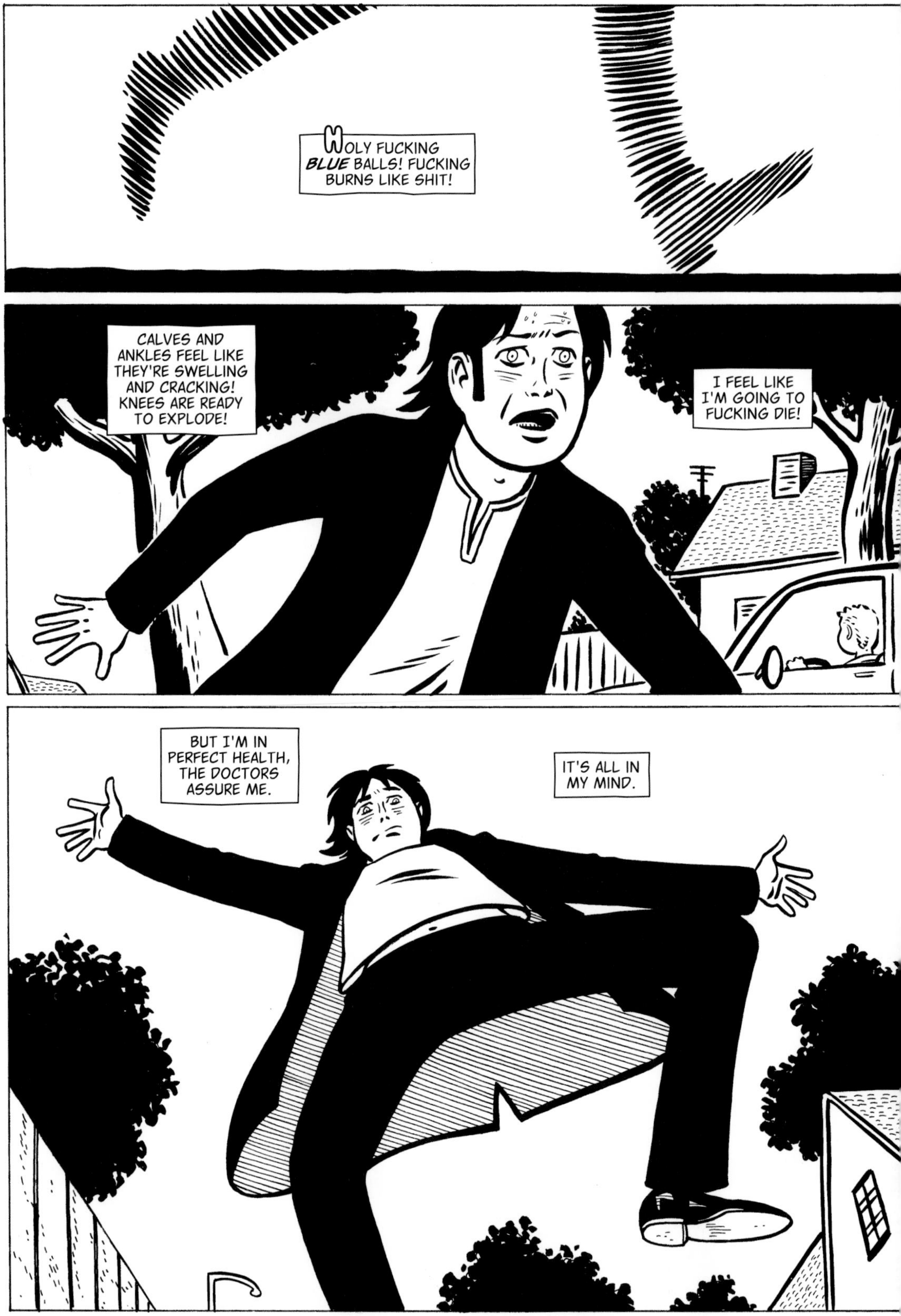
HOLY FUCKING BLUE BALLS! FUCKING BURNS LIKE SHIT!
CALVES AND ANKLES FEEL LIKE THEY'RE SWELLING AND CRACKING! KNEES ARE READY TO EXPLODE!
I FEEL LIKE I'M GOING TO FUCKING DIE!
BUT I'M IN PERFECT HEALTH, THE DOCTORS ASSURE ME.
IT'S ALL IN MY MIND.

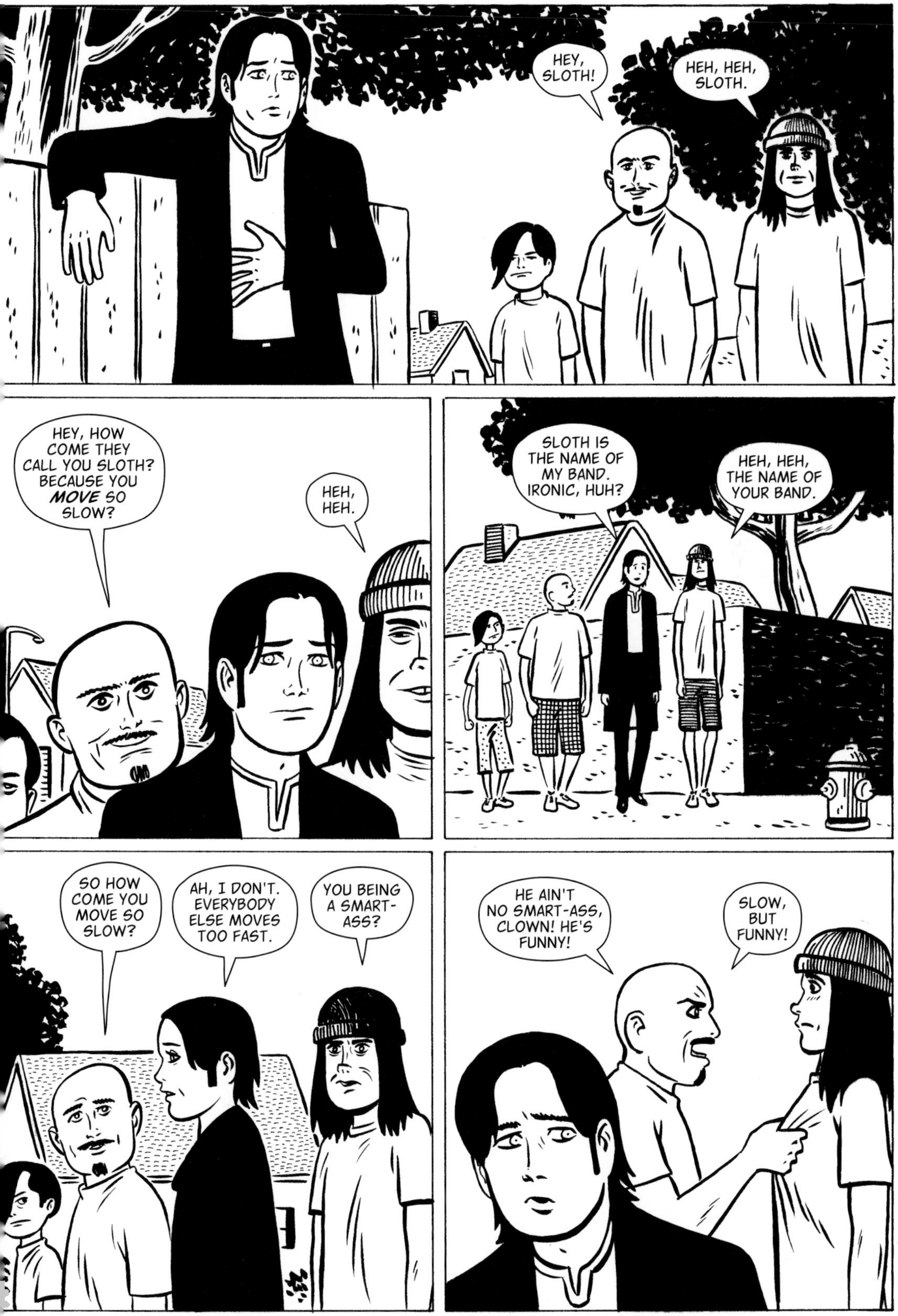
HEY, SLOTH!
HEH, HEH, SLOTH.
HEY, HOW COME THEY CALL YOU SLOTH? BECAUSE YOU *MOVE* SO SLOW?
HEH, HEH.
SLOTH IS THE NAME OF MY BAND. IRONIC, HUH?
HEH, HEH, THE NAME OF YOUR BAND.
SO HOW COME YOU MOVE SO SLOW?
AH, I DON'T. EVERYBODY ELSE MOVES TOO FAST.
YOU BEING A SMART-ASS?
HE AIN'T NO SMART-ASS, CLOWN! HE'S FUNNY!
SLOW, BUT FUNNY!

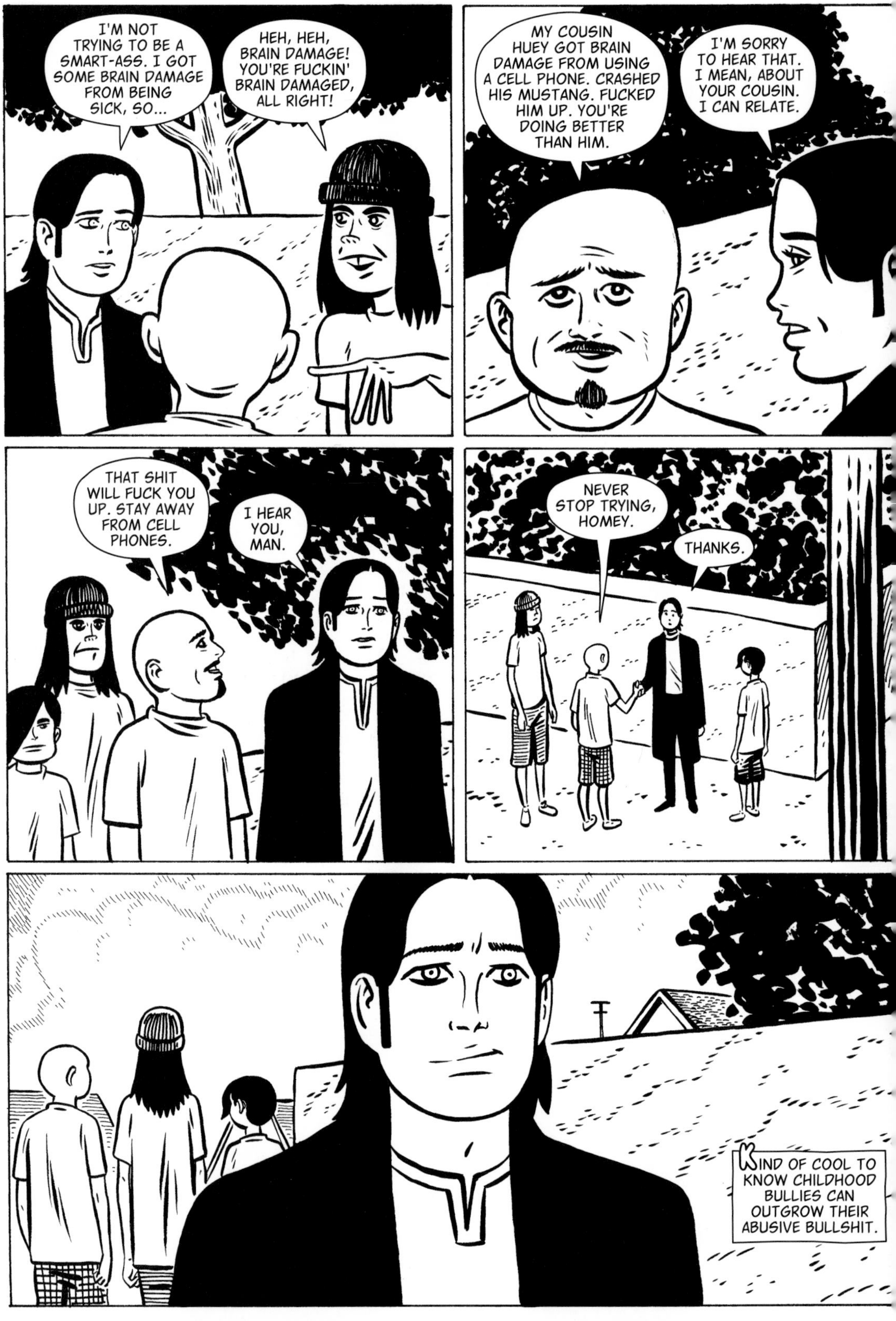
I'M NOT TRYING TO BE A SMART-ASS. I GOT SOME BRAIN DAMAGE FROM BEING SICK, SO...
HEH, HEH, BRAIN DAMAGE! YOU'RE FUCKIN' BRAIN DAMAGED, ALL RIGHT!
MY COUSIN HUEY GOT BRAIN DAMAGE FROM USING A CELL PHONE. CRASHED HIS MUSTANG. FUCKED HIM UP. YOU'RE DOING BETTER THAN HIM.
I'M SORRY TO HEAR THAT. I MEAN, ABOUT YOUR COUSIN. I CAN RELATE.
THAT SHIT WILL FUCK YOU UP. STAY AWAY FROM CELL PHONES.
I HEAR YOU, MAN.
NEVER STOP TRYING, HOMEY.
THANKS.
KIND OF COOL TO KNOW CHILDHOOD BULLIES CAN OUTGROW THEIR ABUSIVE BULLSHIT.

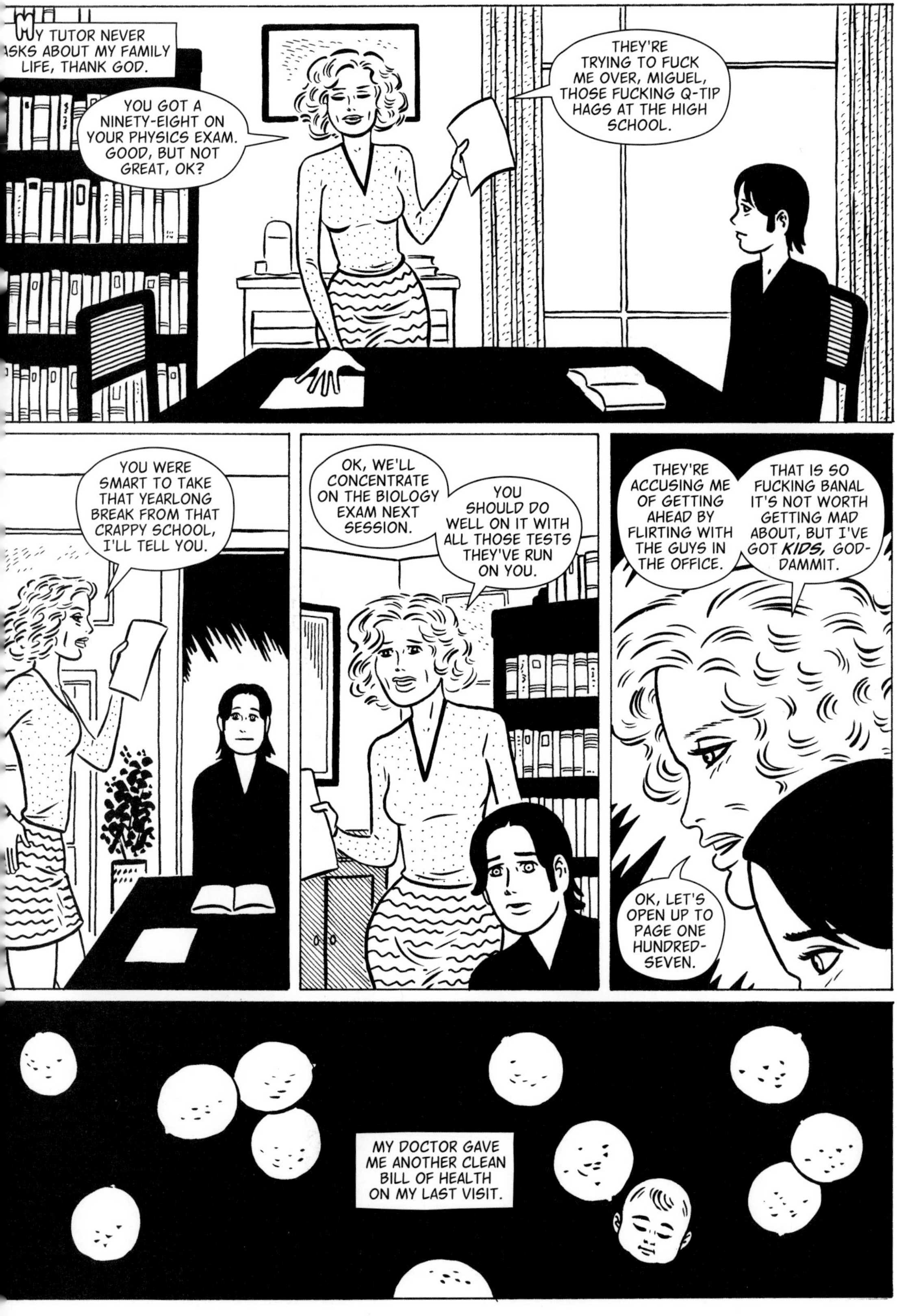
MY TUTOR NEVER ASKS ABOUT MY FAMILY LIFE, THANK GOD.
YOU GOT A NINETY-EIGHT ON YOUR PHYSICS EXAM. GOOD, BUT NOT GREAT, OK?
THEY'RE TRYING TO FUCK ME OVER, MIGUEL, THOSE FUCKING Q-TIP HAGS AT THE HIGH SCHOOL.
YOU WERE SMART TO TAKE THAT YEARLONG BREAK FROM THAT CRAPPY SCHOOL, I'LL TELL YOU.
OK, WE'LL CONCENTRATE ON THE BIOLOGY EXAM NEXT SESSION.
YOU SHOULD DO WELL ON IT WITH ALL THOSE TESTS THEY'VE RUN ON YOU.
THEY'RE ACCUSING ME OF GETTING AHEAD BY FLIRTING WITH THE GUYS IN THE OFFICE.
THAT IS SO FUCKING BANAL IT'S NOT WORTH GETTING MAD ABOUT, BUT I'VE GOT *KIDS,* GOD-DAMMIT.
OK, LET'S OPEN UP TO PAGE ONE HUNDRED-SEVEN.
MY DOCTOR GAVE ME ANOTHER CLEAN BILL OF HEALTH ON MY LAST VISIT.

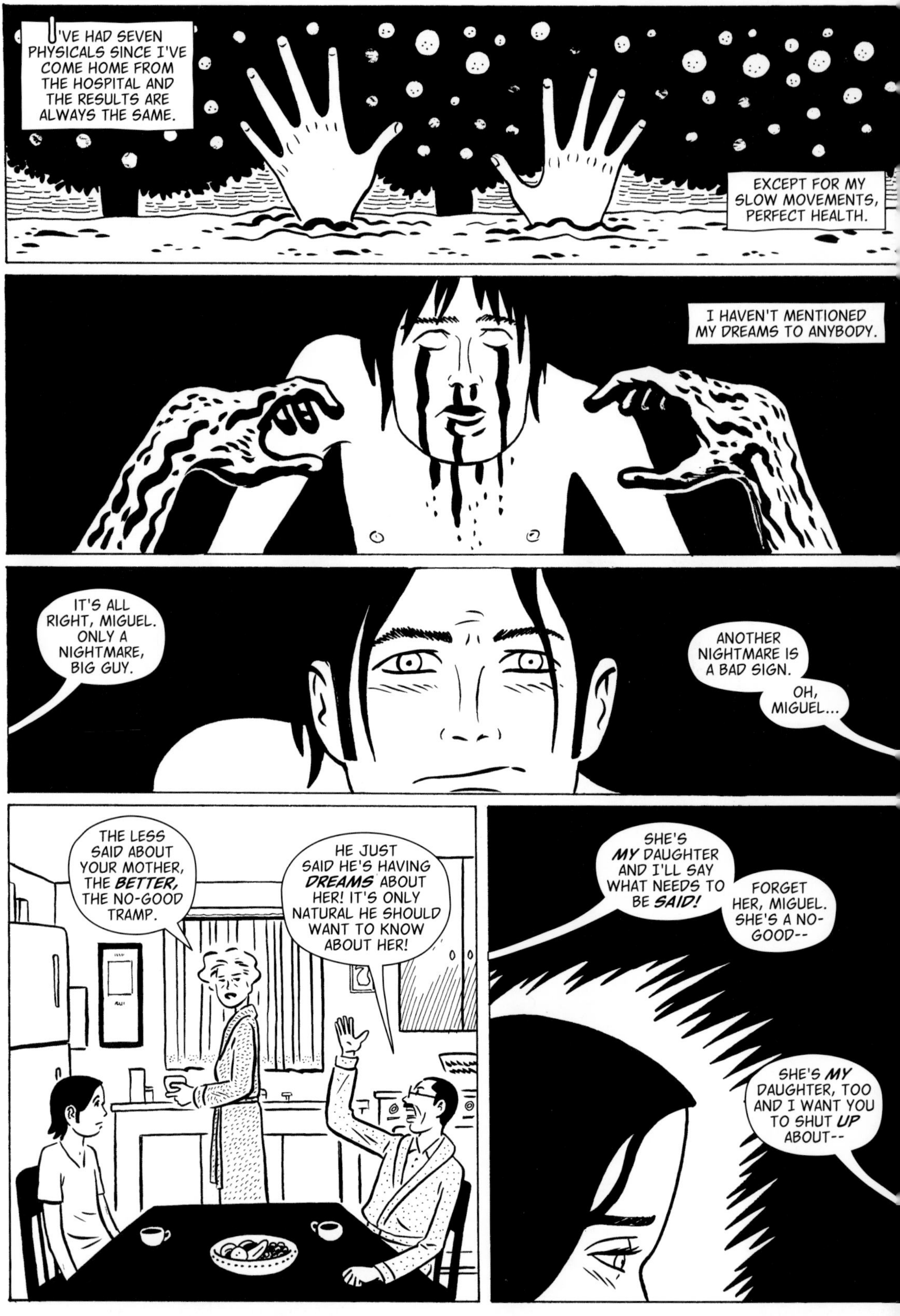
I'VE HAD SEVEN PHYSICALS SINCE I'VE COME HOME FROM THE HOSPITAL AND THE RESULTS ARE ALWAYS THE SAME.
EXCEPT FOR MY SLOW MOVEMENTS, PERFECT HEALTH.
I HAVEN'T MENTIONED MY DREAMS TO ANYBODY.
IT'S ALL RIGHT, MIGUEL. ONLY A NIGHTMARE, BIG GUY.
ANOTHER NIGHTMARE IS A BAD SIGN.
OH, MIGUEL...
THE LESS SAID ABOUT YOUR MOTHER, THE BETTER, THE NO-GOOD TRAMP.
HE JUST SAID HE'S HAVING DREAMS ABOUT HER! IT'S ONLY NATURAL HE SHOULD WANT TO KNOW ABOUT HER!
SHE'S MY DAUGHTER AND I'LL SAY WHAT NEEDS TO BE SAID!
FORGET HER, MIGUEL. SHE'S A NO-GOOD--
SHE'S MY DAUGHTER, TOO AND I WANT YOU TO SHUT UP ABOUT--

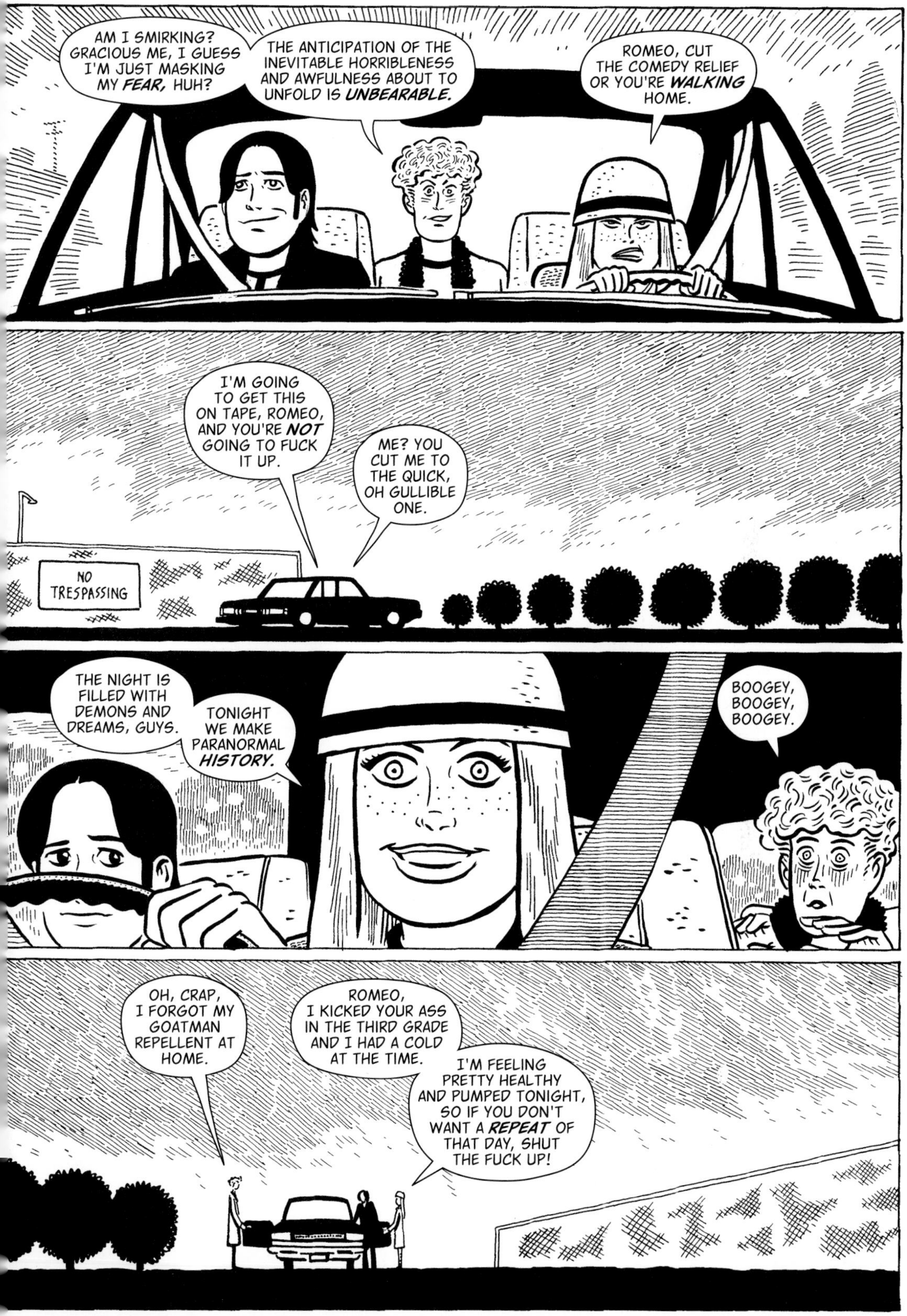
AM I SMIRKING? GRACIOUS ME, I GUESS I'M JUST MASKING MY FEAR, HUH?
THE ANTICIPATION OF THE INEVITABLE HORRIBLENESS AND AWFULNESS ABOUT TO UNFOLD IS UNBEARABLE.
ROMEO, CUT THE COMEDY RELIEF OR YOU'RE WALKING HOME.
I'M GOING TO GET THIS ON TAPE, ROMEO, AND YOU'RE NOT GOING TO FUCK IT UP.
ME? YOU CUT ME TO THE QUICK, OH GULLIBLE ONE.
NO TRESPASSING
THE NIGHT IS FILLED WITH DEMONS AND DREAMS, GUYS.
TONIGHT WE MAKE PARANORMAL HISTORY.
BOOGEY, BOOGEY, BOOGEY.
OH, CRAP, I FORGOT MY GOATMAN REPELLENT AT HOME.
ROMEO, I KICKED YOUR ASS IN THE THIRD GRADE AND I HAD A COLD AT THE TIME.
I'M FEELING PRETTY HEALTHY AND PUMPED TONIGHT, SO IF YOU DON'T WANT A REPEAT OF THAT DAY, SHUT THE FUCK UP!

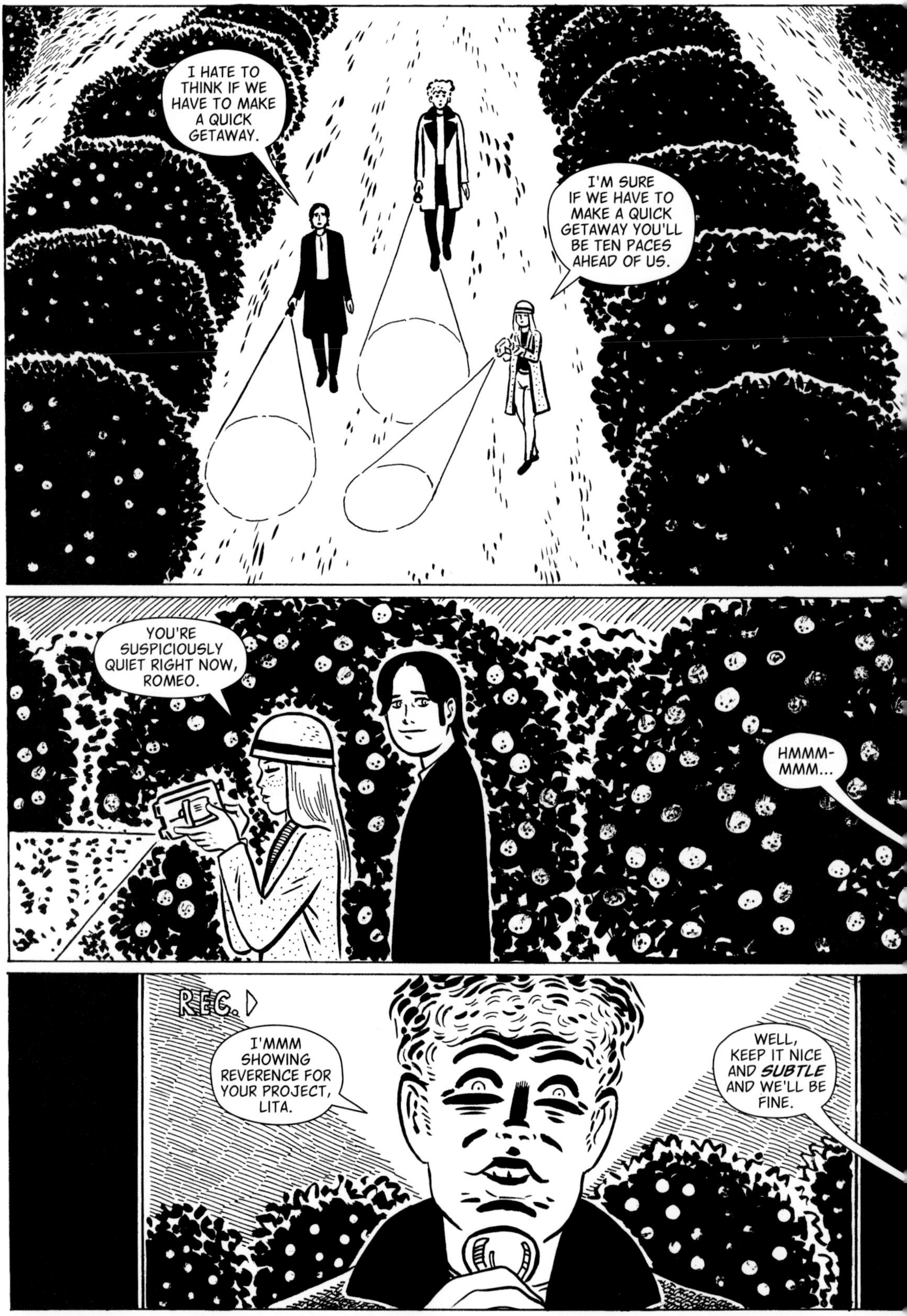
I HATE TO THINK IF WE HAVE TO MAKE A QUICK GETAWAY.
I'M SURE IF WE HAVE TO MAKE A QUICK GETAWAY YOU'LL BE TEN PACES AHEAD OF US.
YOU'RE SUSPICIOUSLY QUIET RIGHT NOW, ROMEO.
HMMM-MMM...
REC.
I'MMM SHOWING REVERENCE FOR YOUR PROJECT, LITA.
WELL, KEEP IT NICE AND *SUBTLE* AND WE'LL BE FINE.

BATTERY'S ALREADY RUNNING LOW. I DON'T WANT TO SHUT IT OFF AND THEN SOMETHING HAPPENS AND I MISS IT.

HEY, IS THIS THE...?

THE SPOT WHERE THE LAST BODY WAS *BURIED*, YEAH.

AS RUMOR HAS IT.

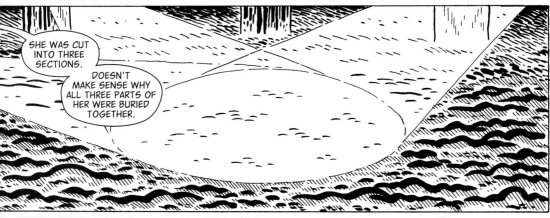

SHE WAS CUT INTO THREE SECTIONS.

DOESN'T MAKE SENSE WHY ALL THREE PARTS OF HER WERE BURIED TOGETHER.

GOD... AND NOT EVEN A MARKER OR ANYTHING.

LIKE SHE WAS NEVER BURIED HERE... LIKE SHE'S JUST TOTALLY *FORGOTTEN*...

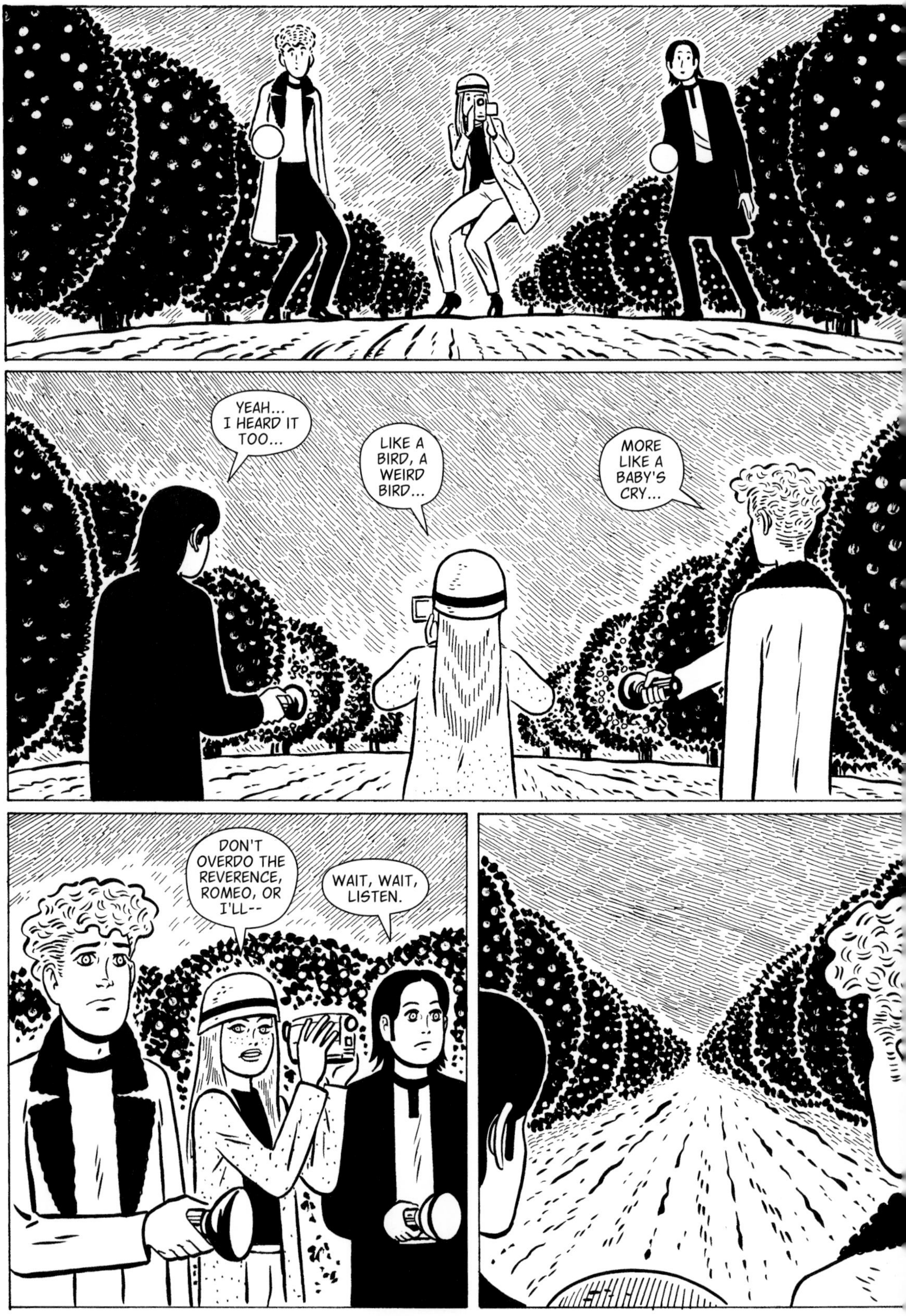
YEAH... I HEARD IT TOO...
LIKE A BIRD, A WEIRD BIRD...
MORE LIKE A BABY'S CRY...
DON'T OVERDO THE REVERENCE, ROMEO, OR I'LL--
WAIT, WAIT, LISTEN.

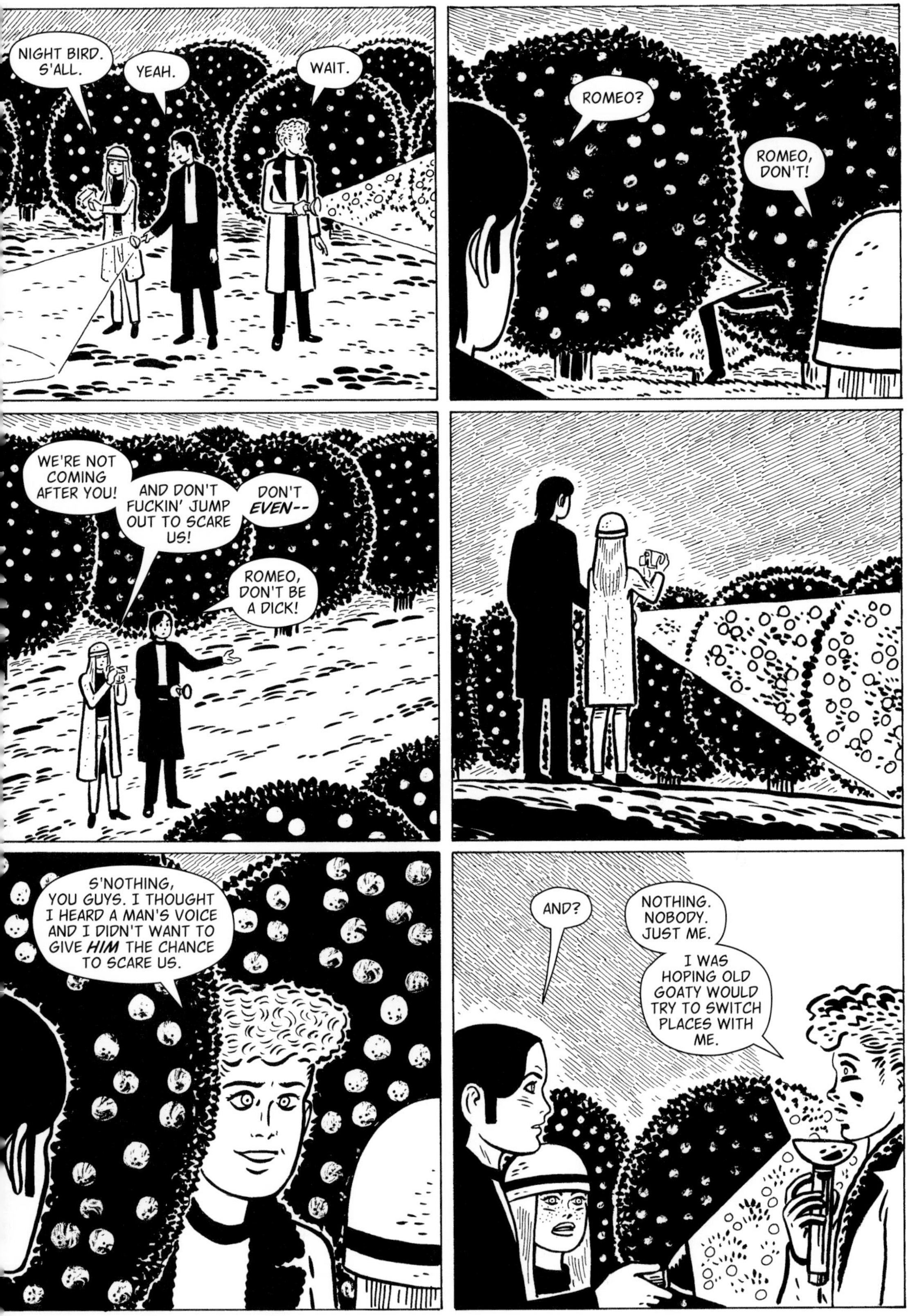
NIGHT BIRD. S'ALL.
YEAH.
WAIT.
ROMEO?
ROMEO, DON'T!
WE'RE NOT COMING AFTER YOU!
AND DON'T FUCKIN' JUMP OUT TO SCARE US!
DON'T EVEN--
ROMEO, DON'T BE A DICK!
S'NOTHING, YOU GUYS. I THOUGHT I HEARD A MAN'S VOICE AND I DIDN'T WANT TO GIVE HIM THE CHANCE TO SCARE US.
AND?
NOTHING. NOBODY. JUST ME.
I WAS HOPING OLD GOATY WOULD TRY TO SWITCH PLACES WITH ME.

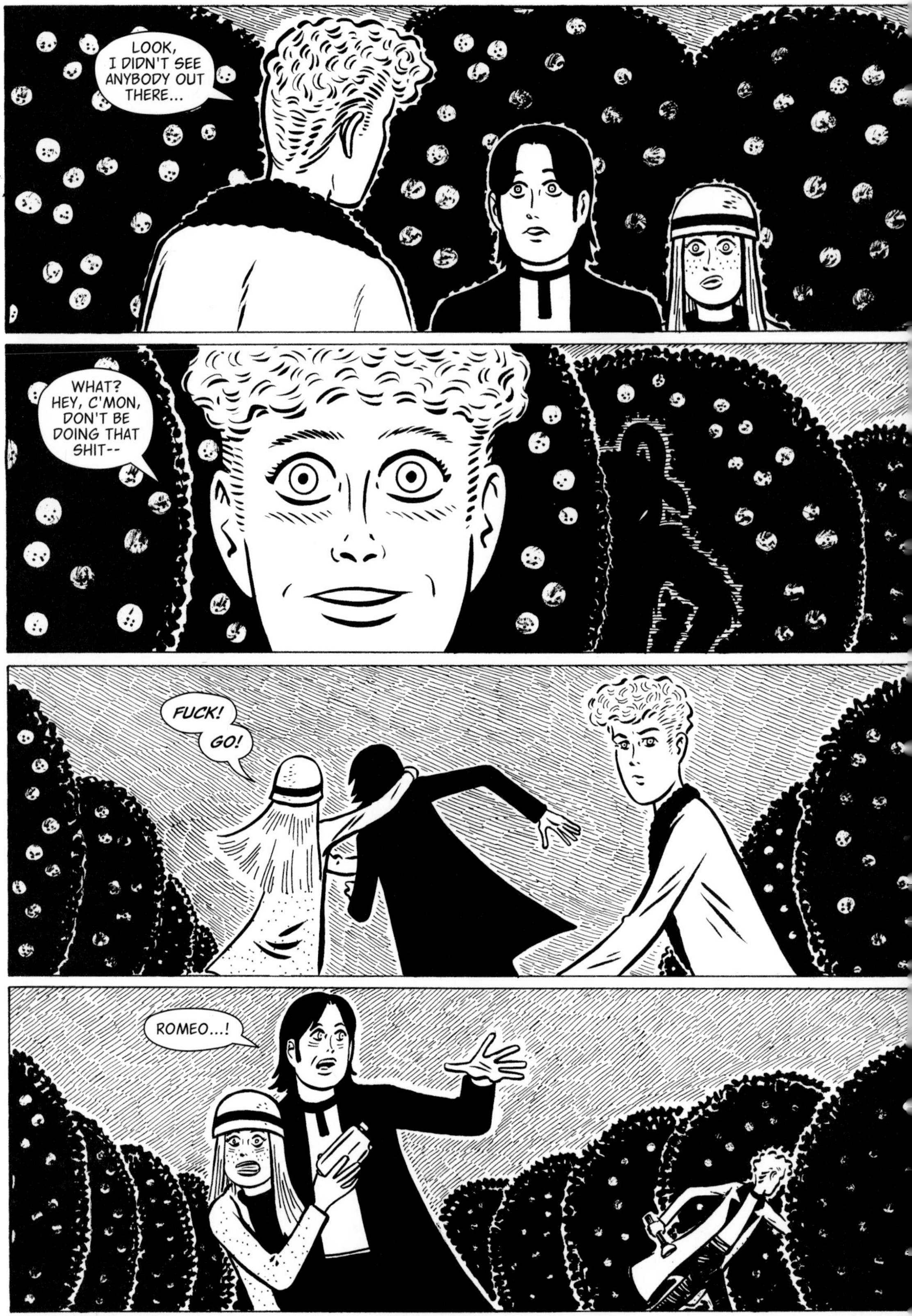
LOOK, I DIDN'T SEE ANYBODY OUT THERE...
WHAT? HEY, C'MON, DON'T BE DOING THAT SHIT--
FUCK!
GO!
ROMEO...!

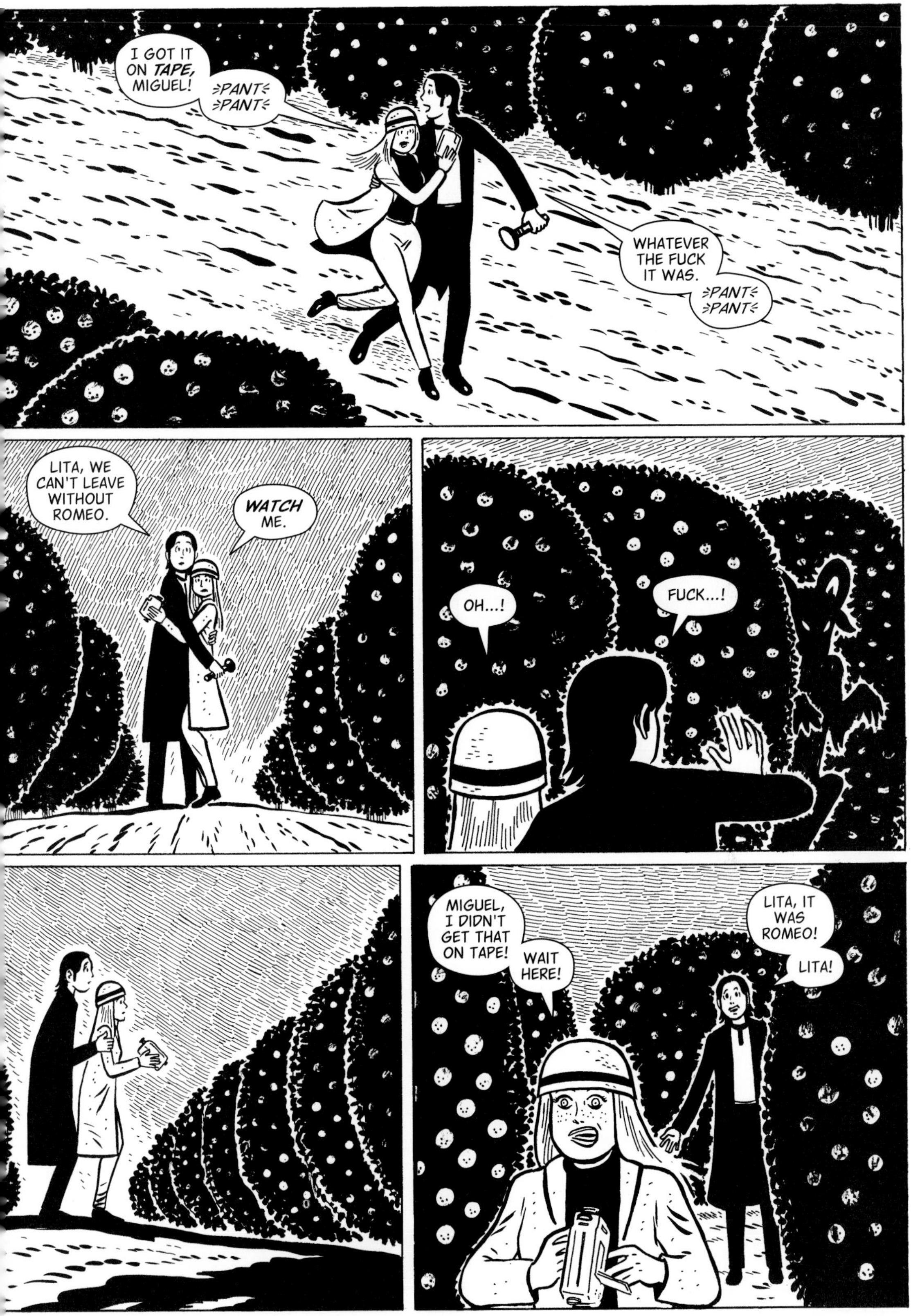

I GOT IT ON *TAPE,* MIGUEL!
PANT PANT
WHATEVER THE FUCK IT WAS.
PANT PANT
LITA, WE CAN'T LEAVE WITHOUT ROMEO.
WATCH ME.
OH...!
FUCK...!
MIGUEL, I DIDN'T GET THAT ON TAPE!
WAIT HERE!
LITA, IT WAS ROMEO!
LITA!

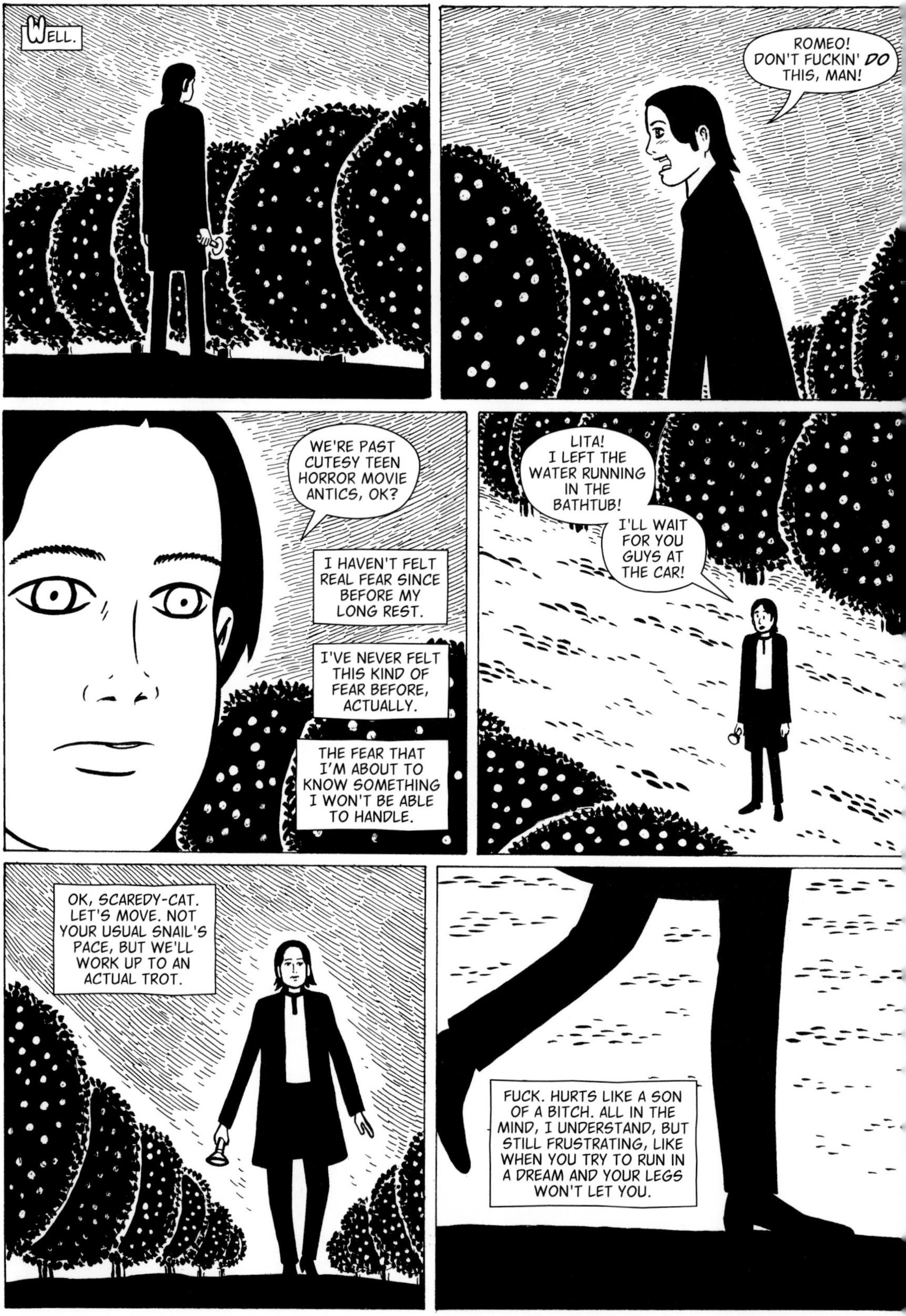
WELL.
ROMEO! DON'T FUCKIN' DO THIS, MAN!
WE'RE PAST CUTESY TEEN HORROR MOVIE ANTICS, OK?
I HAVEN'T FELT REAL FEAR SINCE BEFORE MY LONG REST.
I'VE NEVER FELT THIS KIND OF FEAR BEFORE, ACTUALLY.
THE FEAR THAT I'M ABOUT TO KNOW SOMETHING I WON'T BE ABLE TO HANDLE.
LITA! I LEFT THE WATER RUNNING IN THE BATHTUB!
I'LL WAIT FOR YOU GUYS AT THE CAR!
OK, SCAREDY-CAT. LET'S MOVE. NOT YOUR USUAL SNAIL'S PACE, BUT WE'LL WORK UP TO AN ACTUAL TROT.
FUCK. HURTS LIKE A SON OF A BITCH. ALL IN THE MIND, I UNDERSTAND, BUT STILL FRUSTRATING, LIKE WHEN YOU TRY TO RUN IN A DREAM AND YOUR LEGS WON'T LET YOU.

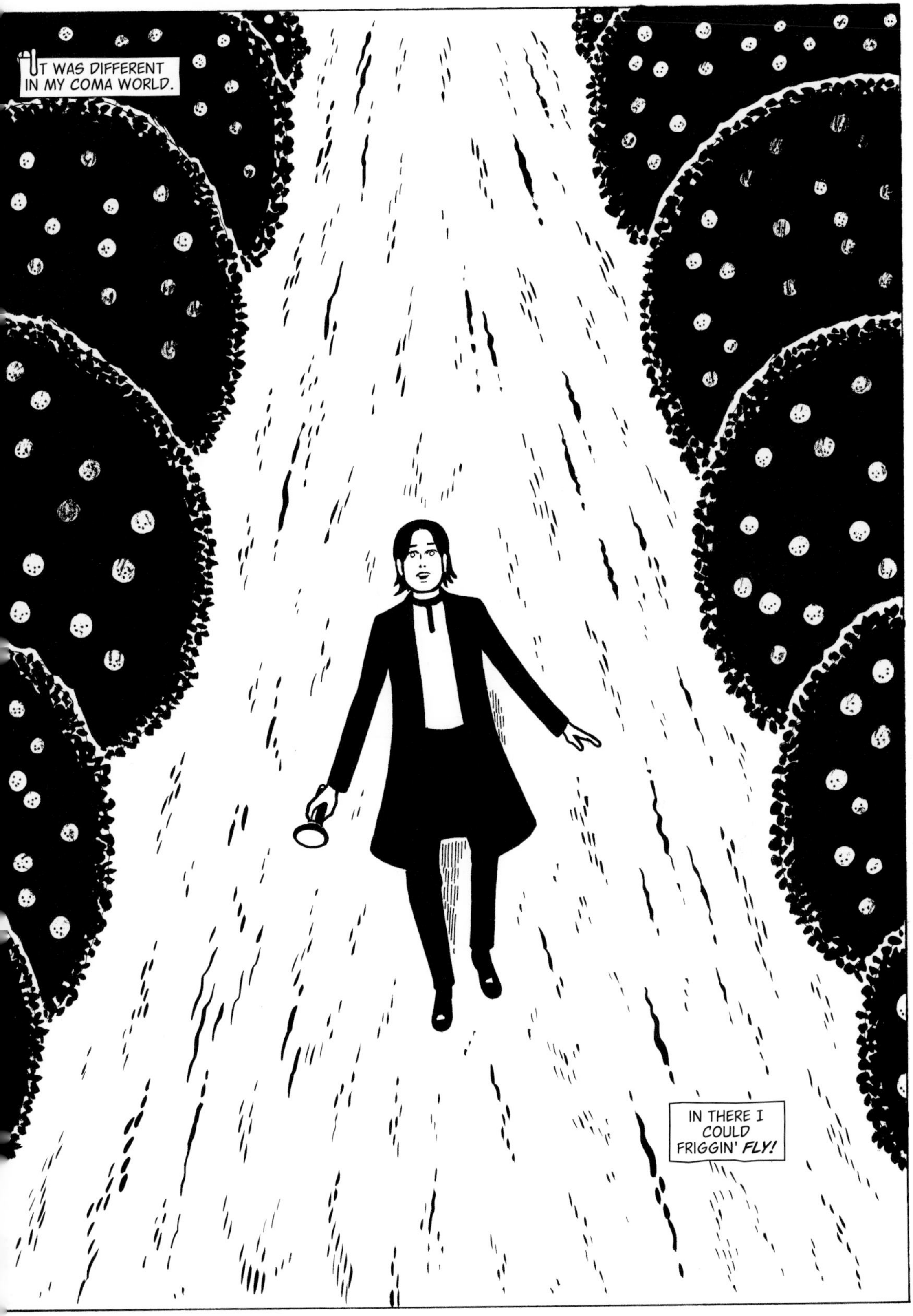
IT WAS DIFFERENT IN MY COMA WORLD.
IN THERE I COULD FRIGGIN' *FLY!*

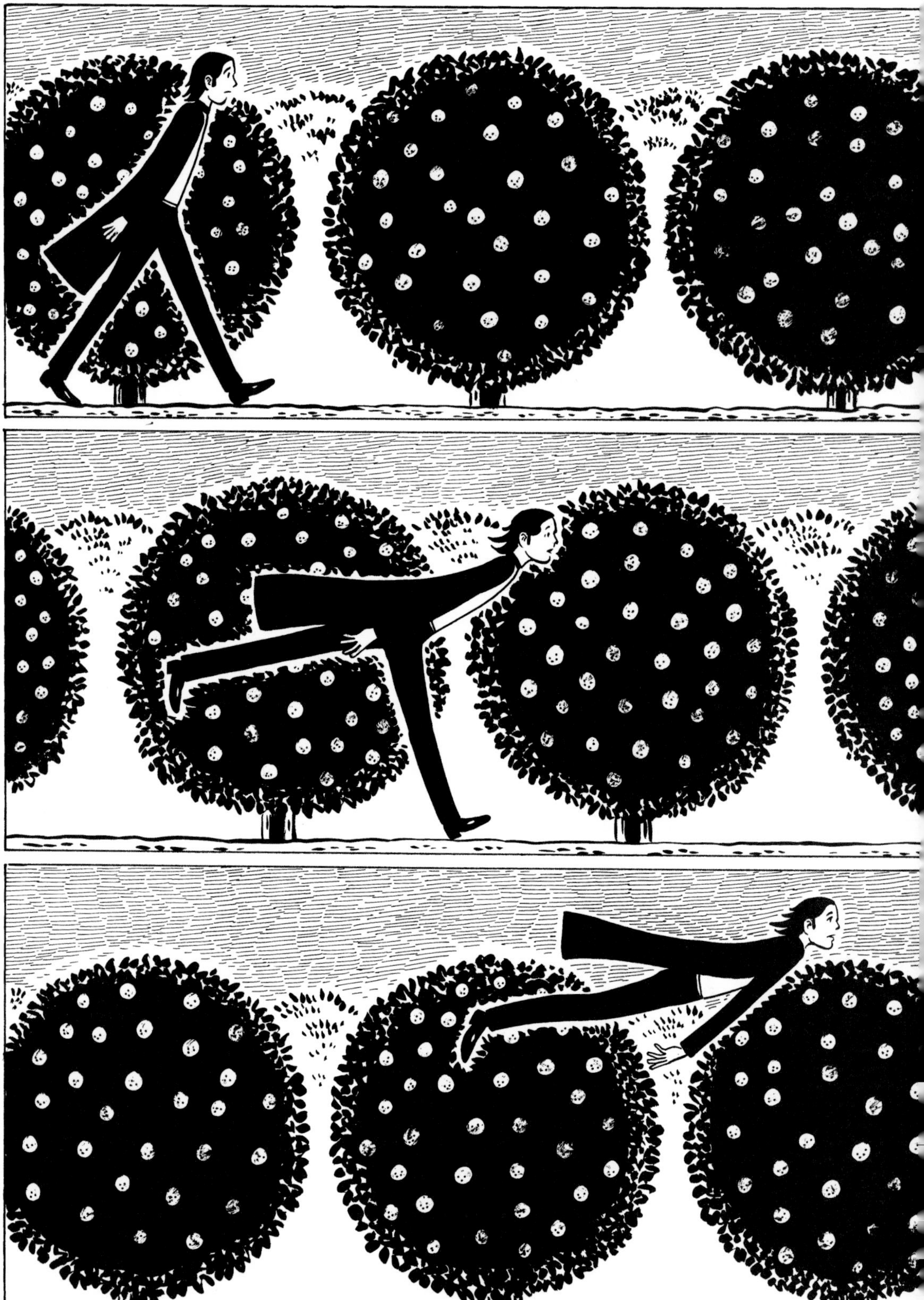

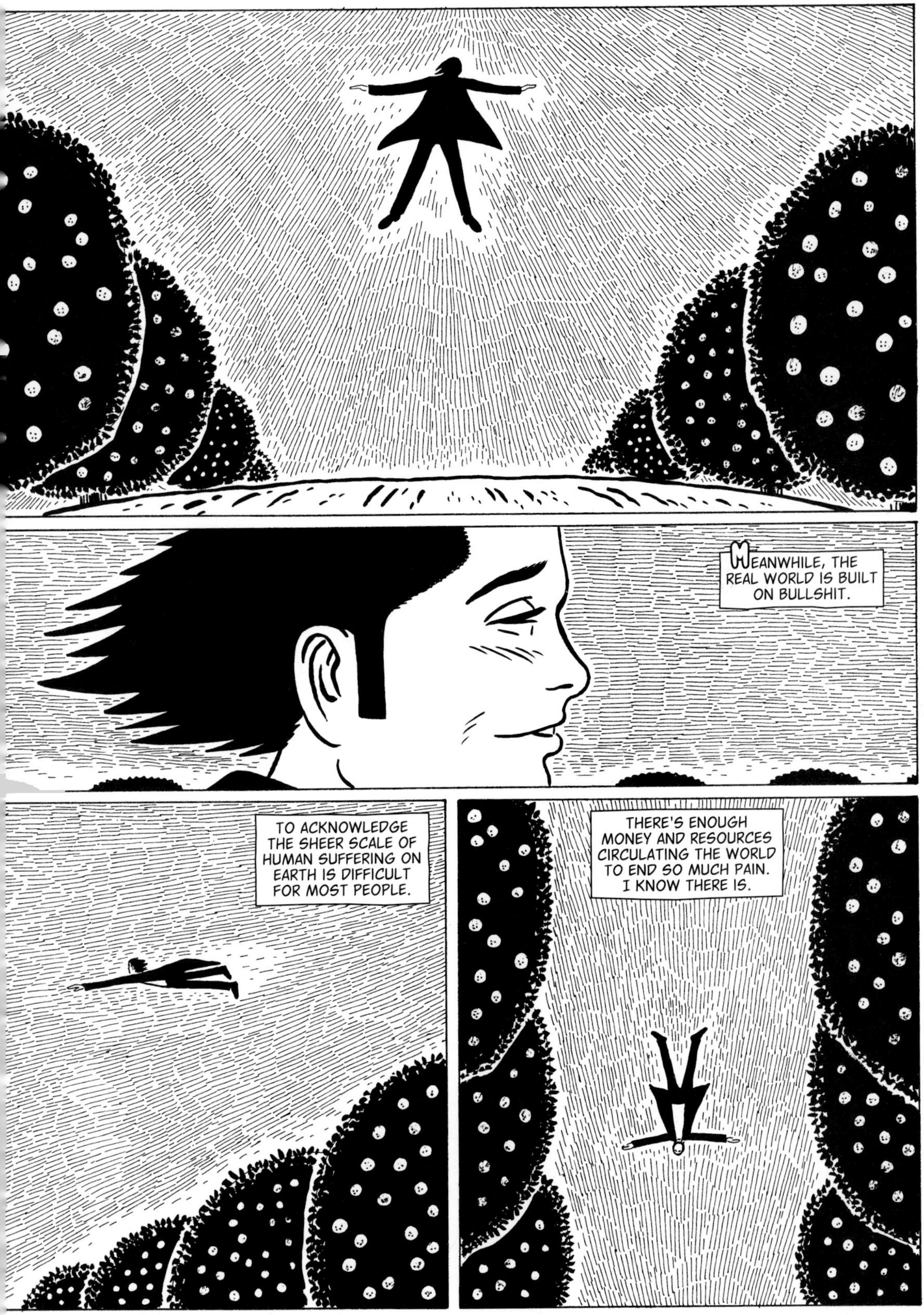
MEANWHILE, THE REAL WORLD IS BUILT ON BULLSHIT.
TO ACKNOWLEDGE THE SHEER SCALE OF HUMAN SUFFERING ON EARTH IS DIFFICULT FOR MOST PEOPLE.
THERE'S ENOUGH MONEY AND RESOURCES CIRCULATING THE WORLD TO END SO MUCH PAIN. I KNOW THERE IS.

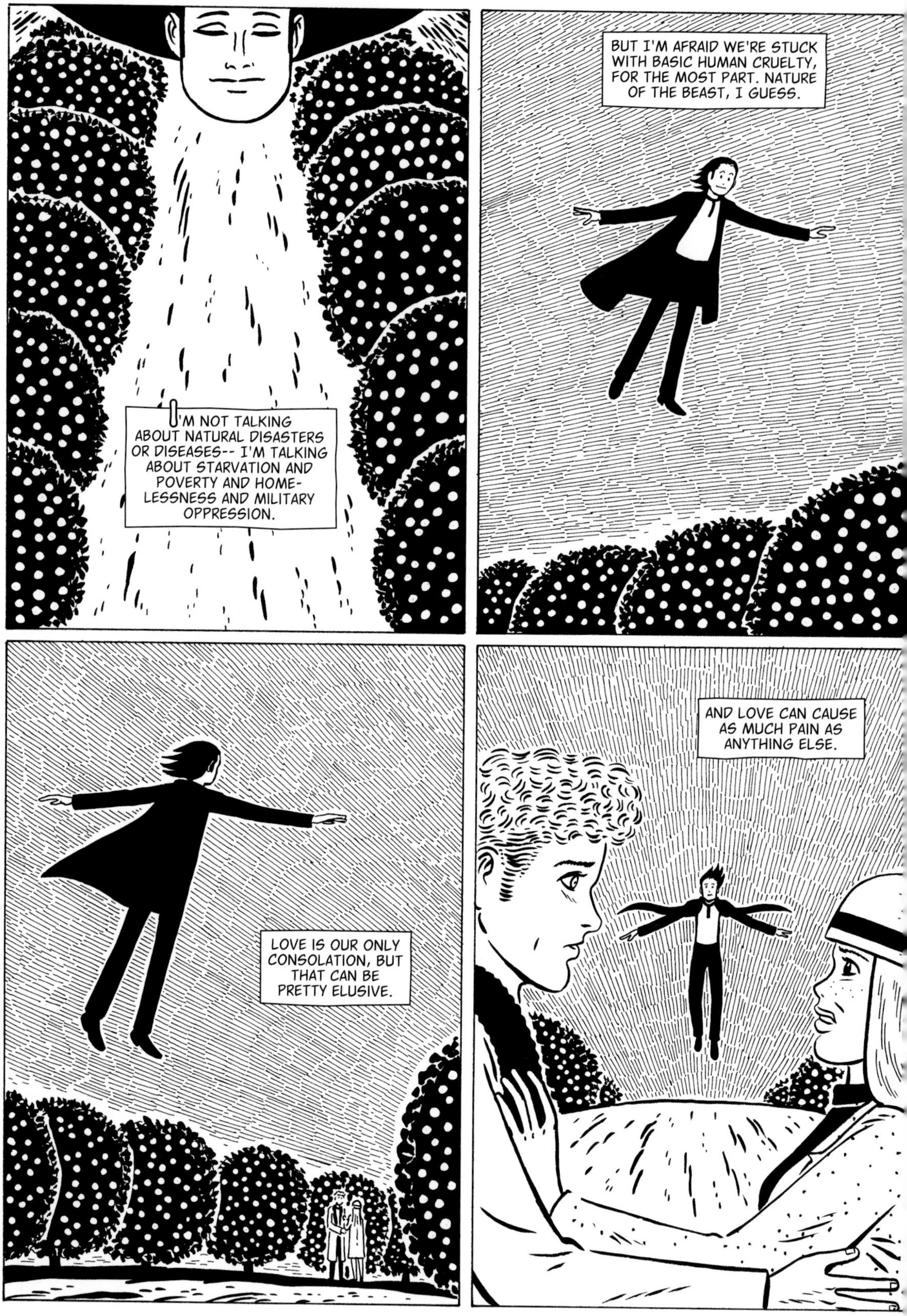
I'M NOT TALKING ABOUT NATURAL DISASTERS OR DISEASES-- I'M TALKING ABOUT STARVATION AND POVERTY AND HOME-LESSNESS AND MILITARY OPPRESSION.
BUT I'M AFRAID WE'RE STUCK WITH BASIC HUMAN CRUELTY, FOR THE MOST PART. NATURE OF THE BEAST, I GUESS.
LOVE IS OUR ONLY CONSOLATION, BUT THAT CAN BE PRETTY ELUSIVE.
AND LOVE CAN CAUSE AS MUCH PAIN AS ANYTHING ELSE.

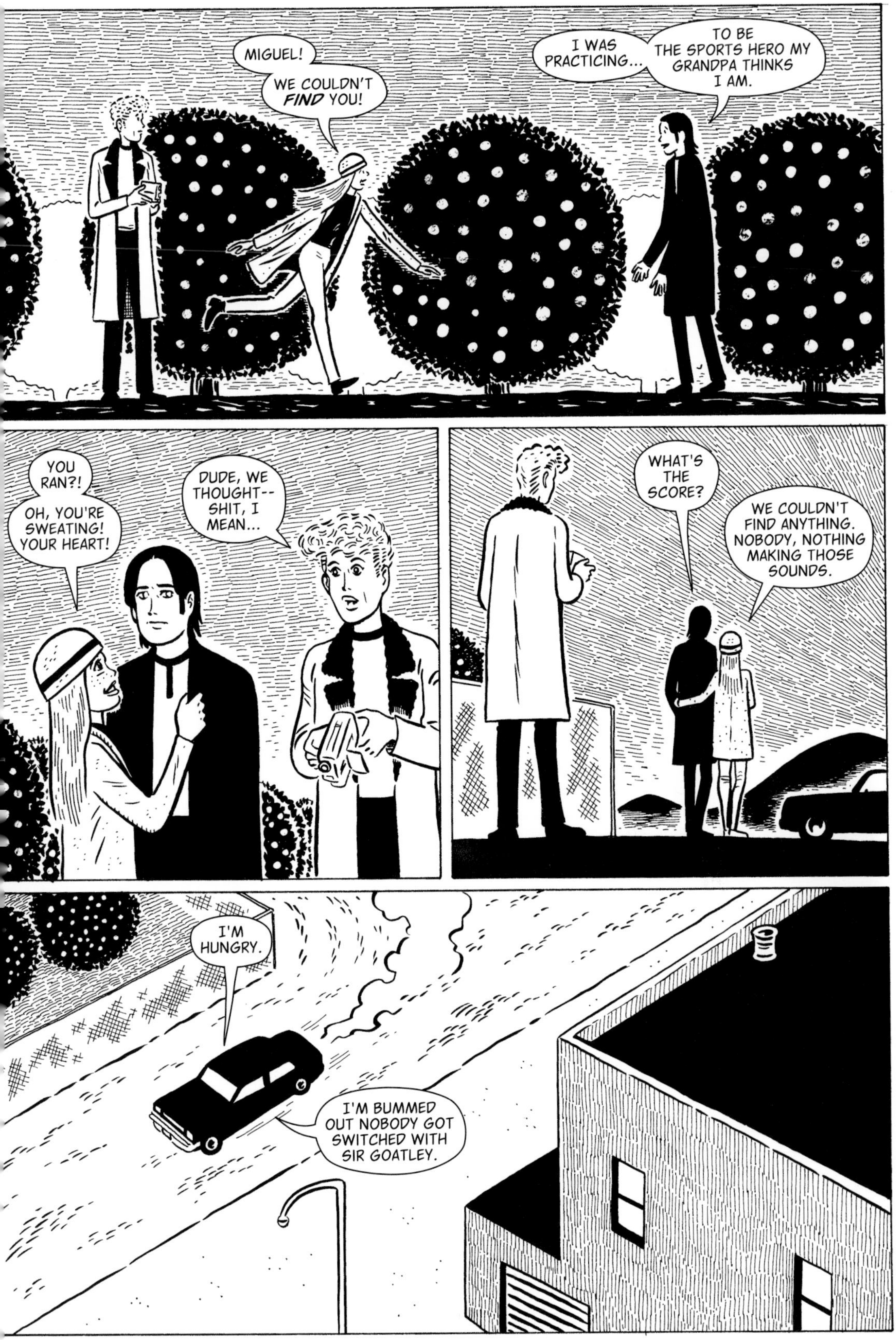
MIGUEL!
WE COULDN'T *FIND* YOU!
I WAS PRACTICING...
TO BE THE SPORTS HERO MY GRANDPA THINKS I AM.
YOU RAN?!
OH, YOU'RE SWEATING! YOUR HEART!
DUDE, WE THOUGHT-- SHIT, I MEAN...
WHAT'S THE SCORE?
WE COULDN'T FIND ANYTHING. NOBODY, NOTHING MAKING THOSE SOUNDS.
I'M HUNGRY.
I'M BUMMED OUT NOBODY GOT SWITCHED WITH SIR GOATLEY.

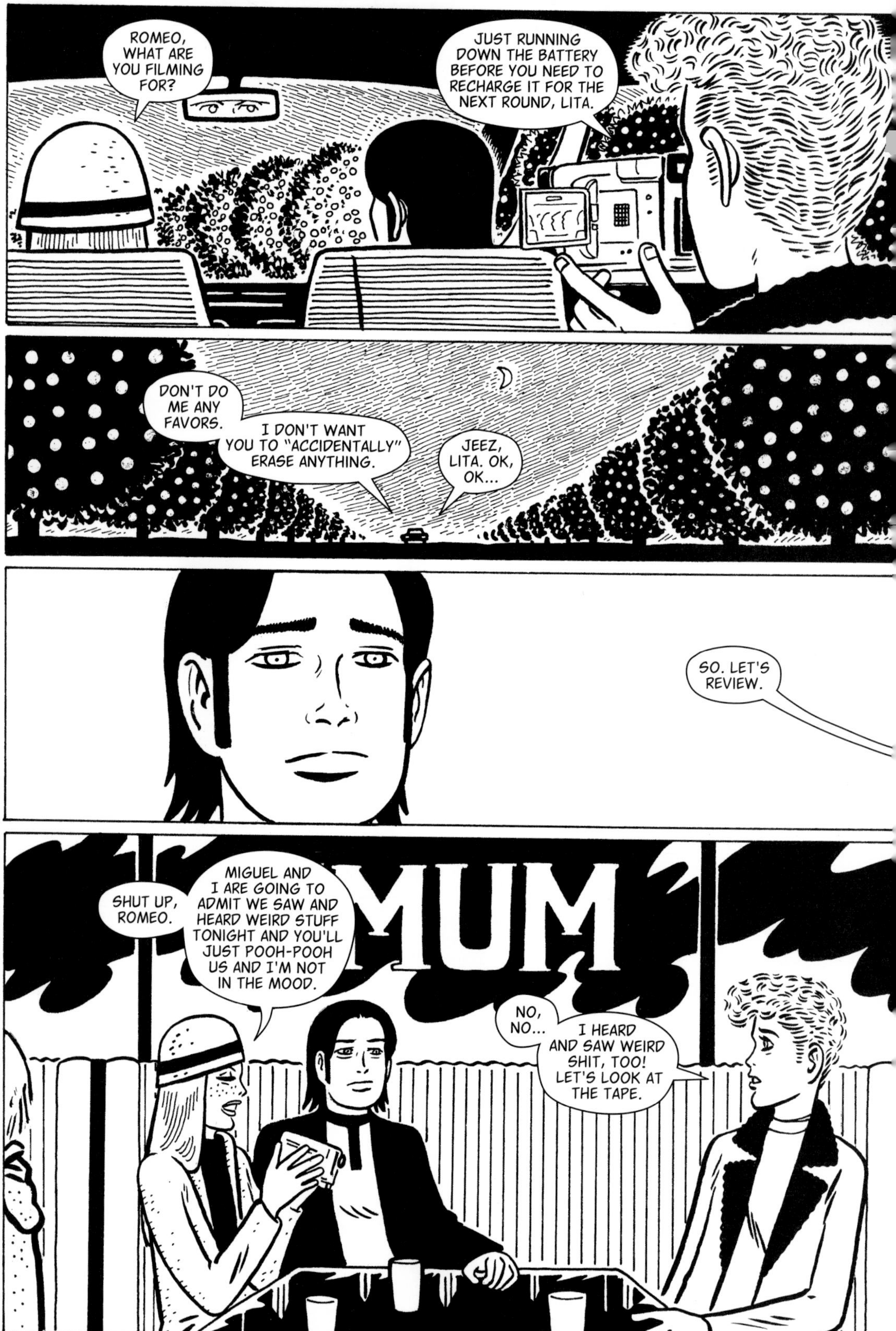
ROMEO, WHAT ARE YOU FILMING FOR?
JUST RUNNING DOWN THE BATTERY BEFORE YOU NEED TO RECHARGE IT FOR THE NEXT ROUND, LITA.
DON'T DO ME ANY FAVORS.
I DON'T WANT YOU TO "ACCIDENTALLY" ERASE ANYTHING.
JEEZ, LITA. OK, OK...
SO. LET'S REVIEW.
MUM
SHUT UP, ROMEO.
MIGUEL AND I ARE GOING TO ADMIT WE SAW AND HEARD WEIRD STUFF TONIGHT AND YOU'LL JUST POOH-POOH US AND I'M NOT IN THE MOOD.
NO, NO...
I HEARD AND SAW WEIRD SHIT, TOO! LET'S LOOK AT THE TAPE.

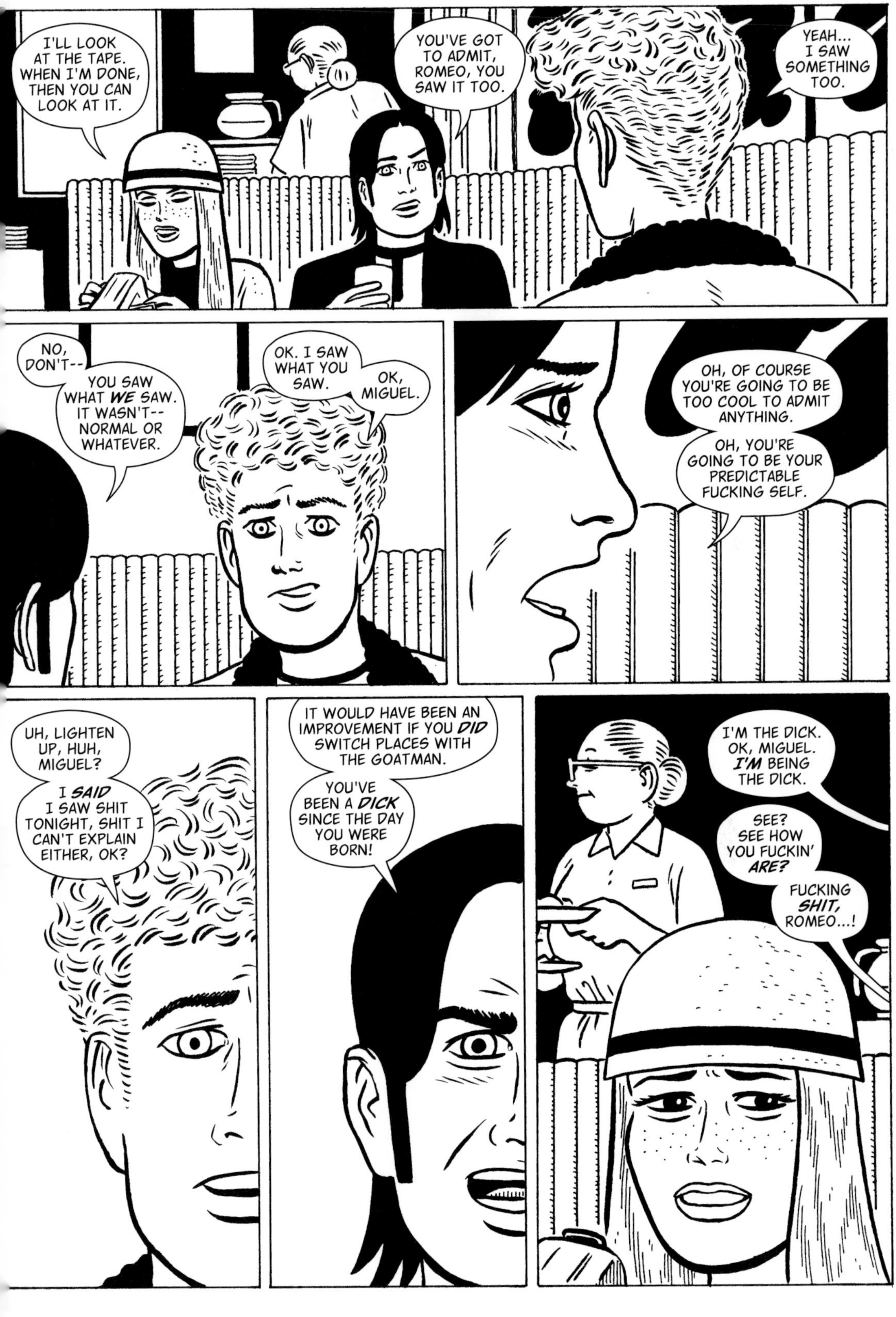

I'LL LOOK AT THE TAPE. WHEN I'M DONE, THEN YOU CAN LOOK AT IT.
YOU'VE GOT TO ADMIT, ROMEO, YOU SAW IT TOO.
YEAH... I SAW SOMETHING TOO.
NO, DON'T--
YOU SAW WHAT *WE* SAW. IT WASN'T-- NORMAL OR WHATEVER.
OK. I SAW WHAT YOU SAW.
OK, MIGUEL.
OH, OF COURSE YOU'RE GOING TO BE TOO COOL TO ADMIT ANYTHING.
OH, YOU'RE GOING TO BE YOUR PREDICTABLE FUCKING SELF.
UH, LIGHTEN UP, HUH, MIGUEL?
I *SAID* I SAW SHIT TONIGHT, SHIT I CAN'T EXPLAIN EITHER, OK?
IT WOULD HAVE BEEN AN IMPROVEMENT IF YOU *DID* SWITCH PLACES WITH THE GOATMAN.
YOU'VE BEEN A *DICK* SINCE THE DAY YOU WERE BORN!
I'M THE DICK. OK, MIGUEL. *I'M* BEING THE DICK.
SEE? SEE HOW YOU FUCKIN' *ARE?*
FUCKING *SHIT,* ROMEO...!

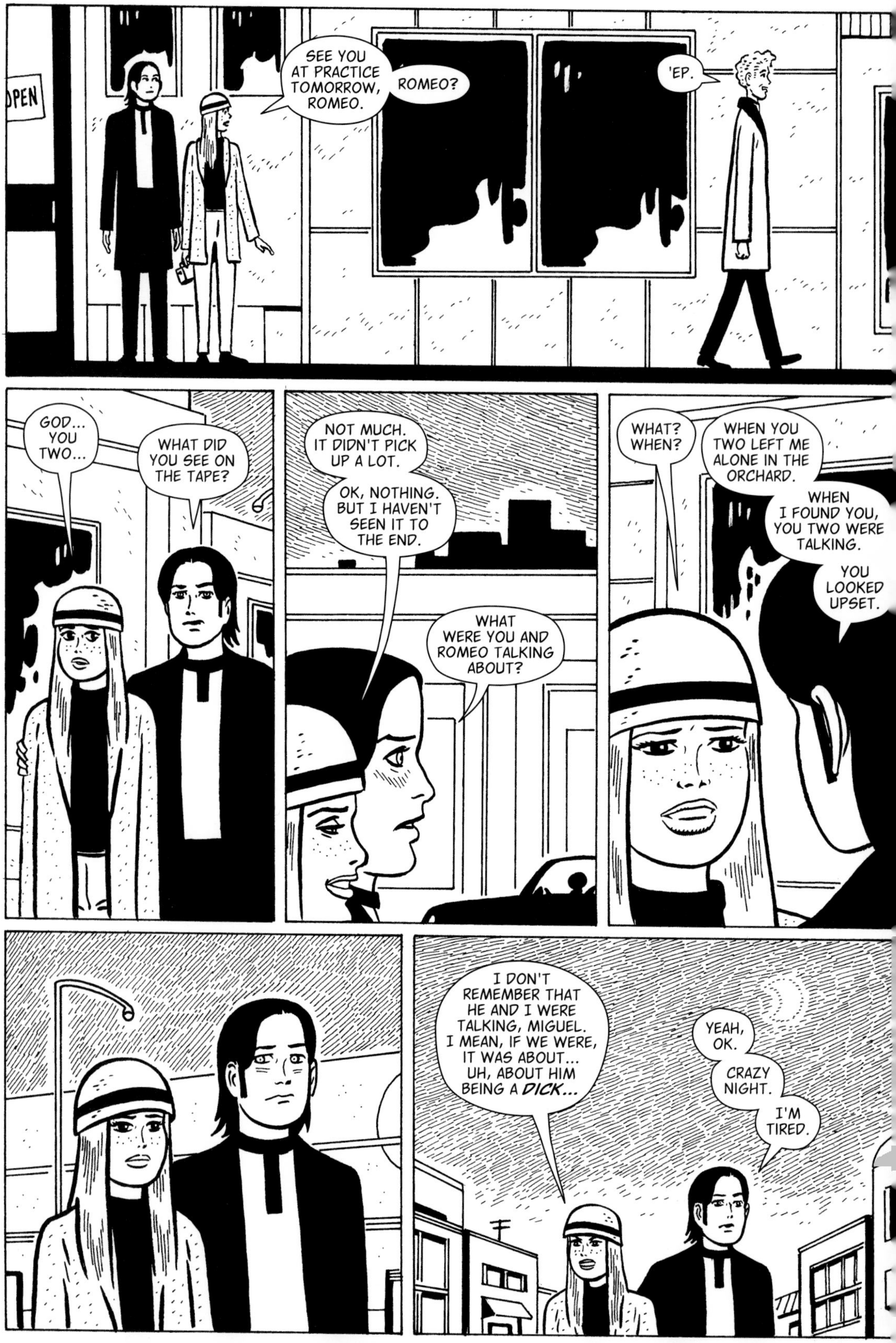
OPEN
SEE YOU AT PRACTICE TOMORROW, ROMEO.
ROMEO?
'EP.
GOD... YOU TWO...
WHAT DID YOU SEE ON THE TAPE?
NOT MUCH. IT DIDN'T PICK UP A LOT.
OK, NOTHING. BUT I HAVEN'T SEEN IT TO THE END.
WHAT WERE YOU AND ROMEO TALKING ABOUT?
WHAT? WHEN?
WHEN YOU TWO LEFT ME ALONE IN THE ORCHARD.
WHEN I FOUND YOU, YOU TWO WERE TALKING.
YOU LOOKED UPSET.
I DON'T REMEMBER THAT HE AND I WERE TALKING, MIGUEL. I MEAN, IF WE WERE, IT WAS ABOUT... UH, ABOUT HIM BEING A *DICK...*
YEAH, OK.
CRAZY NIGHT.
I'M TIRED.

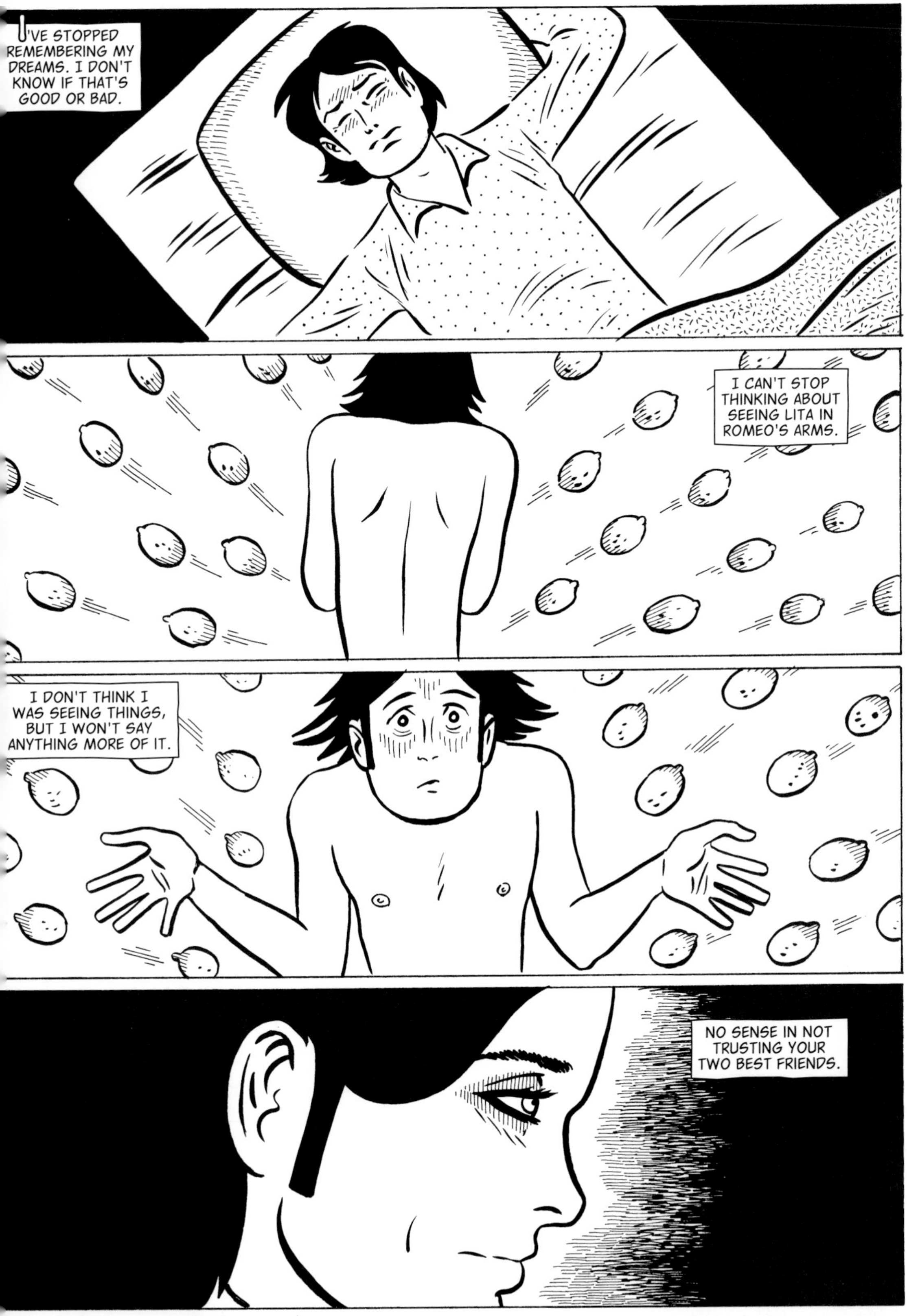
I'VE STOPPED REMEMBERING MY DREAMS. I DON'T KNOW IF THAT'S GOOD OR BAD.
I CAN'T STOP THINKING ABOUT SEEING LITA IN ROMEO'S ARMS.
I DON'T THINK I WAS SEEING THINGS, BUT I WON'T SAY ANYTHING MORE OF IT.
NO SENSE IN NOT TRUSTING YOUR TWO BEST FRIENDS.

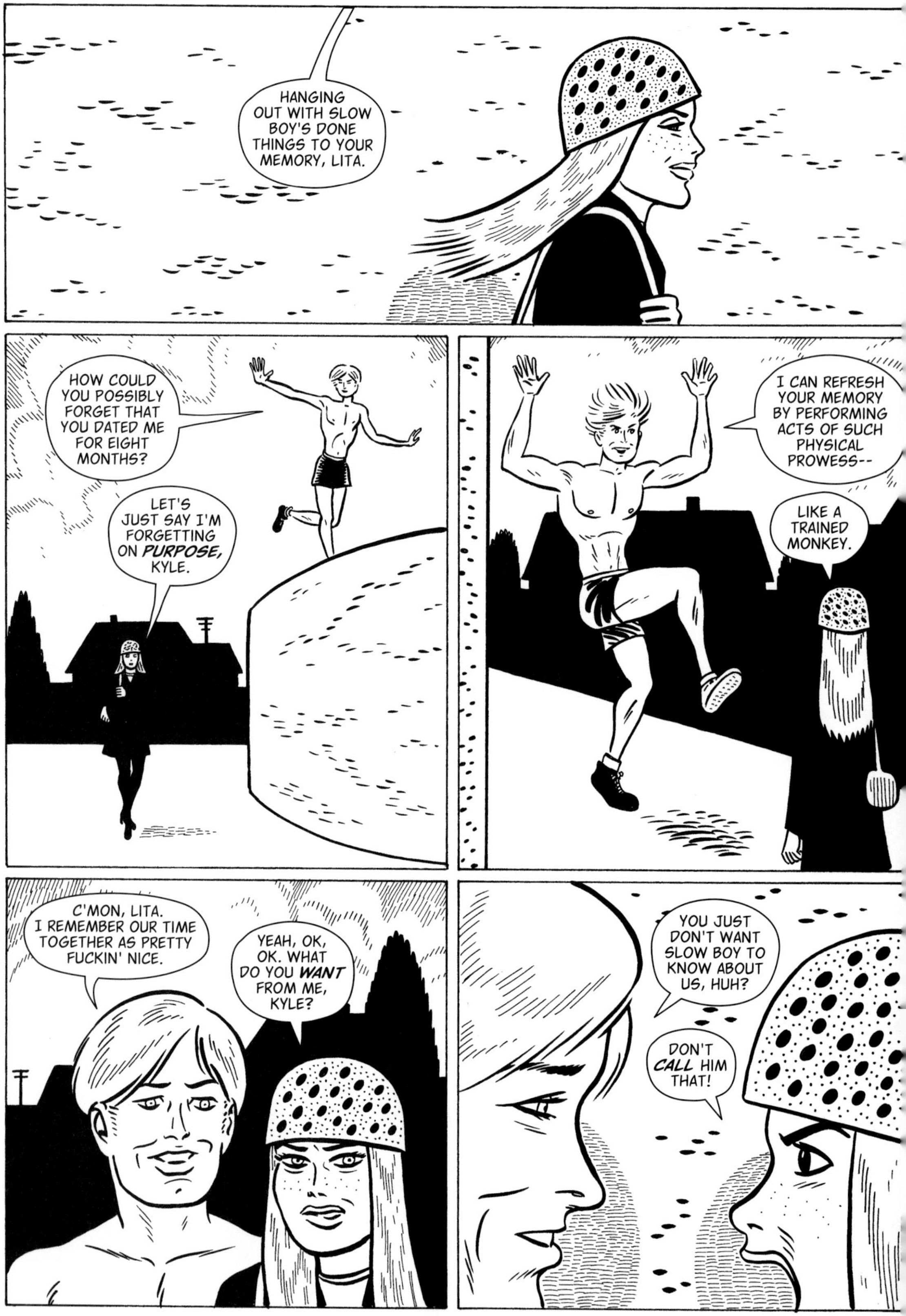
HANGING OUT WITH SLOW BOY'S DONE THINGS TO YOUR MEMORY, LITA.
HOW COULD YOU POSSIBLY FORGET THAT YOU DATED ME FOR EIGHT MONTHS?
LET'S JUST SAY I'M FORGETTING ON *PURPOSE,* KYLE.
I CAN REFRESH YOUR MEMORY BY PERFORMING ACTS OF SUCH PHYSICAL PROWESS--
LIKE A TRAINED MONKEY.
C'MON, LITA. I REMEMBER OUR TIME TOGETHER AS PRETTY FUCKIN' NICE.
YEAH, OK, OK. WHAT DO YOU *WANT* FROM ME, KYLE?
YOU JUST DON'T WANT SLOW BOY TO KNOW ABOUT US, HUH?
DON'T *CALL* HIM THAT!

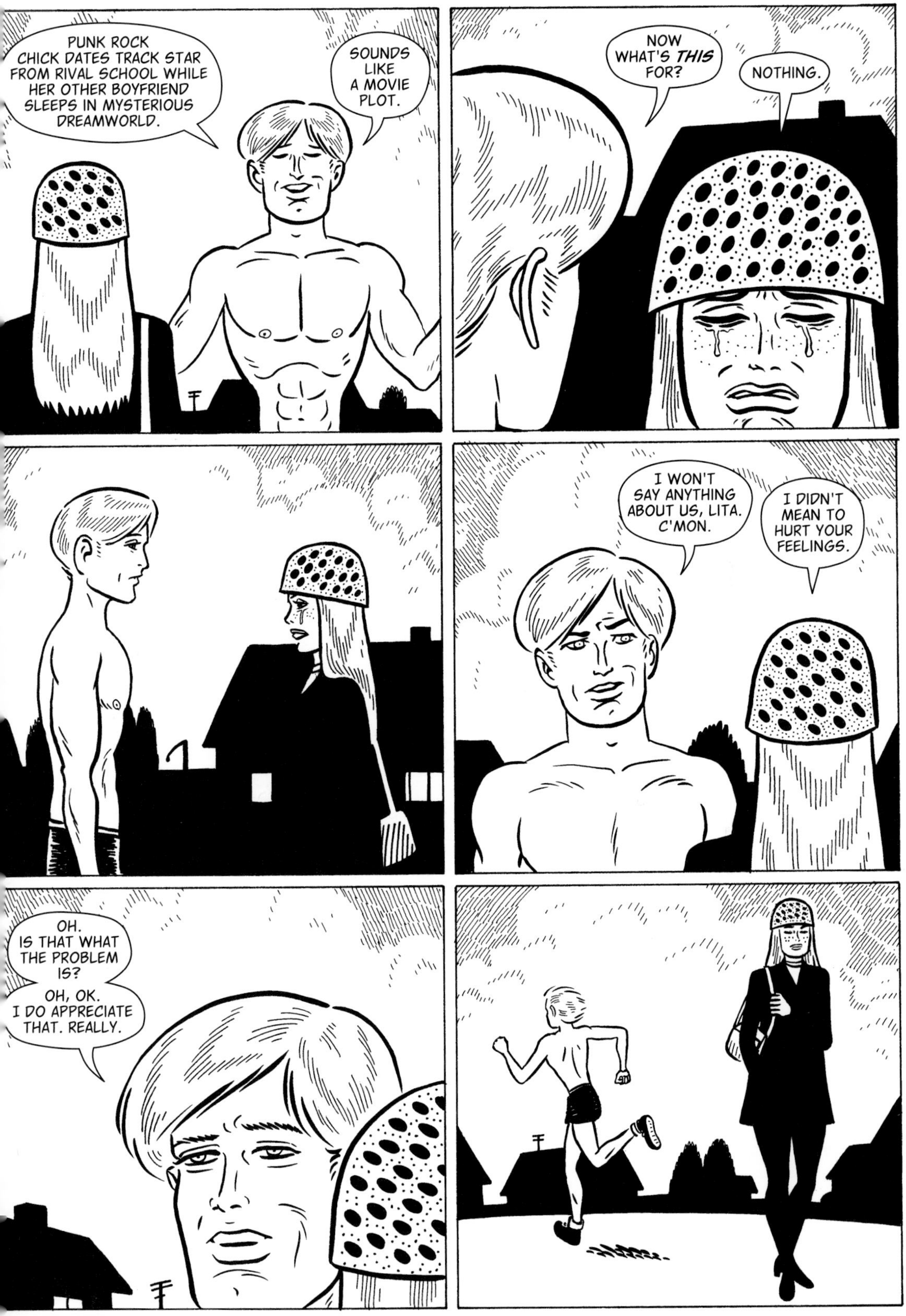
PUNK ROCK CHICK DATES TRACK STAR FROM RIVAL SCHOOL WHILE HER OTHER BOYFRIEND SLEEPS IN MYSTERIOUS DREAMWORLD.
SOUNDS LIKE A MOVIE PLOT.
NOW WHAT'S *THIS* FOR?
NOTHING.
I WON'T SAY ANYTHING ABOUT US, LITA. C'MON.
I DIDN'T MEAN TO HURT YOUR FEELINGS.
OH. IS THAT WHAT THE PROBLEM IS?
OH, OK. I DO APPRECIATE THAT. REALLY.

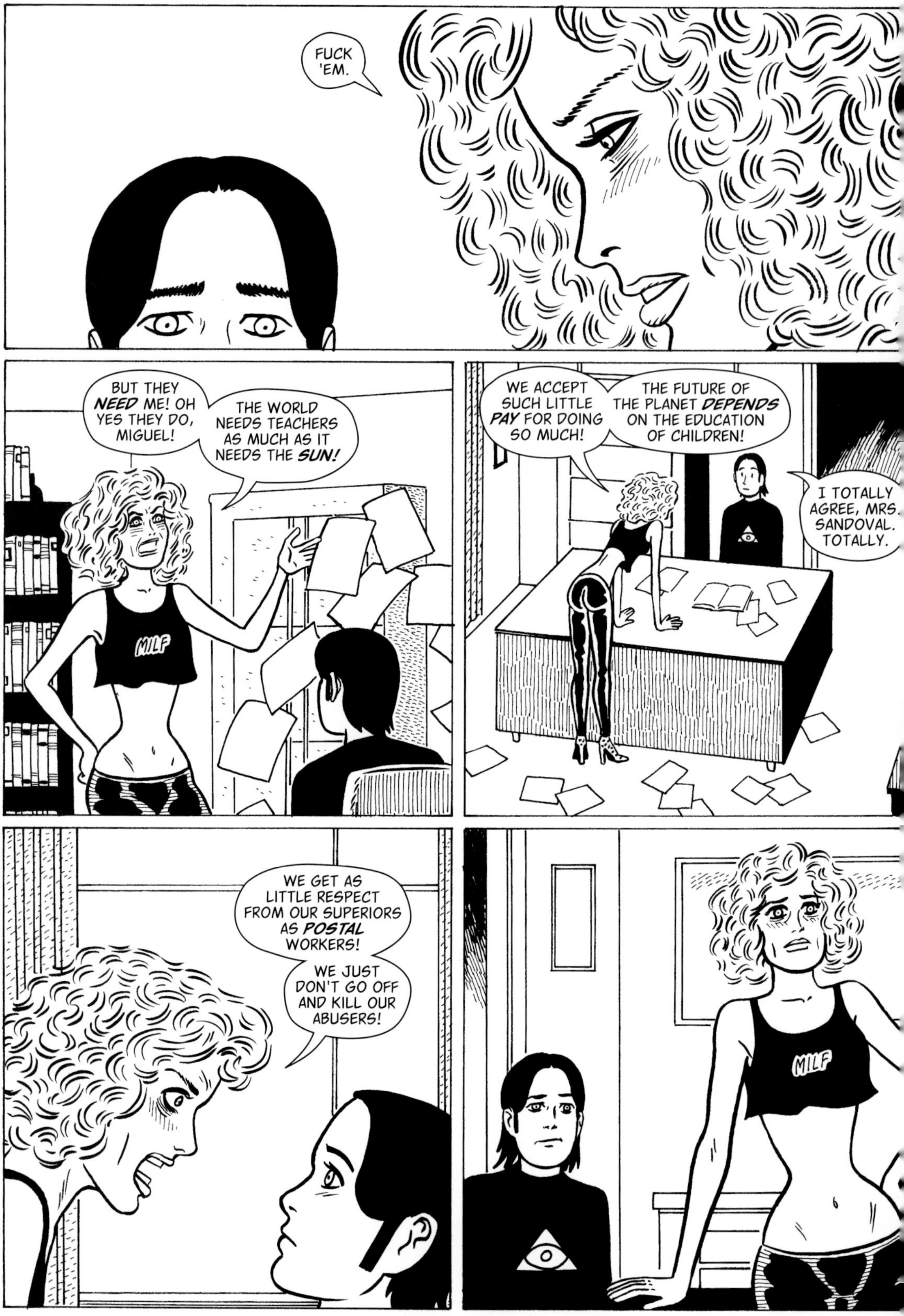
FUCK 'EM.
BUT THEY *NEED* ME! OH YES THEY DO, MIGUEL!
THE WORLD NEEDS TEACHERS AS MUCH AS IT NEEDS THE *SUN!*
MILF
WE ACCEPT SUCH LITTLE *PAY* FOR DOING SO MUCH!
THE FUTURE OF THE PLANET *DEPENDS* ON THE EDUCATION OF CHILDREN!
I TOTALLY AGREE, MRS. SANDOVAL. TOTALLY.
WE GET AS LITTLE RESPECT FROM OUR SUPERIORS AS *POSTAL* WORKERS!
WE JUST DON'T GO OFF AND KILL OUR ABUSERS!
MILF

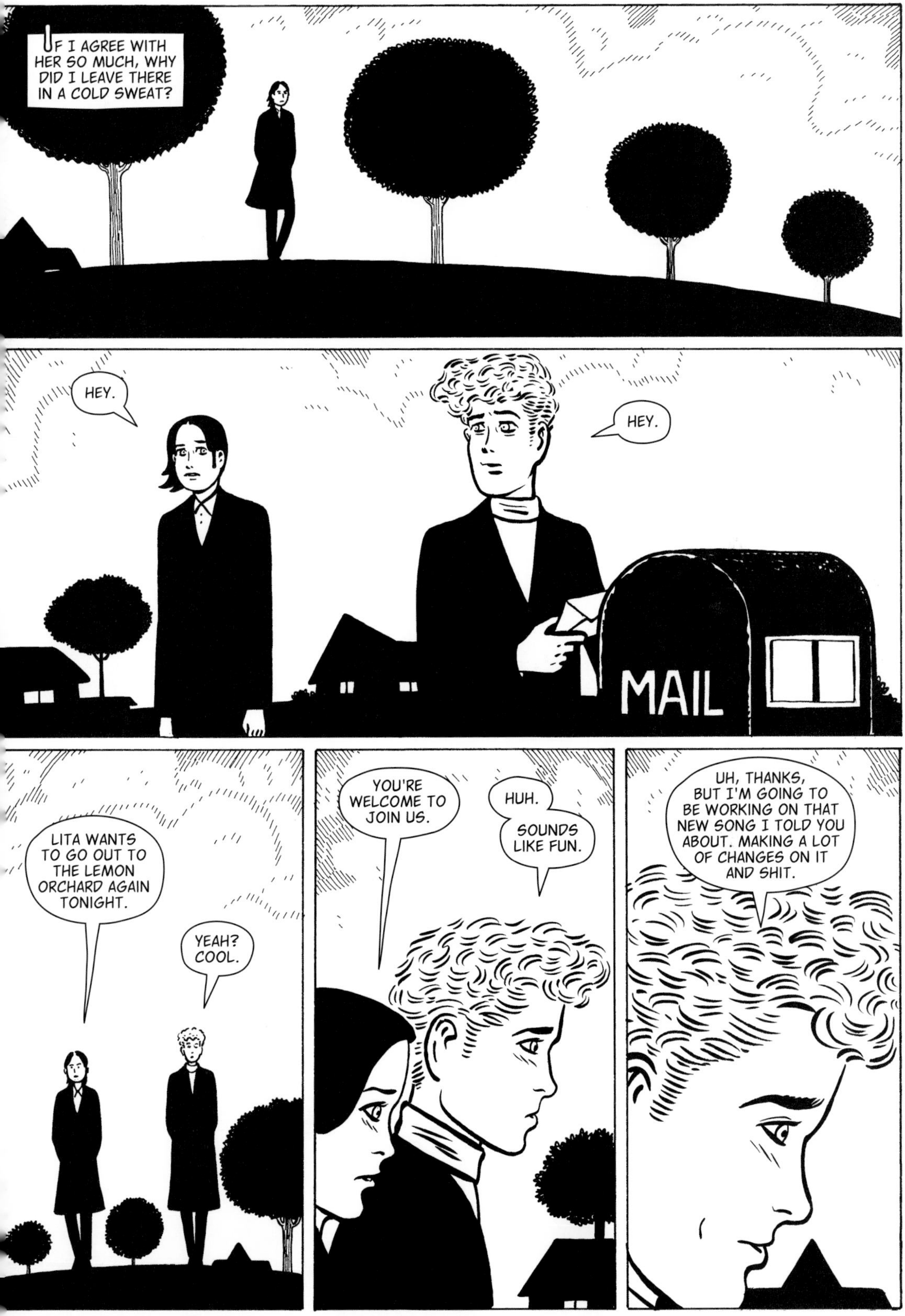
IF I AGREE WITH HER SO MUCH, WHY DID I LEAVE THERE IN A COLD SWEAT?
HEY.
HEY.
MAIL
LITA WANTS TO GO OUT TO THE LEMON ORCHARD AGAIN TONIGHT.
YEAH? COOL.
YOU'RE WELCOME TO JOIN US.
HUH.
SOUNDS LIKE FUN.
UH, THANKS, BUT I'M GOING TO BE WORKING ON THAT NEW SONG I TOLD YOU ABOUT. MAKING A LOT OF CHANGES ON IT AND SHIT.

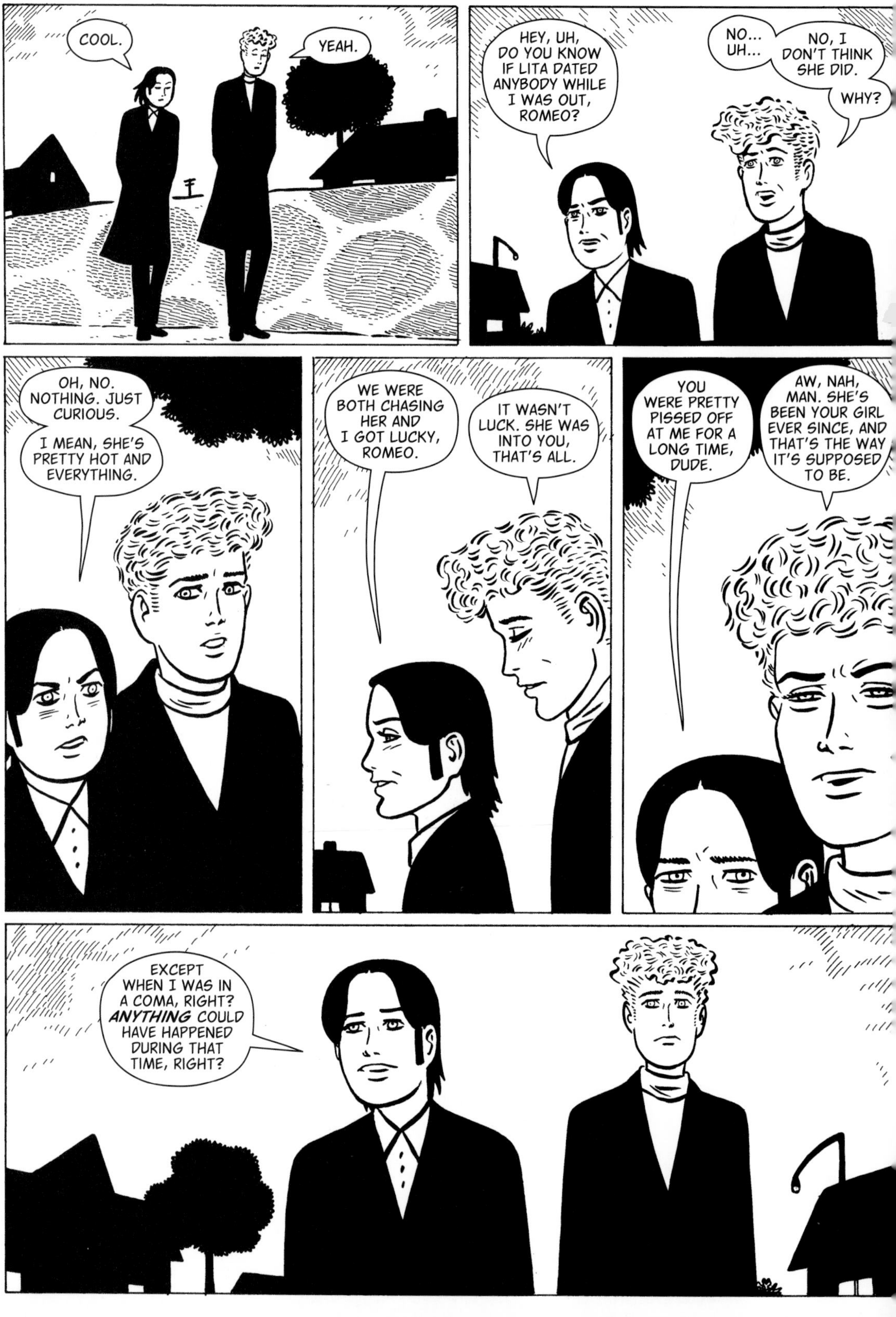
COOL.
YEAH.
HEY, UH, DO YOU KNOW IF LITA DATED ANYBODY WHILE I WAS OUT, ROMEO?
NO... UH...
NO, I DON'T THINK SHE DID.
WHY?
OH, NO. NOTHING. JUST CURIOUS.
I MEAN, SHE'S PRETTY HOT AND EVERYTHING.
WE WERE BOTH CHASING HER AND I GOT LUCKY, ROMEO.
IT WASN'T LUCK. SHE WAS INTO YOU, THAT'S ALL.
YOU WERE PRETTY PISSED OFF AT ME FOR A LONG TIME, DUDE.
AW, NAH, MAN. SHE'S BEEN YOUR GIRL EVER SINCE, AND THAT'S THE WAY IT'S SUPPOSED TO BE.
EXCEPT WHEN I WAS IN A COMA, RIGHT? ANYTHING COULD HAVE HAPPENED DURING THAT TIME, RIGHT?

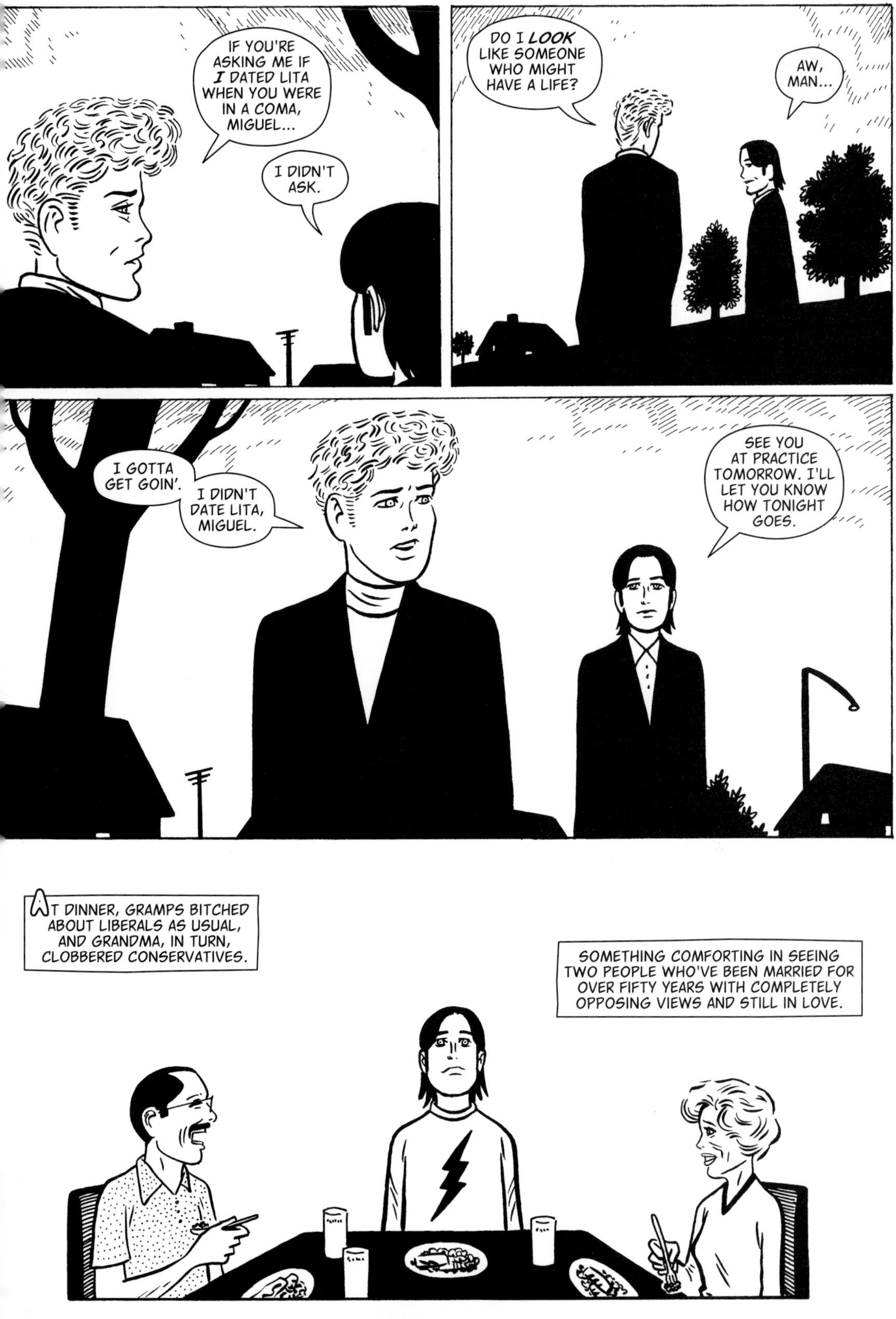
IF YOU'RE ASKING ME IF *I* DATED LITA WHEN YOU WERE IN A COMA, MIGUEL...
I DIDN'T ASK.
DO I ***LOOK*** LIKE SOMEONE WHO MIGHT HAVE A LIFE?
AW, MAN...
I GOTTA GET GOIN'.
I DIDN'T DATE LITA, MIGUEL.
SEE YOU AT PRACTICE TOMORROW. I'LL LET YOU KNOW HOW TONIGHT GOES.
AT DINNER, GRAMPS BITCHED ABOUT LIBERALS AS USUAL, AND GRANDMA, IN TURN, CLOBBERED CONSERVATIVES.
SOMETHING COMFORTING IN SEEING TWO PEOPLE WHO'VE BEEN MARRIED FOR OVER FIFTY YEARS WITH COMPLETELY OPPOSING VIEWS AND STILL IN LOVE.

I WATCHED WHAT WE TAPED AT THE ORCHARD THE OTHER NIGHT, OVER AND OVER, AND DIDN'T SEE ANYTHING UNUSUAL, OK?

OK.

PLAY ▷

I HOOKED IT UP TO THE TV TO SEE IF I WAS MISSING ANYTHING AND I WANT YOU TO SEE.

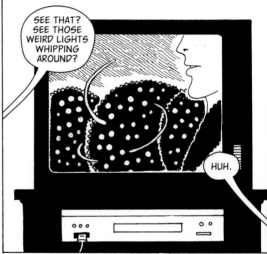

SEE THAT? SEE THOSE WEIRD LIGHTS WHIPPING AROUND?

HUH.

YOU SEE IT A COUPLE MORE TIMES IN DIFFERENT SHOTS.

YEAH...

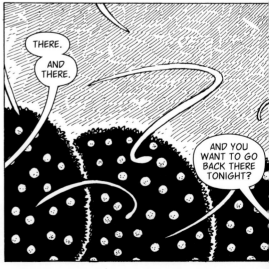

THERE. AND THERE.

AND YOU WANT TO GO BACK THERE TONIGHT?

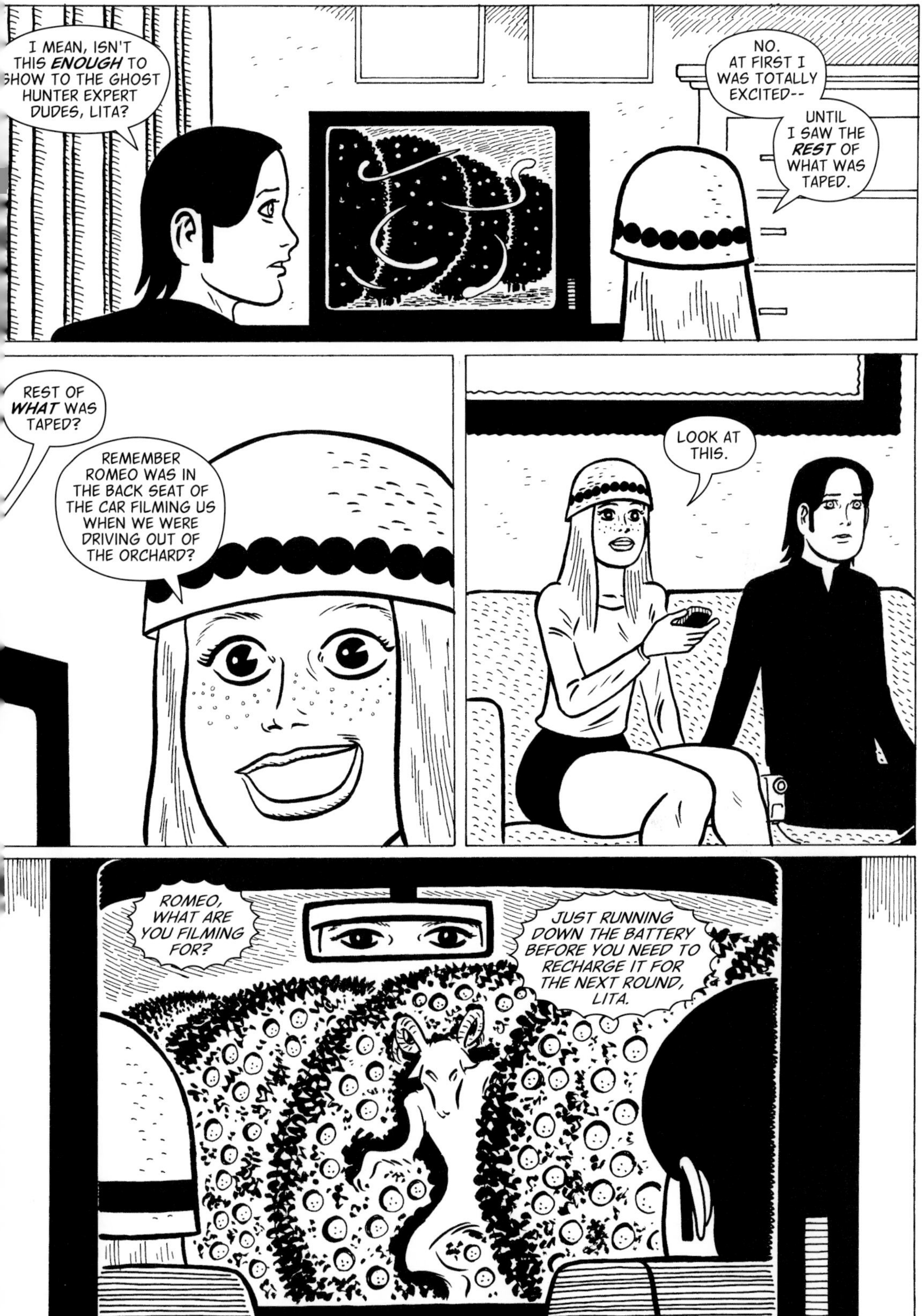
I MEAN, ISN'T THIS **ENOUGH** TO SHOW TO THE GHOST HUNTER EXPERT DUDES, LITA?
NO. AT FIRST I WAS TOTALLY EXCITED--
UNTIL I SAW THE **REST** OF WHAT WAS TAPED.
REST OF **WHAT** WAS TAPED?
REMEMBER ROMEO WAS IN THE BACK SEAT OF THE CAR FILMING US WHEN WE WERE DRIVING OUT OF THE ORCHARD?
LOOK AT THIS.
ROMEO, WHAT ARE YOU FILMING FOR?
JUST RUNNING DOWN THE BATTERY BEFORE YOU NEED TO RECHARGE IT FOR THE NEXT ROUND, LITA.

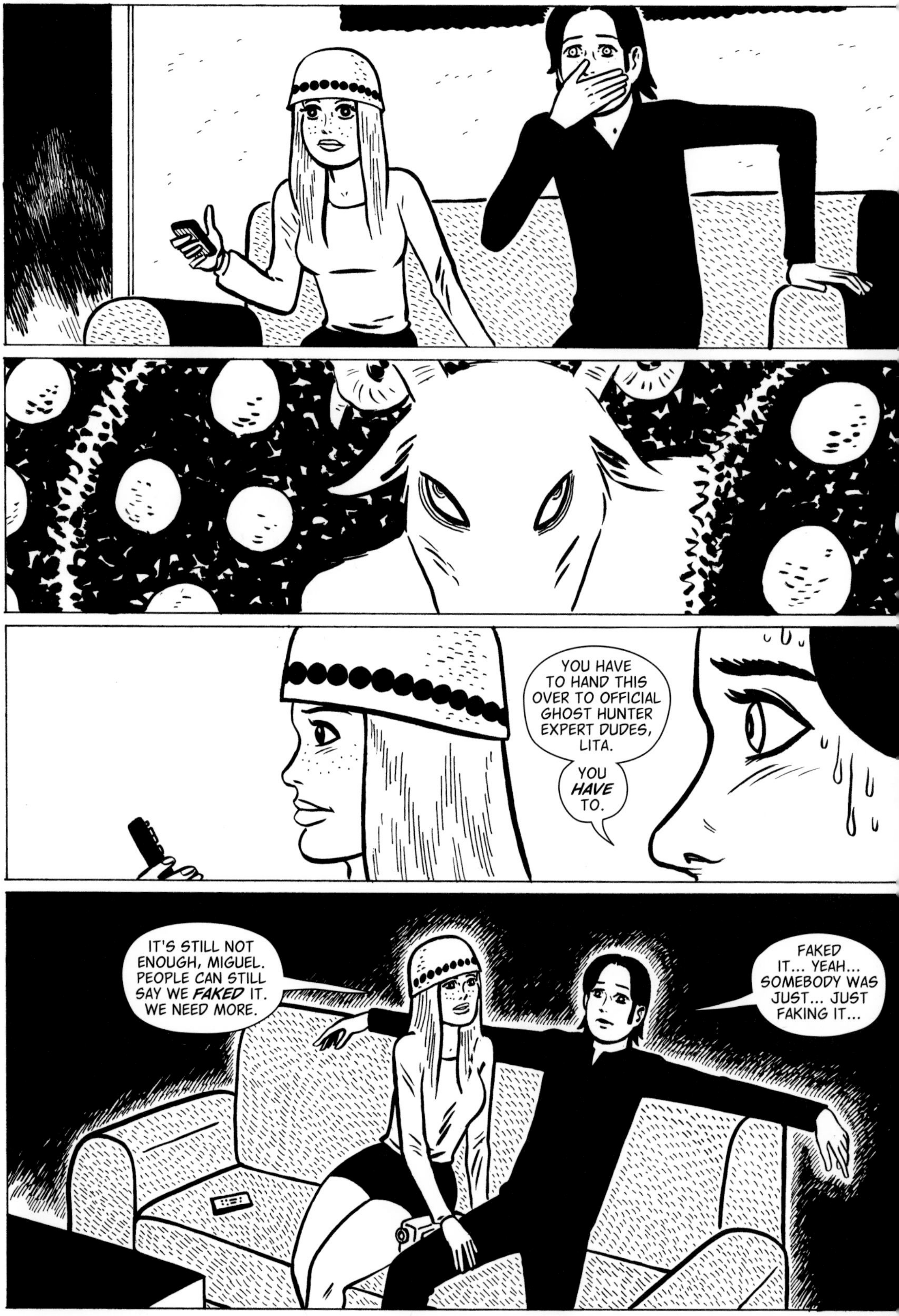
YOU HAVE TO HAND THIS OVER TO OFFICIAL GHOST HUNTER EXPERT DUDES, LITA.
YOU *HAVE* TO.
IT'S STILL NOT ENOUGH, MIGUEL. PEOPLE CAN STILL SAY WE *FAKED* IT. WE NEED MORE.
FAKED IT... YEAH... SOMEBODY WAS JUST... JUST FAKING IT...

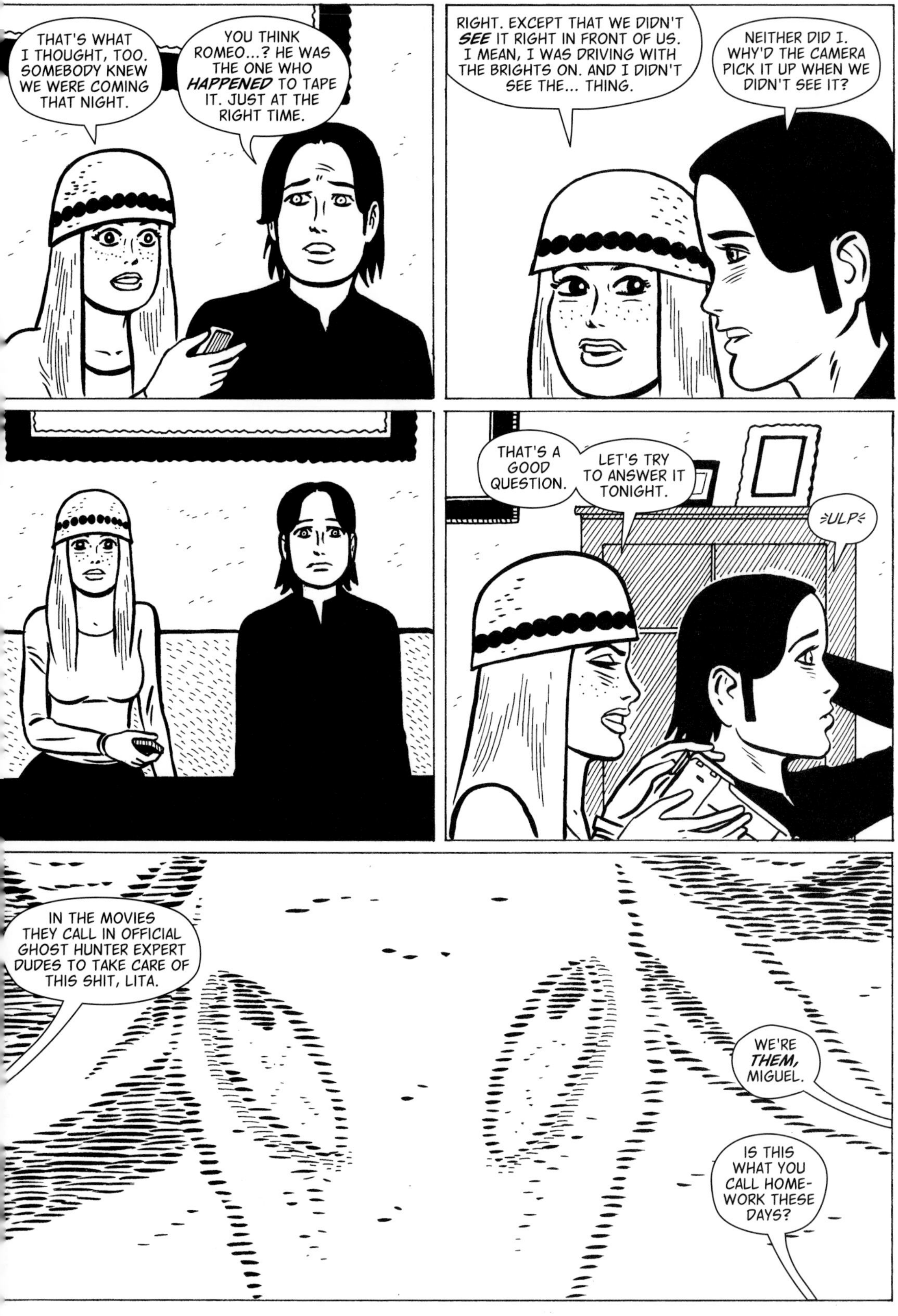
THAT'S WHAT I THOUGHT, TOO. SOMEBODY KNEW WE WERE COMING THAT NIGHT.
YOU THINK ROMEO...? HE WAS THE ONE WHO *HAPPENED* TO TAPE IT. JUST AT THE RIGHT TIME.
RIGHT. EXCEPT THAT WE DIDN'T *SEE* IT RIGHT IN FRONT OF US. I MEAN, I WAS DRIVING WITH THE BRIGHTS ON. AND I DIDN'T SEE THE... THING.
NEITHER DID I. WHY'D THE CAMERA PICK IT UP WHEN WE DIDN'T SEE IT?
THAT'S A GOOD QUESTION.
LET'S TRY TO ANSWER IT TONIGHT.
ULP
IN THE MOVIES THEY CALL IN OFFICIAL GHOST HUNTER EXPERT DUDES TO TAKE CARE OF THIS SHIT, LITA.
WE'RE *THEM,* MIGUEL.
IS THIS WHAT YOU CALL HOME-WORK THESE DAYS?

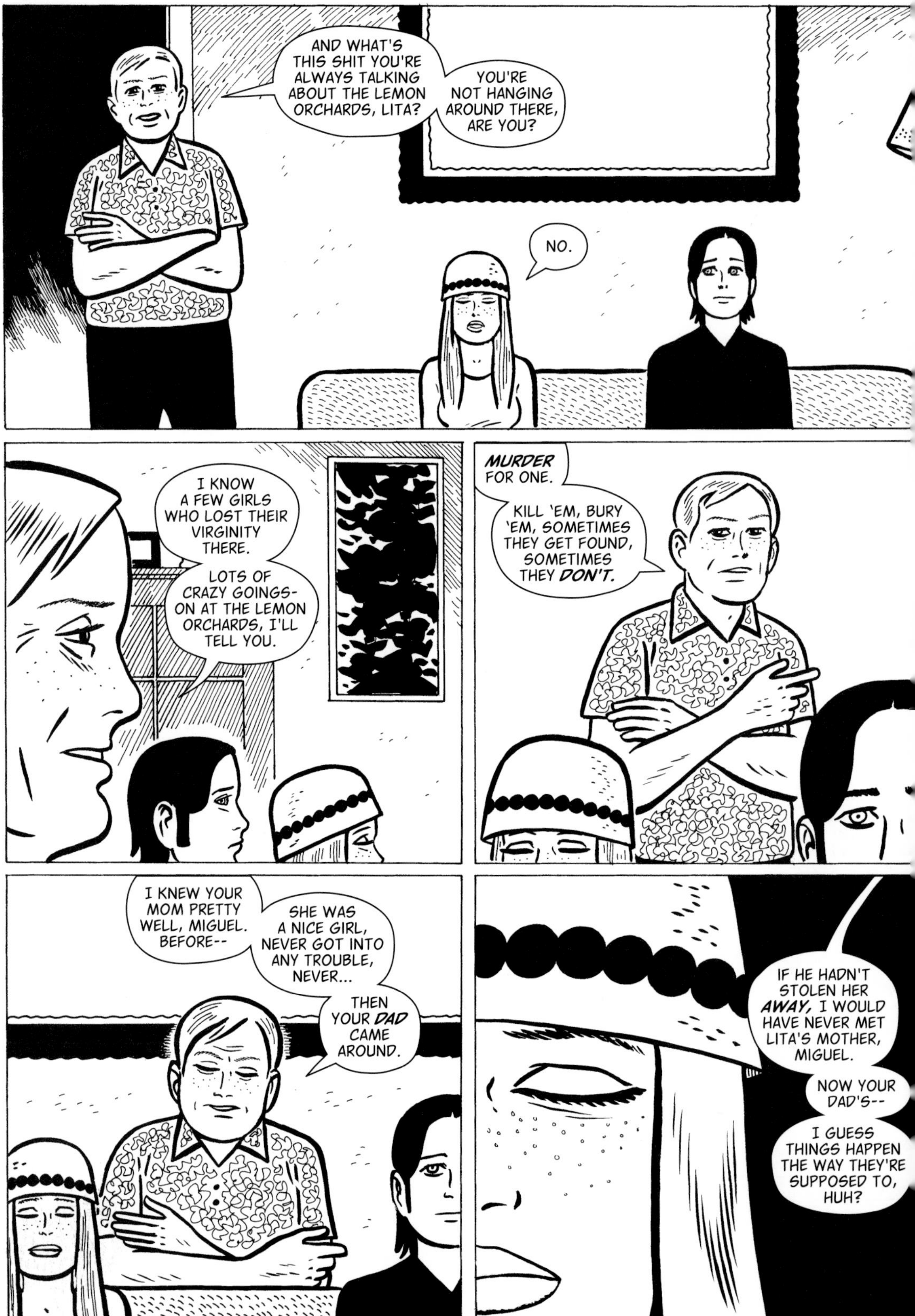
AND WHAT'S THIS SHIT YOU'RE ALWAYS TALKING ABOUT THE LEMON ORCHARDS, LITA?
YOU'RE NOT HANGING AROUND THERE, ARE YOU?
NO.
I KNOW A FEW GIRLS WHO LOST THEIR VIRGINITY THERE.
LOTS OF CRAZY GOINGS-ON AT THE LEMON ORCHARDS, I'LL TELL YOU.
MURDER FOR ONE.
KILL 'EM, BURY 'EM, SOMETIMES THEY GET FOUND, SOMETIMES THEY DON'T.
I KNEW YOUR MOM PRETTY WELL, MIGUEL. BEFORE--
SHE WAS A NICE GIRL, NEVER GOT INTO ANY TROUBLE, NEVER...
THEN YOUR DAD CAME AROUND.
IF HE HADN'T STOLEN HER AWAY, I WOULD HAVE NEVER MET LITA'S MOTHER, MIGUEL.
NOW YOUR DAD'S--
I GUESS THINGS HAPPEN THE WAY THEY'RE SUPPOSED TO, HUH?

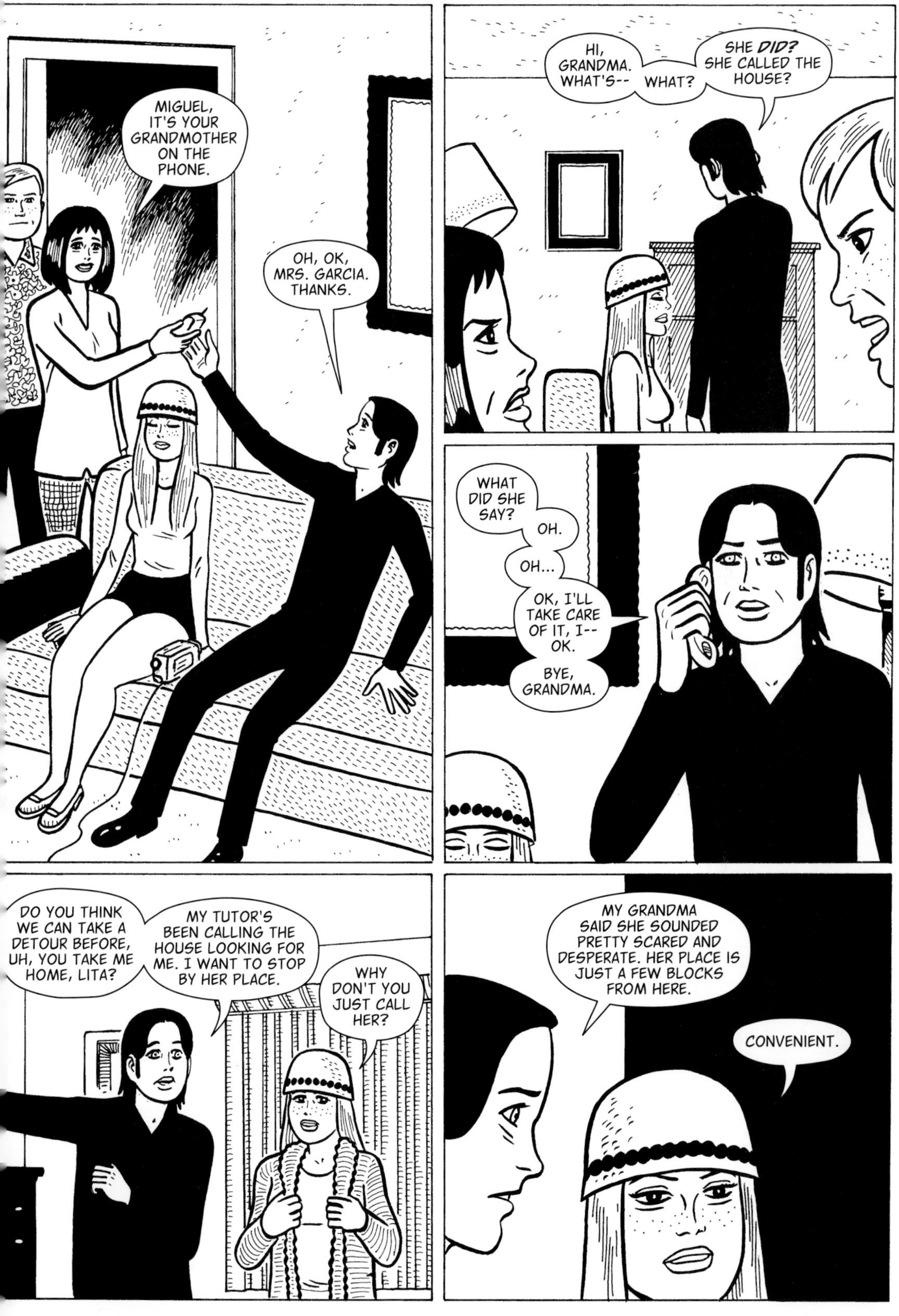
MIGUEL, IT'S YOUR GRANDMOTHER ON THE PHONE.
OH, OK, MRS. GARCIA. THANKS.
HI, GRANDMA. WHAT'S--
WHAT?
SHE *DID?* SHE CALLED THE HOUSE?
WHAT DID SHE SAY?
OH.
OH...
OK, I'LL TAKE CARE OF IT, I-- OK.
BYE, GRANDMA.
DO YOU THINK WE CAN TAKE A DETOUR BEFORE, UH, YOU TAKE ME HOME, LITA?
MY TUTOR'S BEEN CALLING THE HOUSE LOOKING FOR ME. I WANT TO STOP BY HER PLACE.
WHY DON'T YOU JUST CALL HER?
MY GRANDMA SAID SHE SOUNDED PRETTY SCARED AND DESPERATE. HER PLACE IS JUST A FEW BLOCKS FROM HERE.
CONVENIENT.

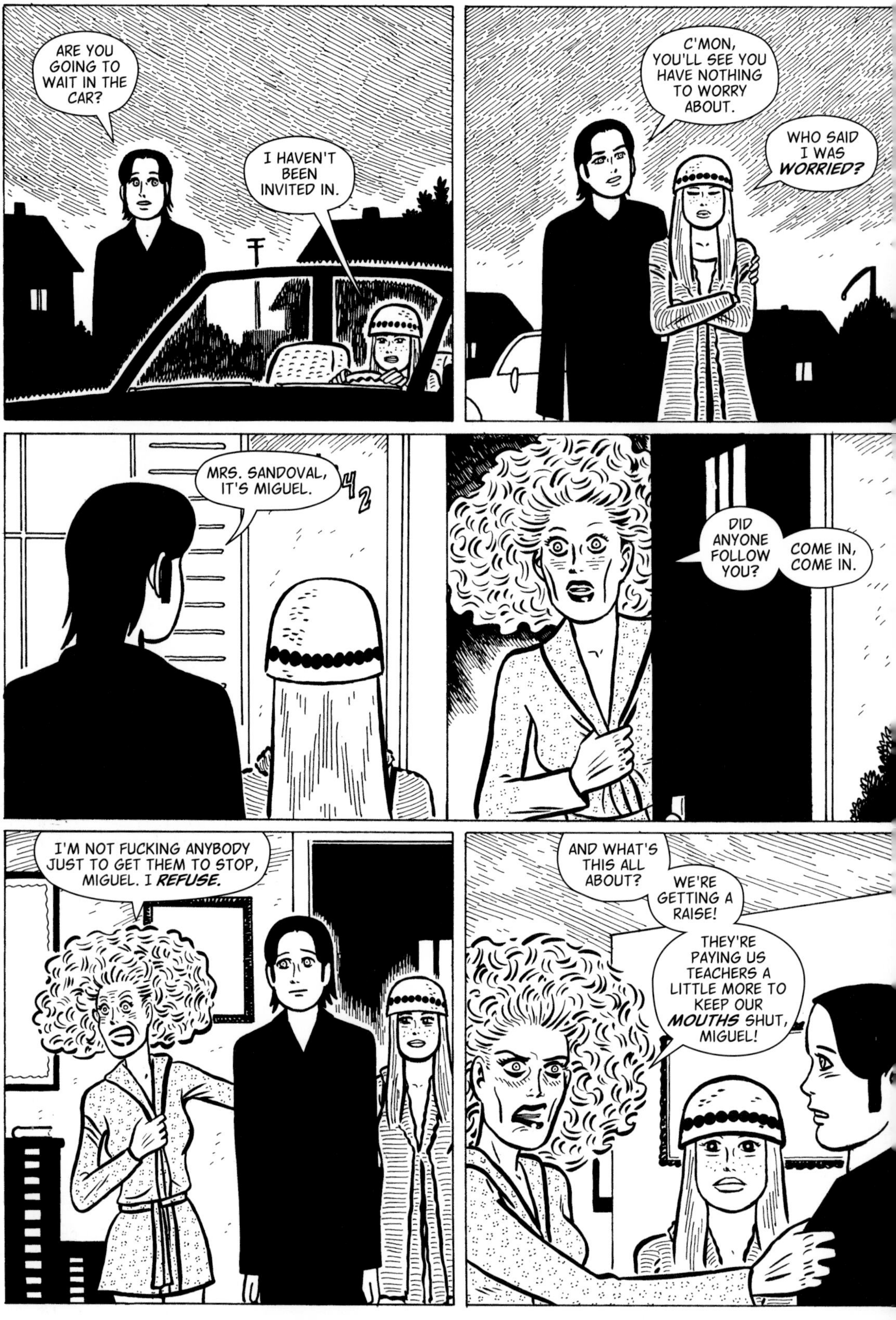
ARE YOU GOING TO WAIT IN THE CAR?
I HAVEN'T BEEN INVITED IN.
C'MON, YOU'LL SEE YOU HAVE NOTHING TO WORRY ABOUT.
WHO SAID I WAS WORRIED?
MRS. SANDOVAL, IT'S MIGUEL.
42
DID ANYONE FOLLOW YOU?
COME IN, COME IN.
I'M NOT FUCKING ANYBODY JUST TO GET THEM TO STOP, MIGUEL. I REFUSE.
AND WHAT'S THIS ALL ABOUT?
WE'RE GETTING A RAISE!
THEY'RE PAYING US TEACHERS A LITTLE MORE TO KEEP OUR MOUTHS SHUT, MIGUEL!

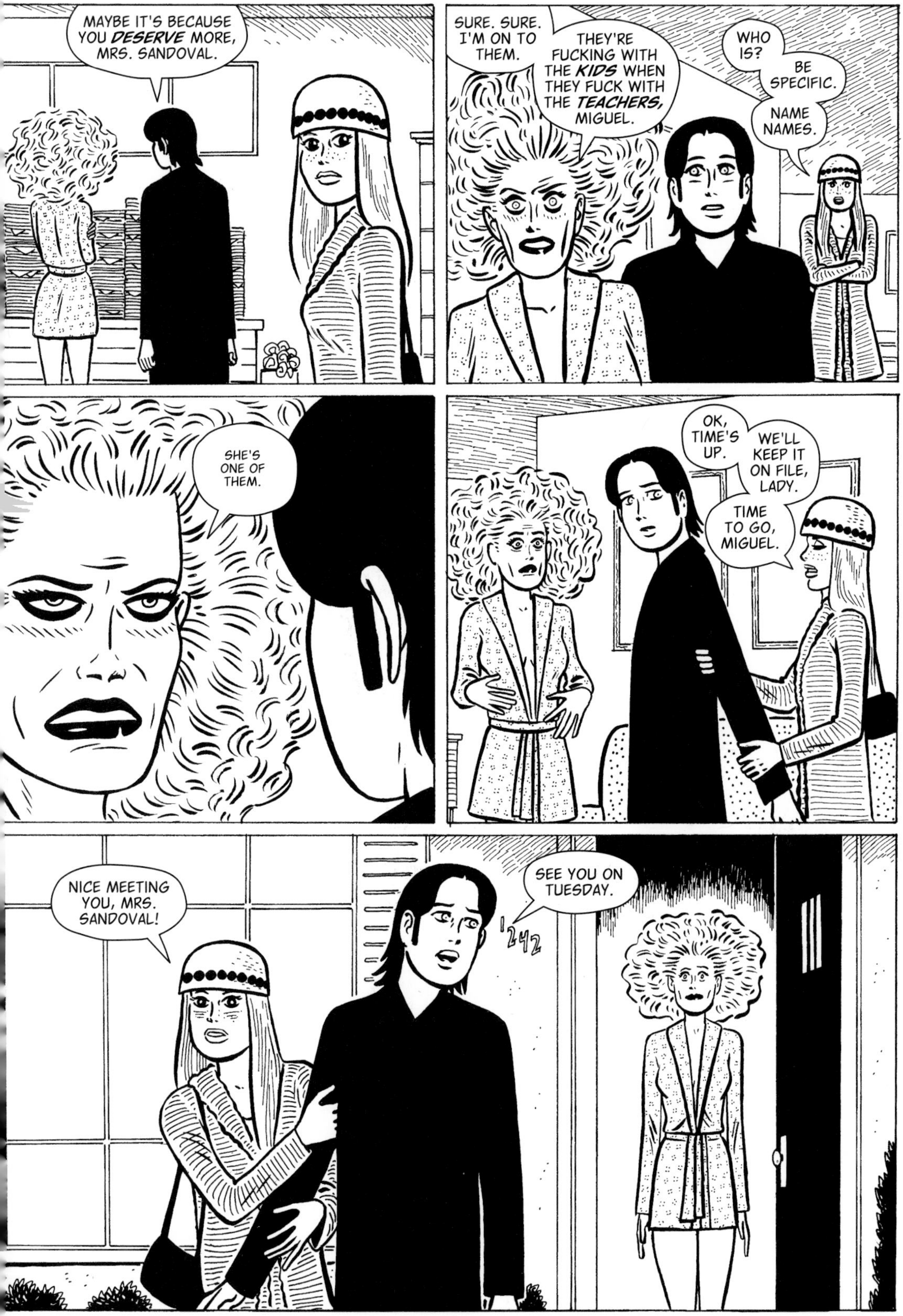
MAYBE IT'S BECAUSE YOU *DESERVE* MORE, MRS. SANDOVAL.
SURE. SURE. I'M ON TO THEM.
THEY'RE FUCKING WITH THE *KIDS* WHEN THEY FUCK WITH THE *TEACHERS,* MIGUEL.
WHO IS?
BE SPECIFIC.
NAME NAMES.
SHE'S ONE OF THEM.
OK, TIME'S UP.
WE'LL KEEP IT ON FILE, LADY.
TIME TO GO, MIGUEL.
NICE MEETING YOU, MRS. SANDOVAL!
SEE YOU ON TUESDAY.

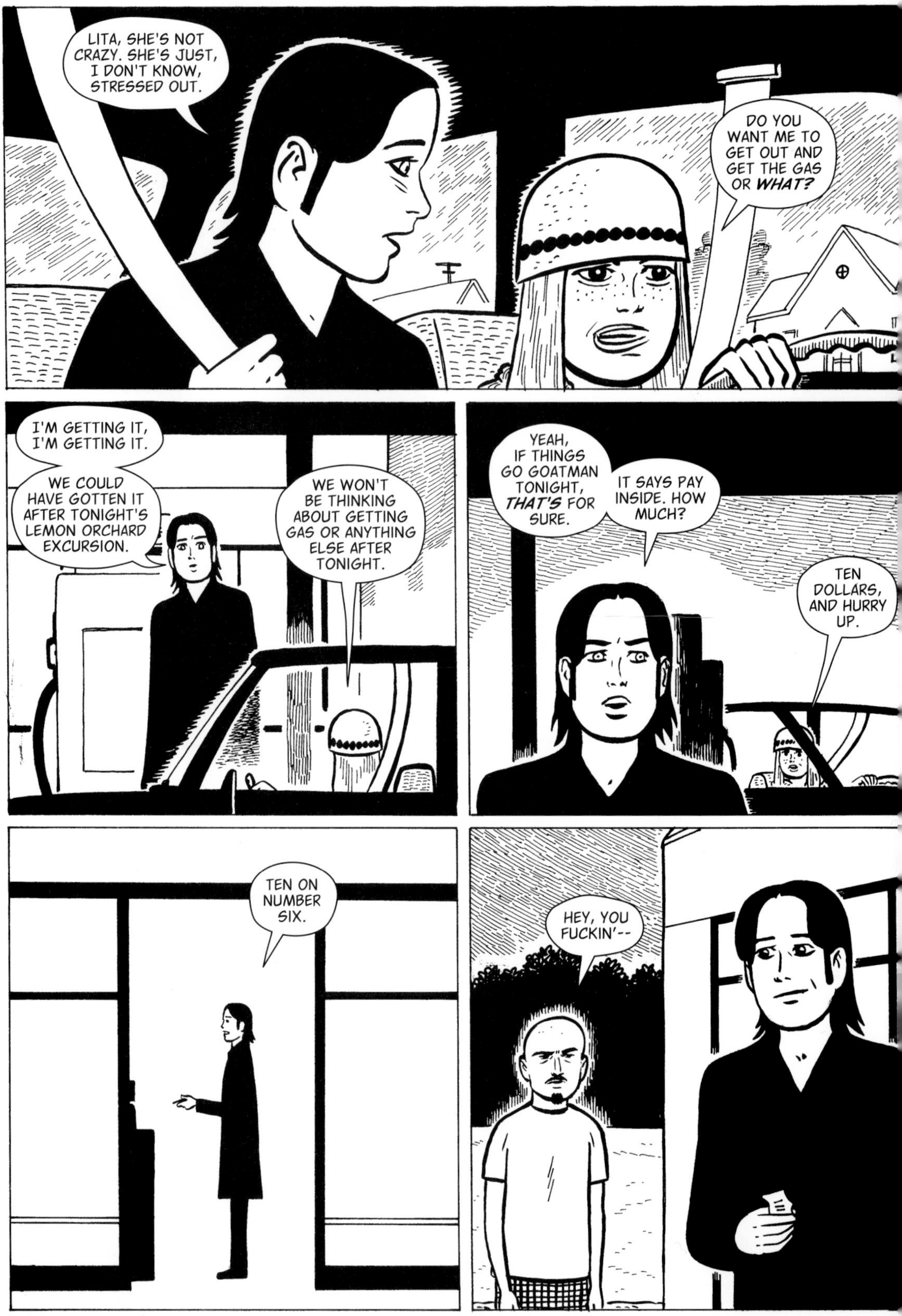
LITA, SHE'S NOT CRAZY. SHE'S JUST, I DON'T KNOW, STRESSED OUT.
DO YOU WANT ME TO GET OUT AND GET THE GAS OR *WHAT?*
I'M GETTING IT, I'M GETTING IT.
WE COULD HAVE GOTTEN IT AFTER TONIGHT'S LEMON ORCHARD EXCURSION.
WE WON'T BE THINKING ABOUT GETTING GAS OR ANYTHING ELSE AFTER TONIGHT.
YEAH, IF THINGS GO GOATMAN TONIGHT, *THAT'S* FOR SURE.
IT SAYS PAY INSIDE. HOW MUCH?
TEN DOLLARS, AND HURRY UP.
TEN ON NUMBER SIX.
HEY, YOU FUCKIN'--

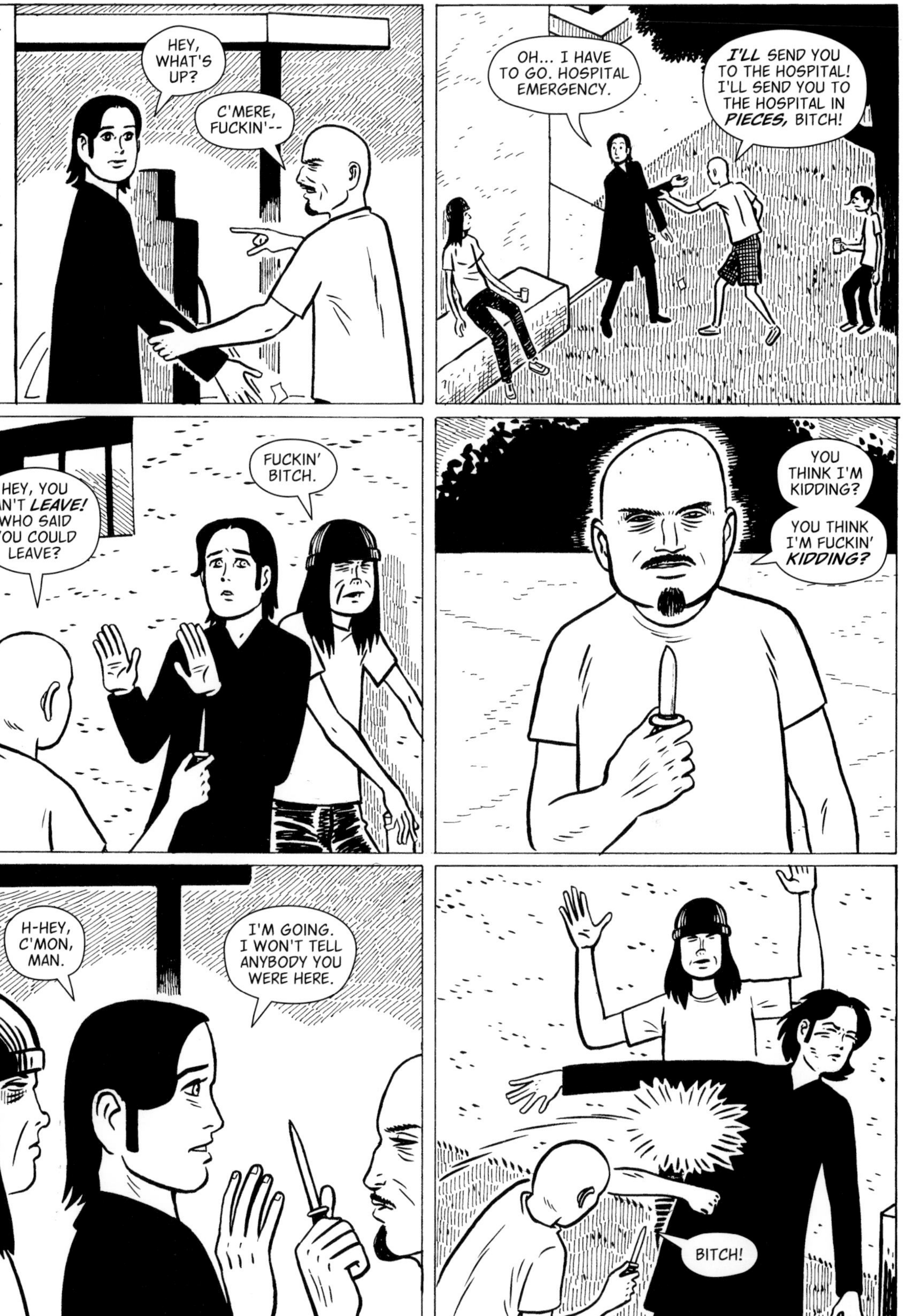
HEY, WHAT'S UP?
C'MERE, FUCKIN'--
OH... I HAVE TO GO. HOSPITAL EMERGENCY.
I'LL SEND YOU TO THE HOSPITAL! I'LL SEND YOU TO THE HOSPITAL IN PIECES, BITCH!
HEY, YOU CAN'T LEAVE! WHO SAID YOU COULD LEAVE?
FUCKIN' BITCH.
YOU THINK I'M KIDDING?
YOU THINK I'M FUCKIN' KIDDING?
H-HEY, C'MON, MAN.
I'M GOING. I WON'T TELL ANYBODY YOU WERE HERE.
BITCH!

WHAT'D YOU DO, FALL IN THE *TOILET?*

THAT TUTOR OF YOURS IS THE MOST HEARTBREAKING PERSON I'VE EVER SEEN.

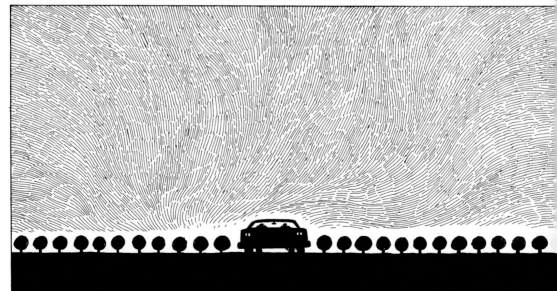

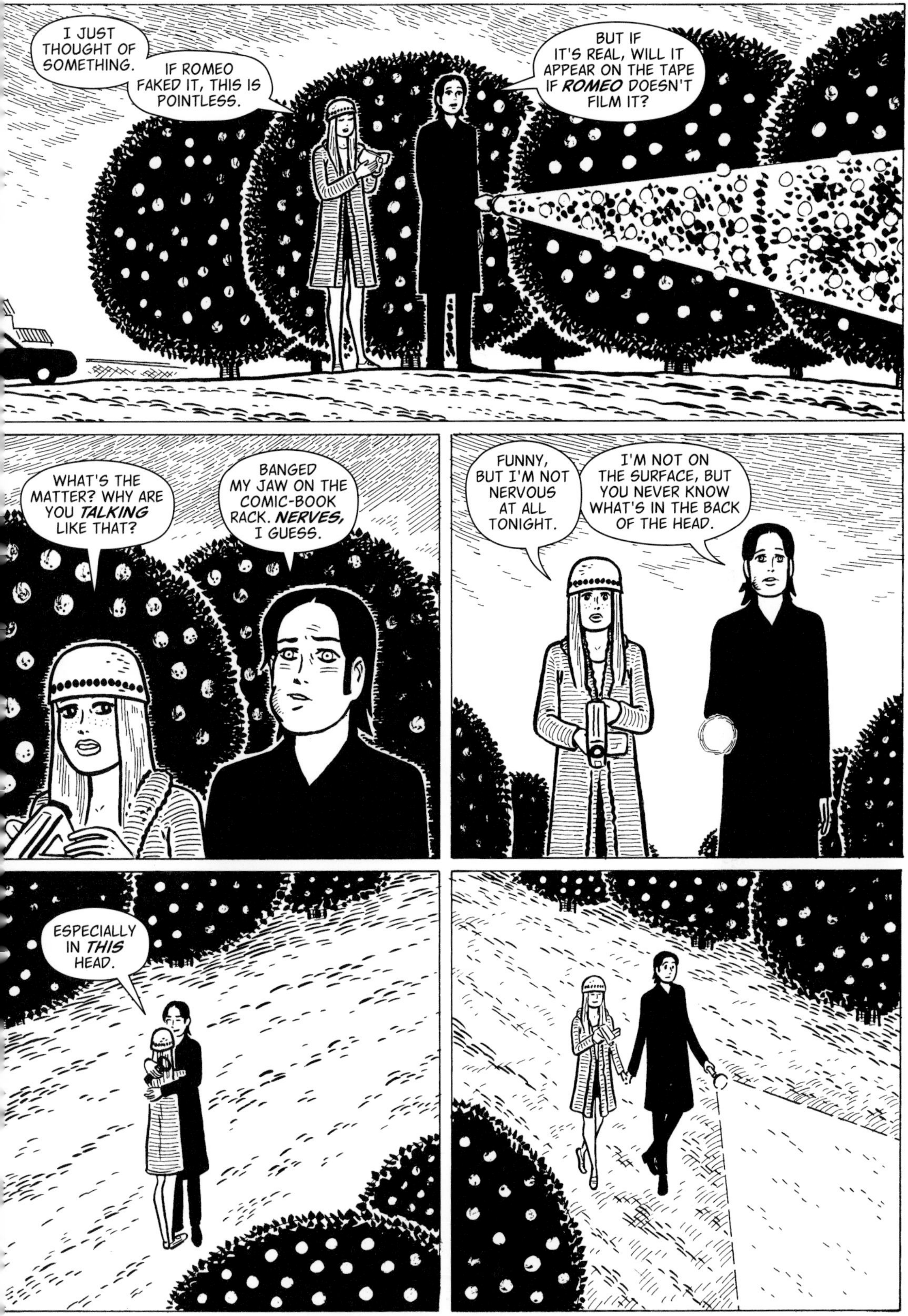
I JUST THOUGHT OF SOMETHING.
IF ROMEO FAKED IT, THIS IS POINTLESS.
BUT IF IT'S REAL, WILL IT APPEAR ON THE TAPE IF *ROMEO* DOESN'T FILM IT?
WHAT'S THE MATTER? WHY ARE YOU *TALKING* LIKE THAT?
BANGED MY JAW ON THE COMIC-BOOK RACK. *NERVES,* I GUESS.
FUNNY, BUT I'M NOT NERVOUS AT ALL TONIGHT.
I'M NOT ON THE SURFACE, BUT YOU NEVER KNOW WHAT'S IN THE BACK OF THE HEAD.
ESPECIALLY IN *THIS* HEAD.

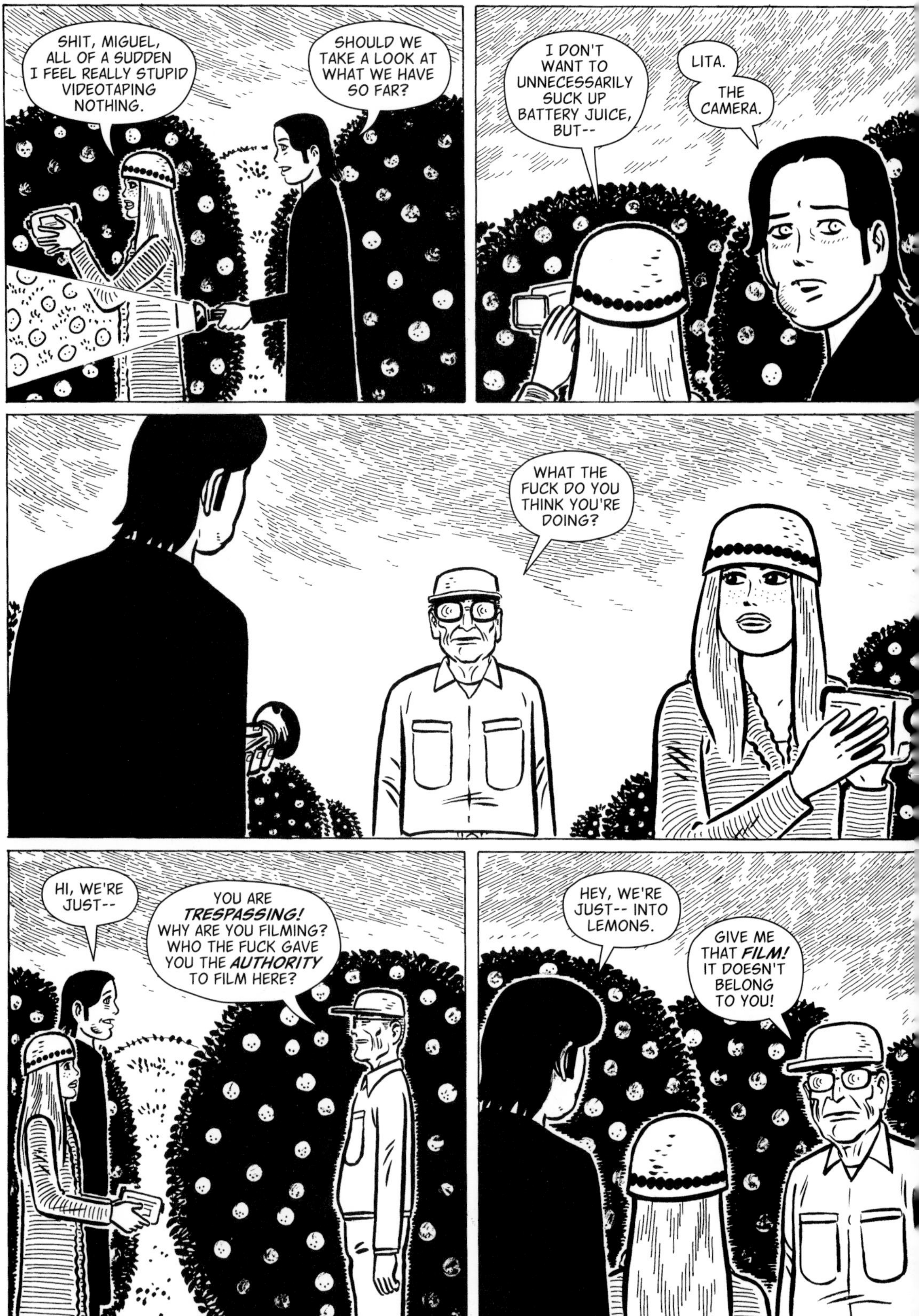
SHIT, MIGUEL, ALL OF A SUDDEN I FEEL REALLY STUPID VIDEOTAPING NOTHING.
SHOULD WE TAKE A LOOK AT WHAT WE HAVE SO FAR?
I DON'T WANT TO UNNECESSARILY SUCK UP BATTERY JUICE, BUT--
LITA.
THE CAMERA.
WHAT THE FUCK DO YOU THINK YOU'RE DOING?
HI, WE'RE JUST--
YOU ARE *TRESPASSING!* WHY ARE YOU FILMING? WHO THE FUCK GAVE YOU THE *AUTHORITY* TO FILM HERE?
HEY, WE'RE JUST-- INTO LEMONS.
GIVE ME THAT *FILM!* IT DOESN'T BELONG TO YOU!

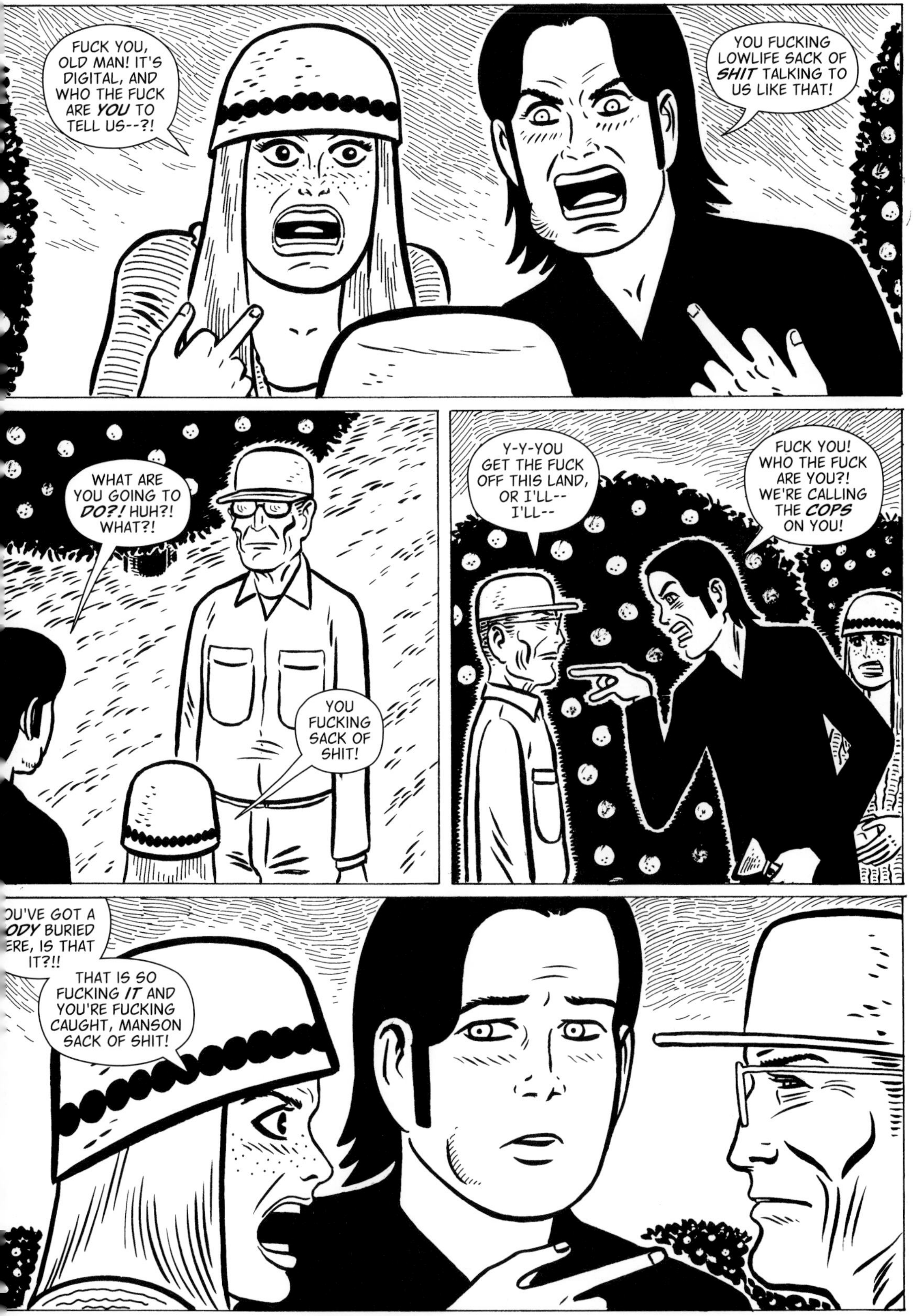
FUCK YOU, OLD MAN! IT'S DIGITAL, AND WHO THE FUCK ARE *YOU* TO TELL US--?!
YOU FUCKING LOWLIFE SACK OF *SHIT* TALKING TO US LIKE THAT!
WHAT ARE YOU GOING TO *DO?!* HUH?! WHAT?!
YOU FUCKING SACK OF SHIT!
Y-Y-YOU GET THE FUCK OFF THIS LAND, OR I'LL-- I'LL--
FUCK YOU! WHO THE FUCK ARE YOU?! WE'RE CALLING THE *COPS* ON YOU!
OU'VE GOT A ODY BURIED ERE, IS THAT IT?!!
THAT IS SO FUCKING *IT* AND YOU'RE FUCKING CAUGHT, MANSON SACK OF SHIT!

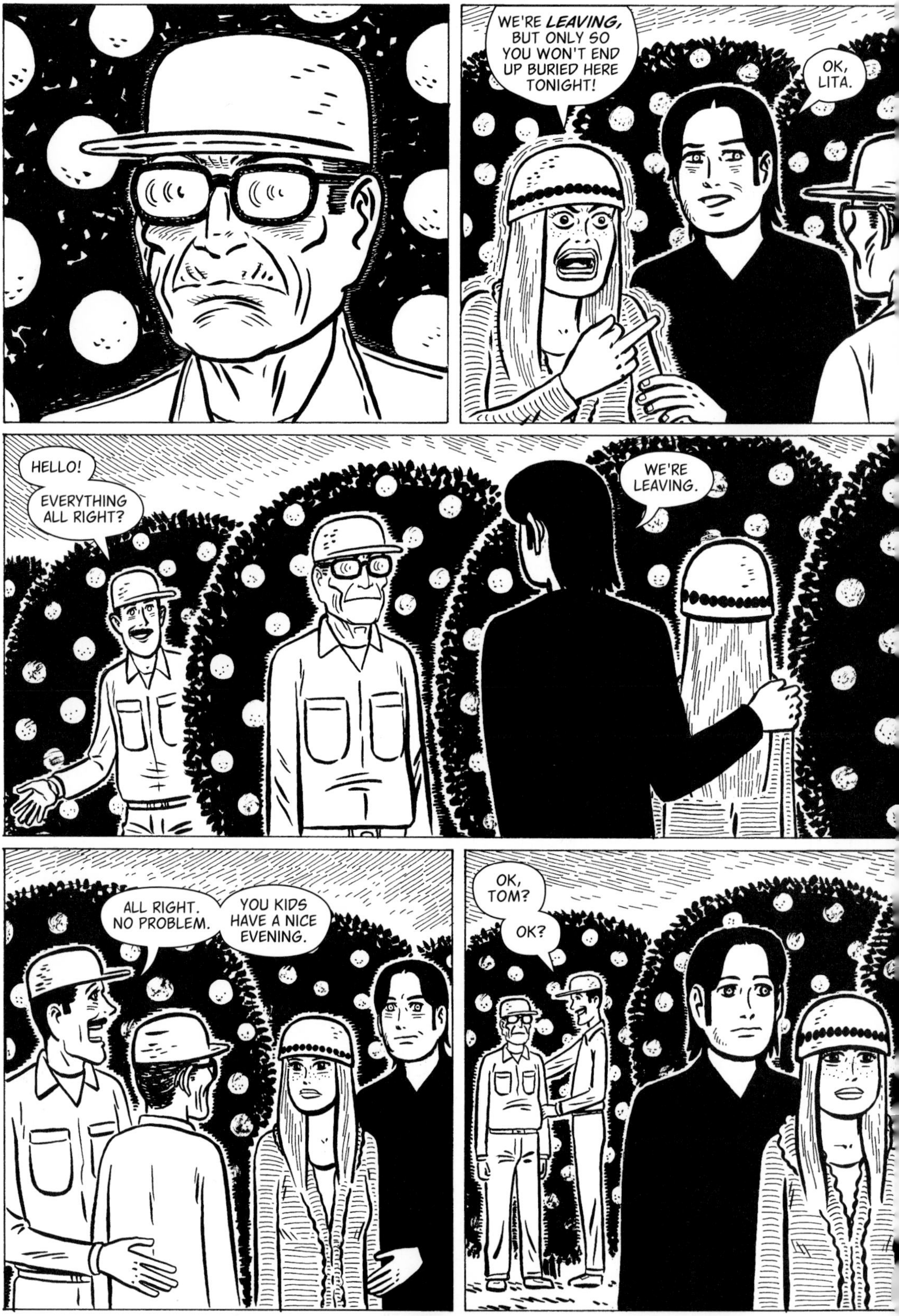
WE'RE *LEAVING,* BUT ONLY SO YOU WON'T END UP BURIED HERE TONIGHT!
OK, LITA.
HELLO!
EVERYTHING ALL RIGHT?
WE'RE LEAVING.
ALL RIGHT. NO PROBLEM.
YOU KIDS HAVE A NICE EVENING.
OK, TOM?
OK?

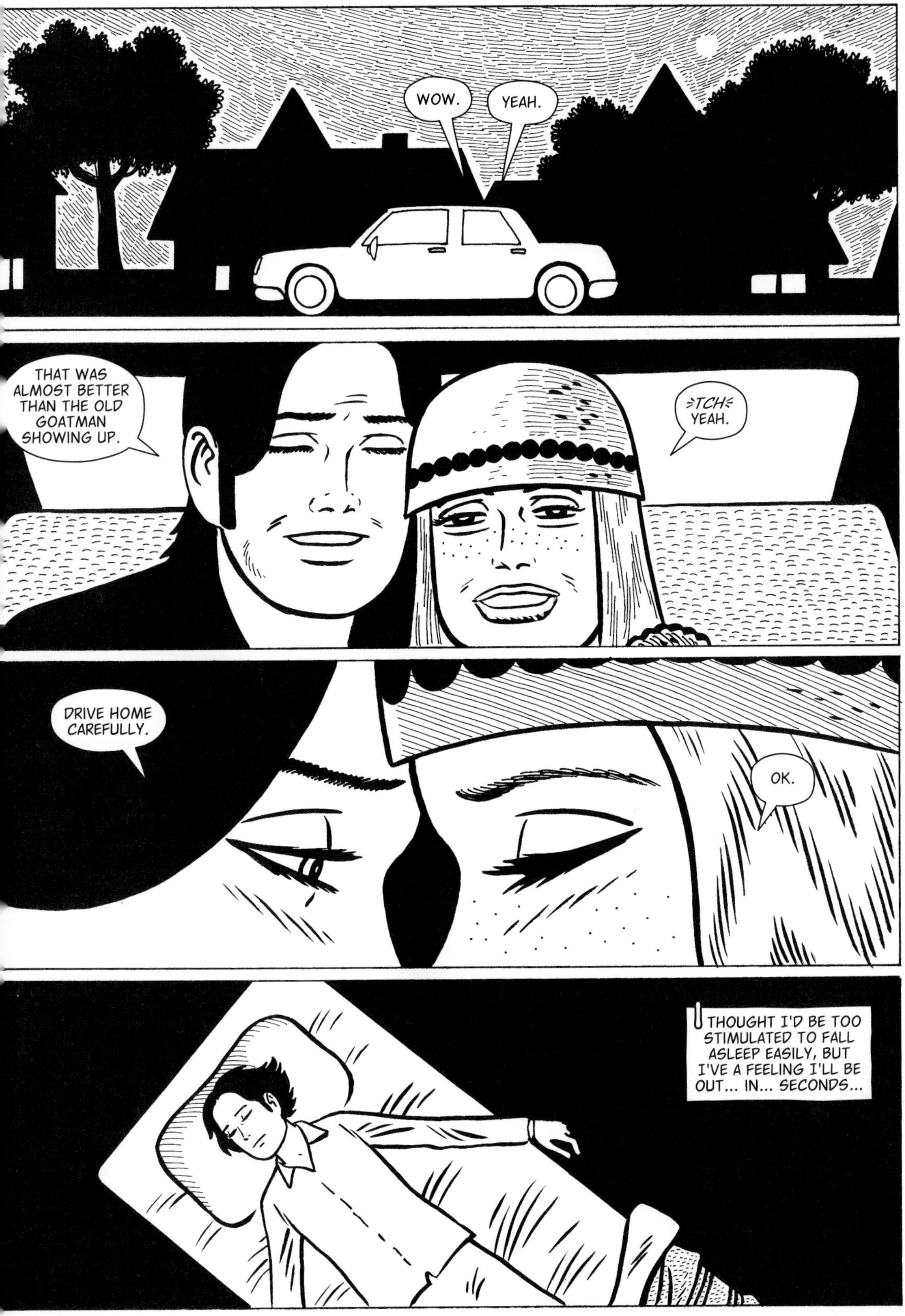
WOW.
YEAH.
THAT WAS ALMOST BETTER THAN THE OLD GOATMAN SHOWING UP.
TCH YEAH.
DRIVE HOME CAREFULLY.
OK.
I THOUGHT I'D BE TOO STIMULATED TO FALL ASLEEP EASILY, BUT I'VE A FEELING I'LL BE OUT... IN... SECONDS...

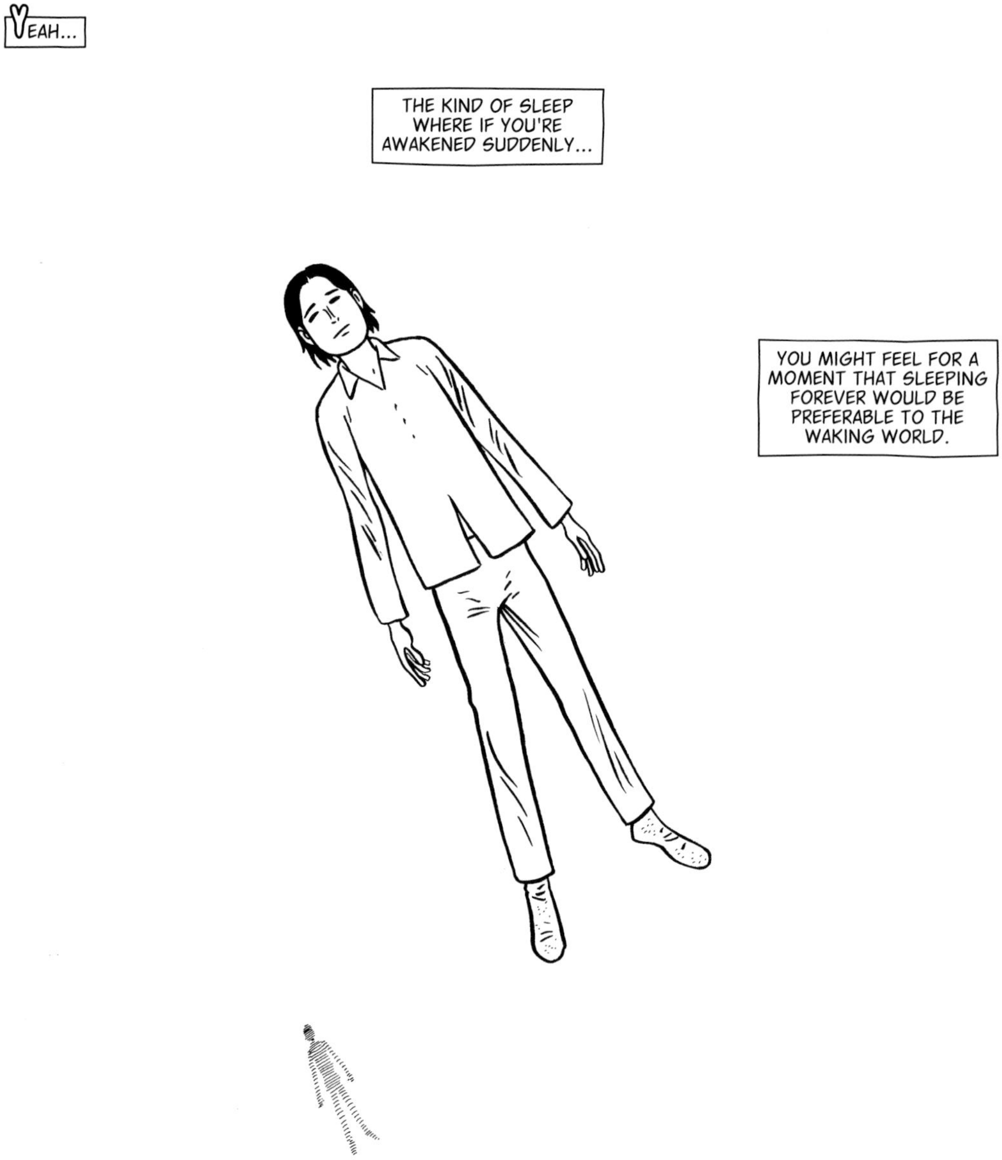
YEAH...
THE KIND OF SLEEP WHERE IF YOU'RE AWAKENED SUDDENLY...
YOU MIGHT FEEL FOR A MOMENT THAT SLEEPING FOREVER WOULD BE PREFERABLE TO THE WAKING WORLD.

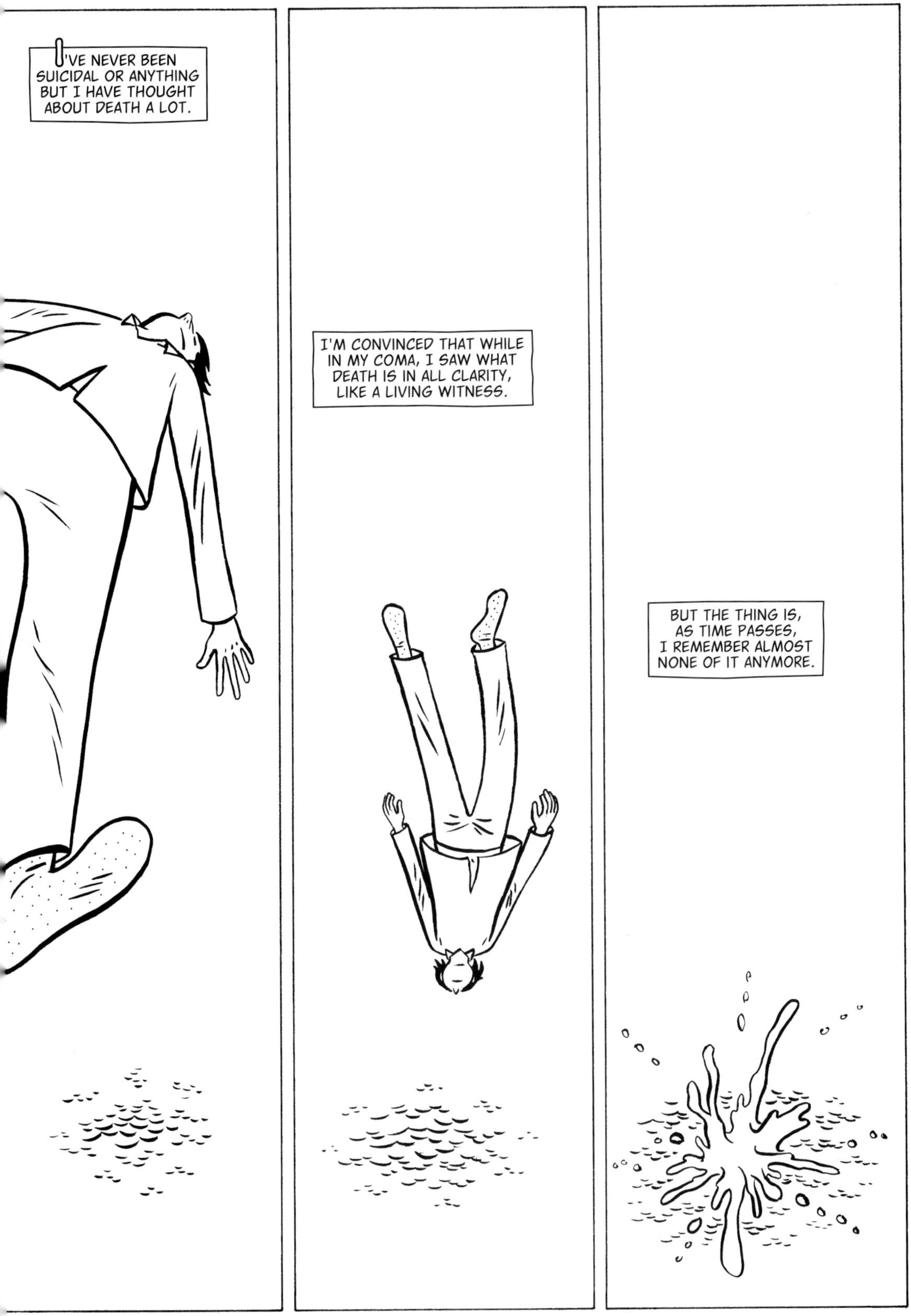
I'VE NEVER BEEN SUICIDAL OR ANYTHING BUT I HAVE THOUGHT ABOUT DEATH A LOT.
I'M CONVINCED THAT WHILE IN MY COMA, I SAW WHAT DEATH IS IN ALL CLARITY, LIKE A LIVING WITNESS.
BUT THE THING IS, AS TIME PASSES, I REMEMBER ALMOST NONE OF IT ANYMORE.

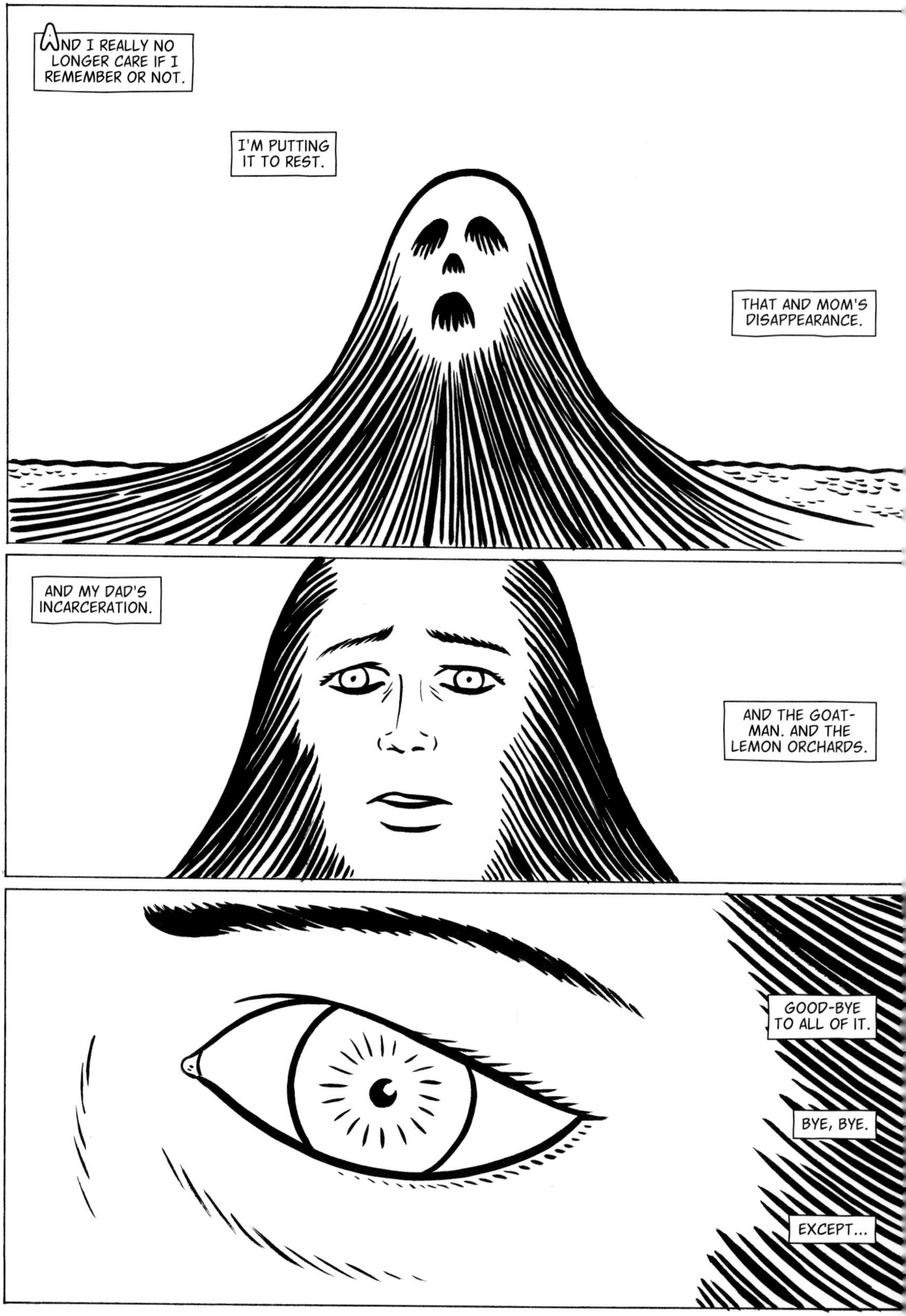
AND I REALLY NO LONGER CARE IF I REMEMBER OR NOT.
I'M PUTTING IT TO REST.
THAT AND MOM'S DISAPPEARANCE.
AND MY DAD'S INCARCERATION.
AND THE GOAT-MAN. AND THE LEMON ORCHARDS.
GOOD-BYE TO ALL OF IT.
BYE, BYE.
EXCEPT...

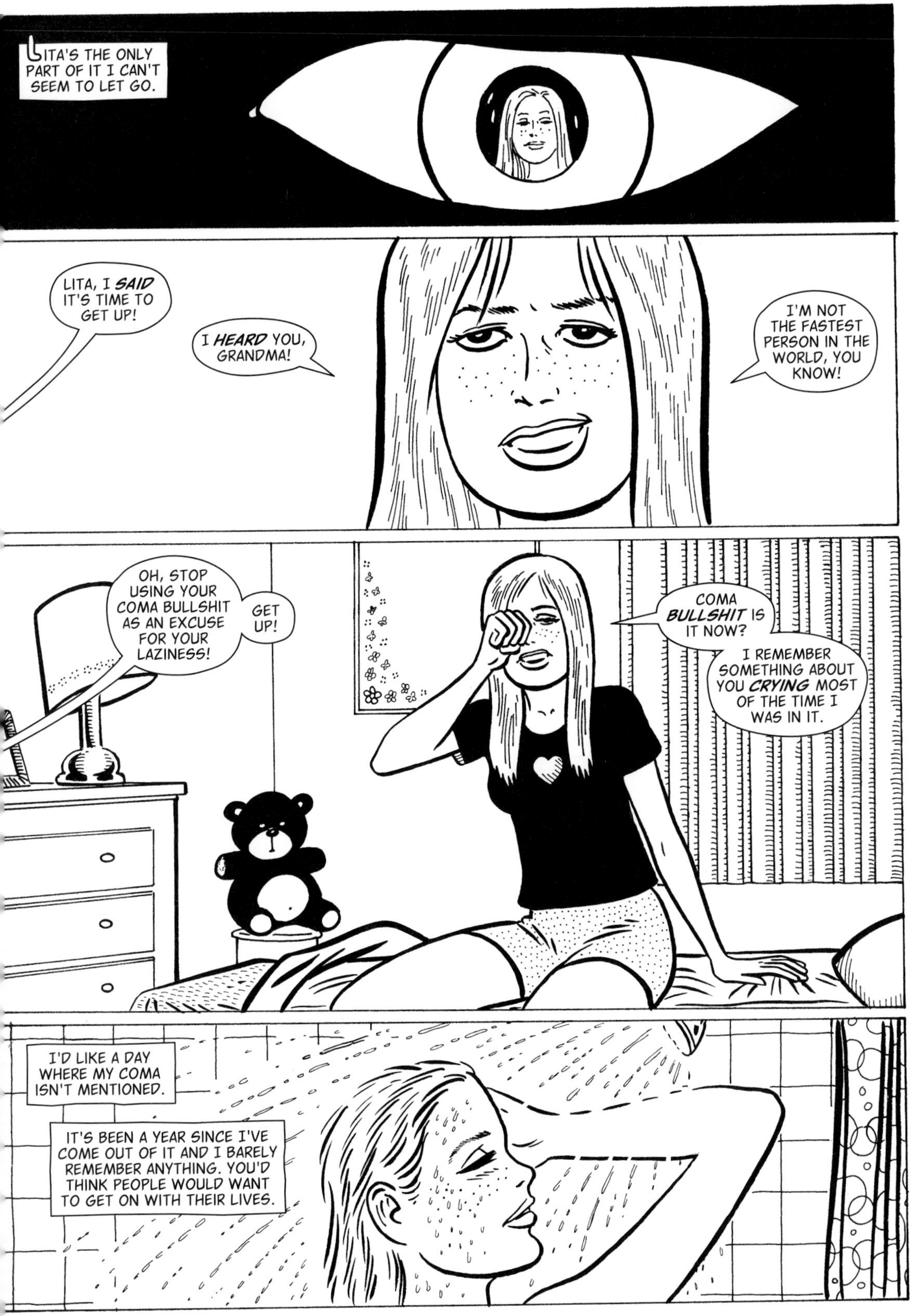
LITA'S THE ONLY PART OF IT I CAN'T SEEM TO LET GO.
LITA, I *SAID* IT'S TIME TO GET UP!
I *HEARD* YOU, GRANDMA!
I'M NOT THE FASTEST PERSON IN THE WORLD, YOU KNOW!
OH, STOP USING YOUR COMA BULLSHIT AS AN EXCUSE FOR YOUR LAZINESS!
GET UP!
COMA *BULLSHIT* IS IT NOW?
I REMEMBER SOMETHING ABOUT YOU *CRYING* MOST OF THE TIME I WAS IN IT.
I'D LIKE A DAY WHERE MY COMA ISN'T MENTIONED.
IT'S BEEN A YEAR SINCE I'VE COME OUT OF IT AND I BARELY REMEMBER ANYTHING. YOU'D THINK PEOPLE WOULD WANT TO GET ON WITH THEIR LIVES.

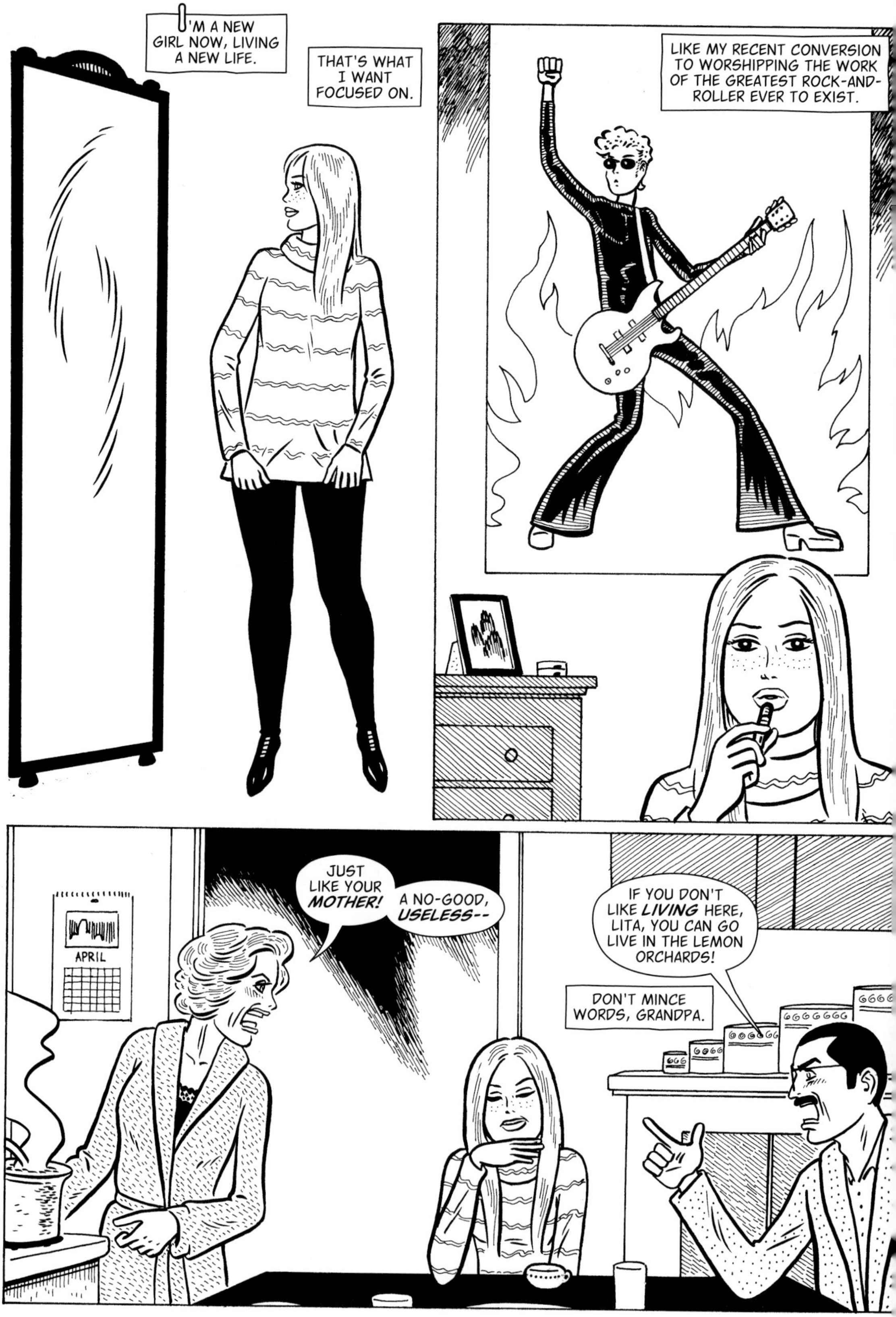
I'M A NEW GIRL NOW, LIVING A NEW LIFE.
THAT'S WHAT I WANT FOCUSED ON.
LIKE MY RECENT CONVERSION TO WORSHIPPING THE WORK OF THE GREATEST ROCK-AND-ROLLER EVER TO EXIST.
APRIL
JUST LIKE YOUR MOTHER!
A NO-GOOD, USELESS--
IF YOU DON'T LIKE LIVING HERE, LITA, YOU CAN GO LIVE IN THE LEMON ORCHARDS!
DON'T MINCE WORDS, GRANDPA.

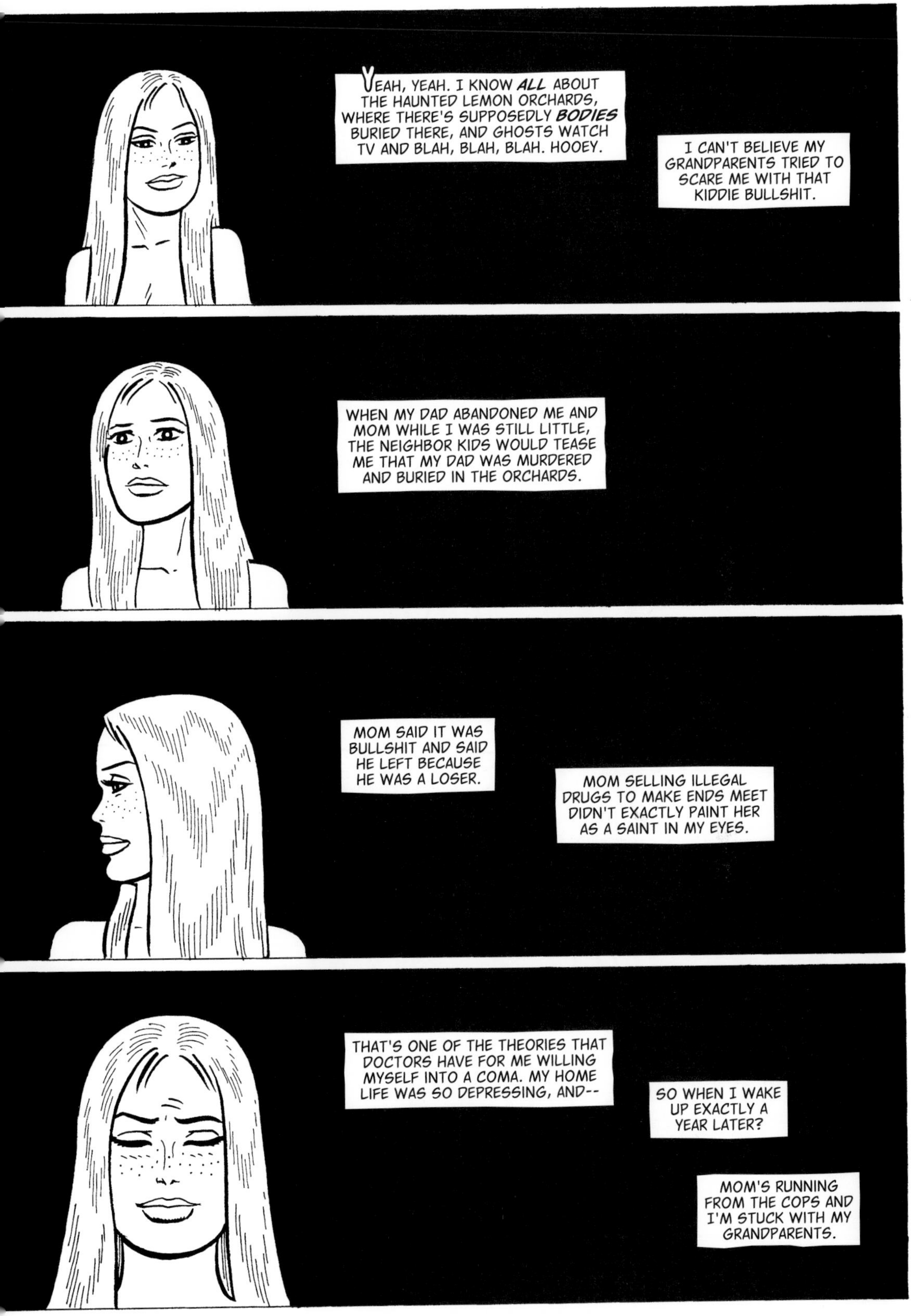
YEAH, YEAH. I KNOW ALL ABOUT THE HAUNTED LEMON ORCHARDS, WHERE THERE'S SUPPOSEDLY BODIES BURIED THERE, AND GHOSTS WATCH TV AND BLAH, BLAH, BLAH. HOOEY.
I CAN'T BELIEVE MY GRANDPARENTS TRIED TO SCARE ME WITH THAT KIDDIE BULLSHIT.
WHEN MY DAD ABANDONED ME AND MOM WHILE I WAS STILL LITTLE, THE NEIGHBOR KIDS WOULD TEASE ME THAT MY DAD WAS MURDERED AND BURIED IN THE ORCHARDS.
MOM SAID IT WAS BULLSHIT AND SAID HE LEFT BECAUSE HE WAS A LOSER.
MOM SELLING ILLEGAL DRUGS TO MAKE ENDS MEET DIDN'T EXACTLY PAINT HER AS A SAINT IN MY EYES.
THAT'S ONE OF THE THEORIES THAT DOCTORS HAVE FOR ME WILLING MYSELF INTO A COMA. MY HOME LIFE WAS SO DEPRESSING, AND--
SO WHEN I WAKE UP EXACTLY A YEAR LATER?
MOM'S RUNNING FROM THE COPS AND I'M STUCK WITH MY GRANDPARENTS.

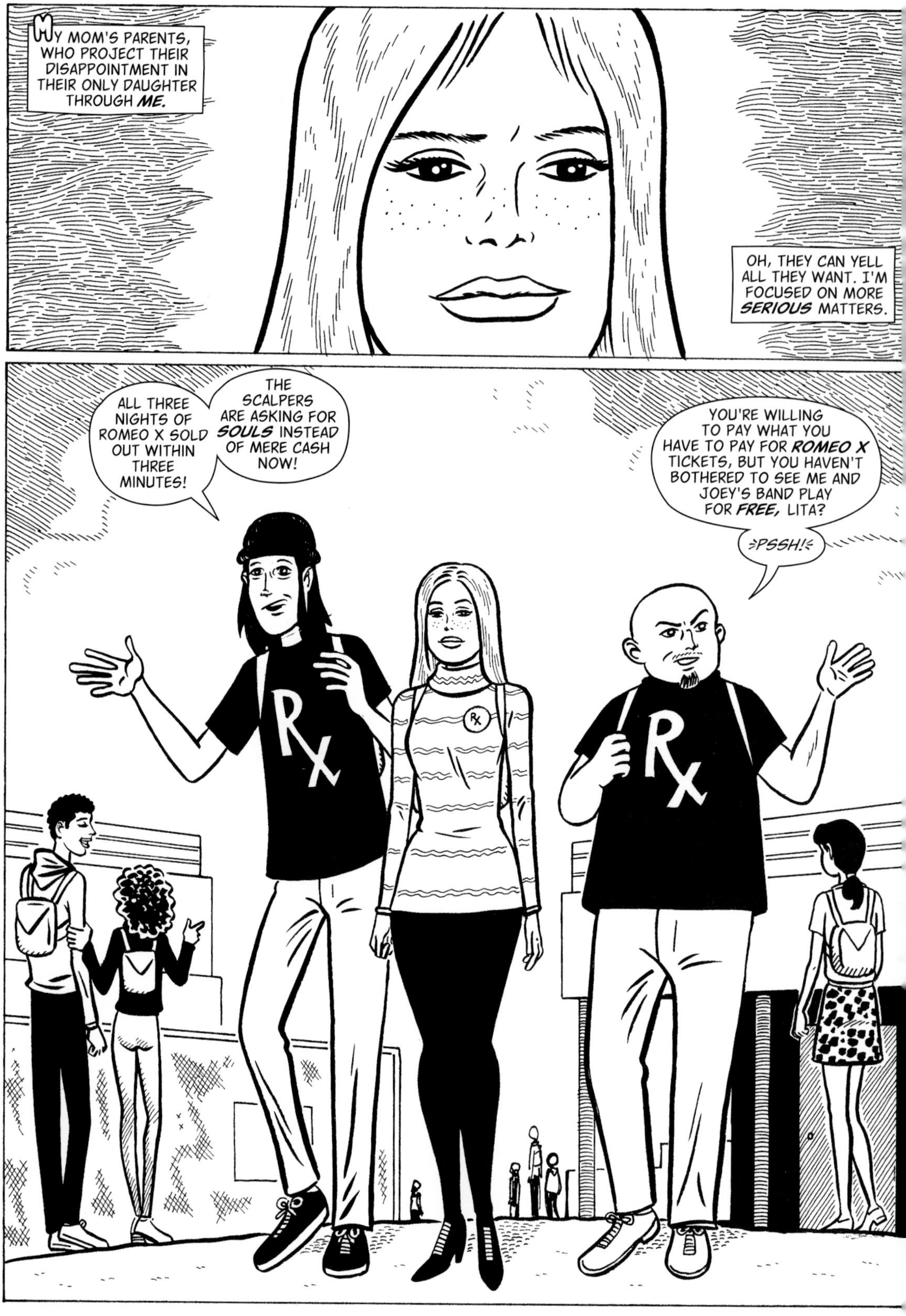
MY MOM'S PARENTS, WHO PROJECT THEIR DISAPPOINTMENT IN THEIR ONLY DAUGHTER THROUGH ME.
OH, THEY CAN YELL ALL THEY WANT. I'M FOCUSED ON MORE SERIOUS MATTERS.
ALL THREE NIGHTS OF ROMEO X SOLD OUT WITHIN THREE MINUTES!
THE SCALPERS ARE ASKING FOR SOULS INSTEAD OF MERE CASH NOW!
YOU'RE WILLING TO PAY WHAT YOU HAVE TO PAY FOR ROMEO X TICKETS, BUT YOU HAVEN'T BOTHERED TO SEE ME AND JOEY'S BAND PLAY FOR FREE, LITA?
PSSH!
Rx
Rx

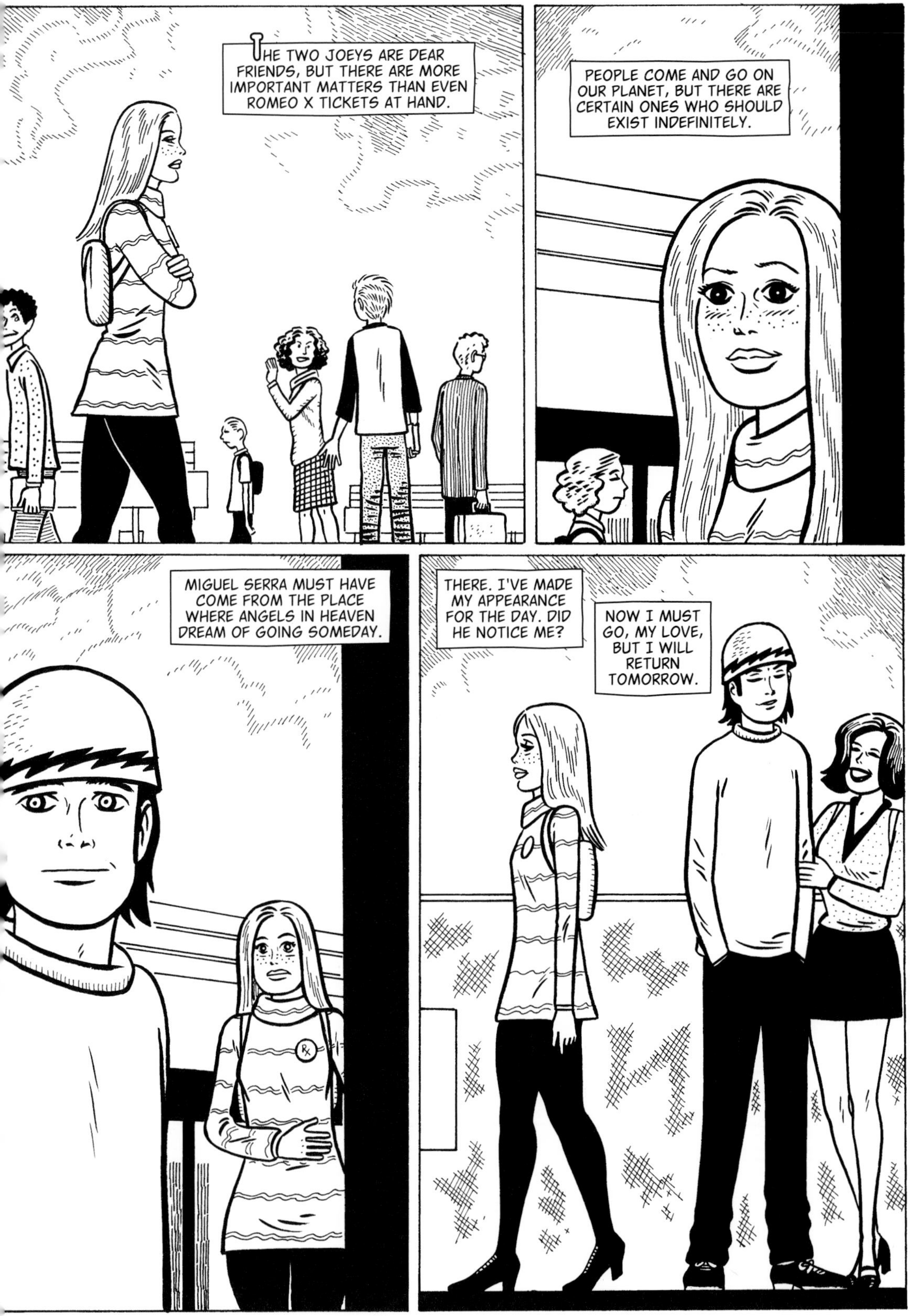
THE TWO JOEYS ARE DEAR FRIENDS, BUT THERE ARE MORE IMPORTANT MATTERS THAN EVEN ROMEO X TICKETS AT HAND.
PEOPLE COME AND GO ON OUR PLANET, BUT THERE ARE CERTAIN ONES WHO SHOULD EXIST INDEFINITELY.
MIGUEL SERRA MUST HAVE COME FROM THE PLACE WHERE ANGELS IN HEAVEN DREAM OF GOING SOMEDAY.
THERE. I'VE MADE MY APPEARANCE FOR THE DAY. DID HE NOTICE ME?
NOW I MUST GO, MY LOVE, BUT I WILL RETURN TOMORROW.

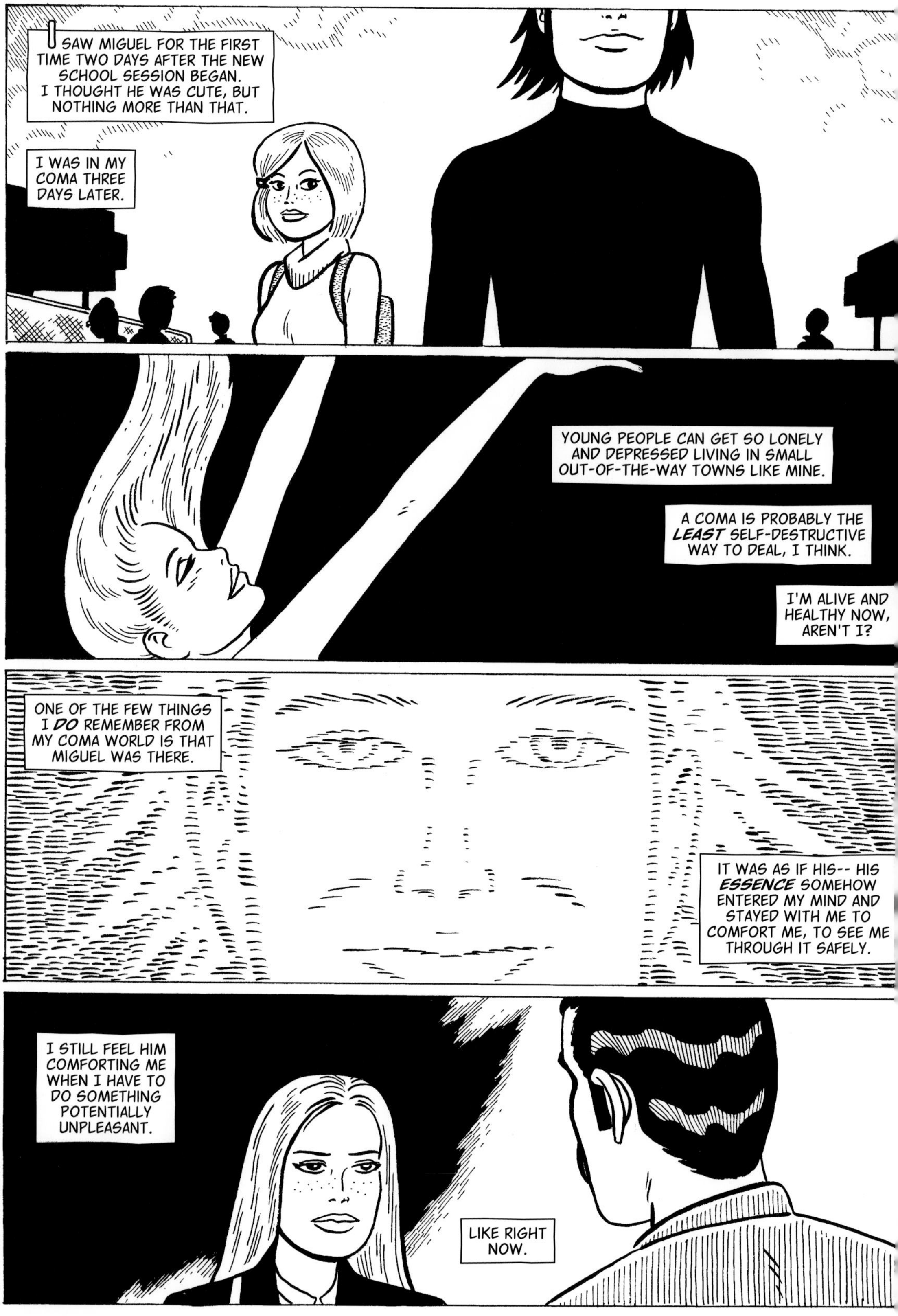
I SAW MIGUEL FOR THE FIRST TIME TWO DAYS AFTER THE NEW SCHOOL SESSION BEGAN. I THOUGHT HE WAS CUTE, BUT NOTHING MORE THAN THAT.
I WAS IN MY COMA THREE DAYS LATER.
YOUNG PEOPLE CAN GET SO LONELY AND DEPRESSED LIVING IN SMALL OUT-OF-THE-WAY TOWNS LIKE MINE.
A COMA IS PROBABLY THE *LEAST* SELF-DESTRUCTIVE WAY TO DEAL, I THINK.
I'M ALIVE AND HEALTHY NOW, AREN'T I?
ONE OF THE FEW THINGS I *DO* REMEMBER FROM MY COMA WORLD IS THAT MIGUEL WAS THERE.
IT WAS AS IF HIS-- HIS *ESSENCE* SOMEHOW ENTERED MY MIND AND STAYED WITH ME TO COMFORT ME, TO SEE ME THROUGH IT SAFELY.
I STILL FEEL HIM COMFORTING ME WHEN I HAVE TO DO SOMETHING POTENTIALLY UNPLEASANT.
LIKE RIGHT NOW.

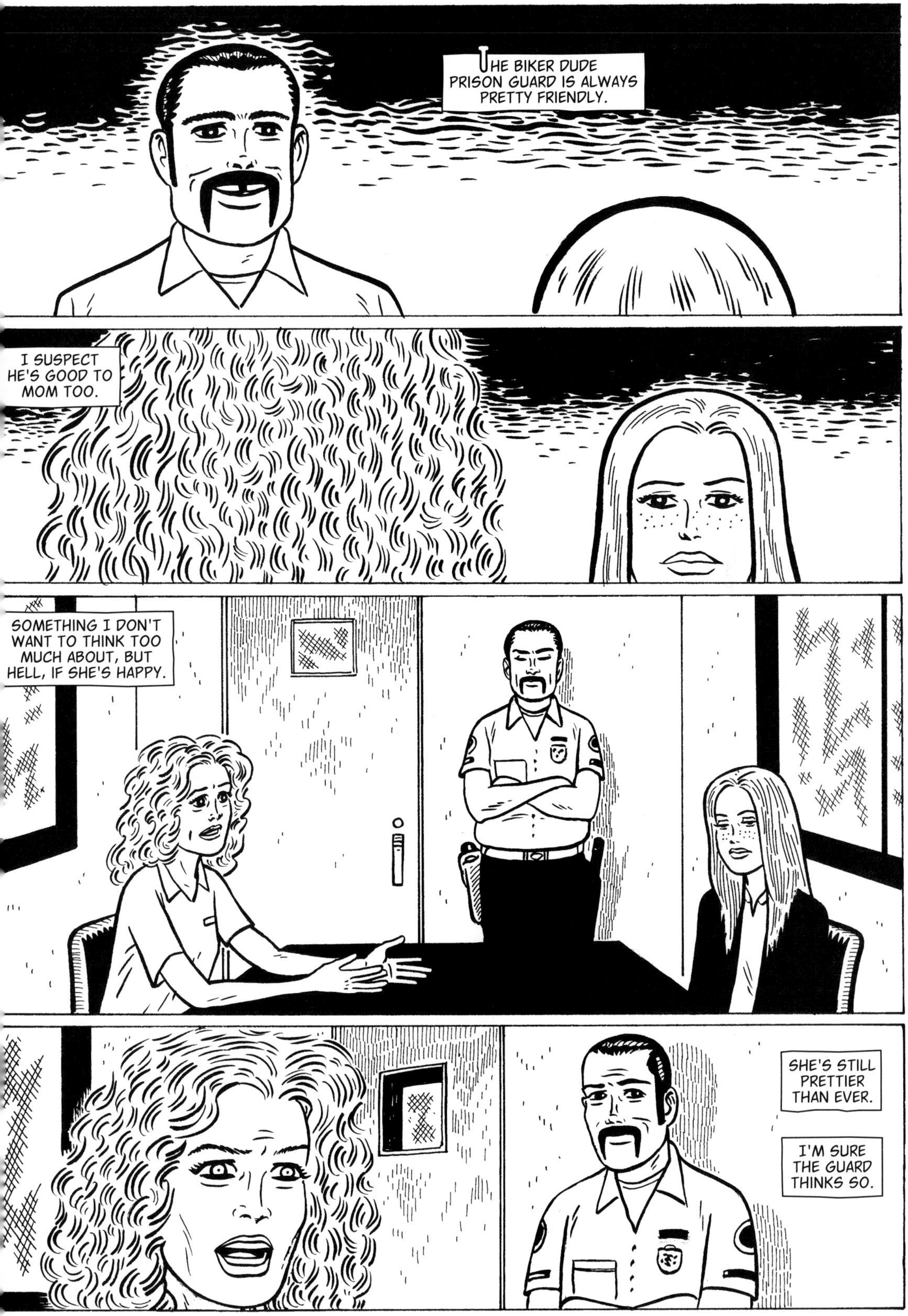
THE BIKER DUDE PRISON GUARD IS ALWAYS PRETTY FRIENDLY.
I SUSPECT HE'S GOOD TO MOM TOO.
SOMETHING I DON'T WANT TO THINK TOO MUCH ABOUT, BUT HELL, IF SHE'S HAPPY.
SHE'S STILL PRETTIER THAN EVER.
I'M SURE THE GUARD THINKS SO.

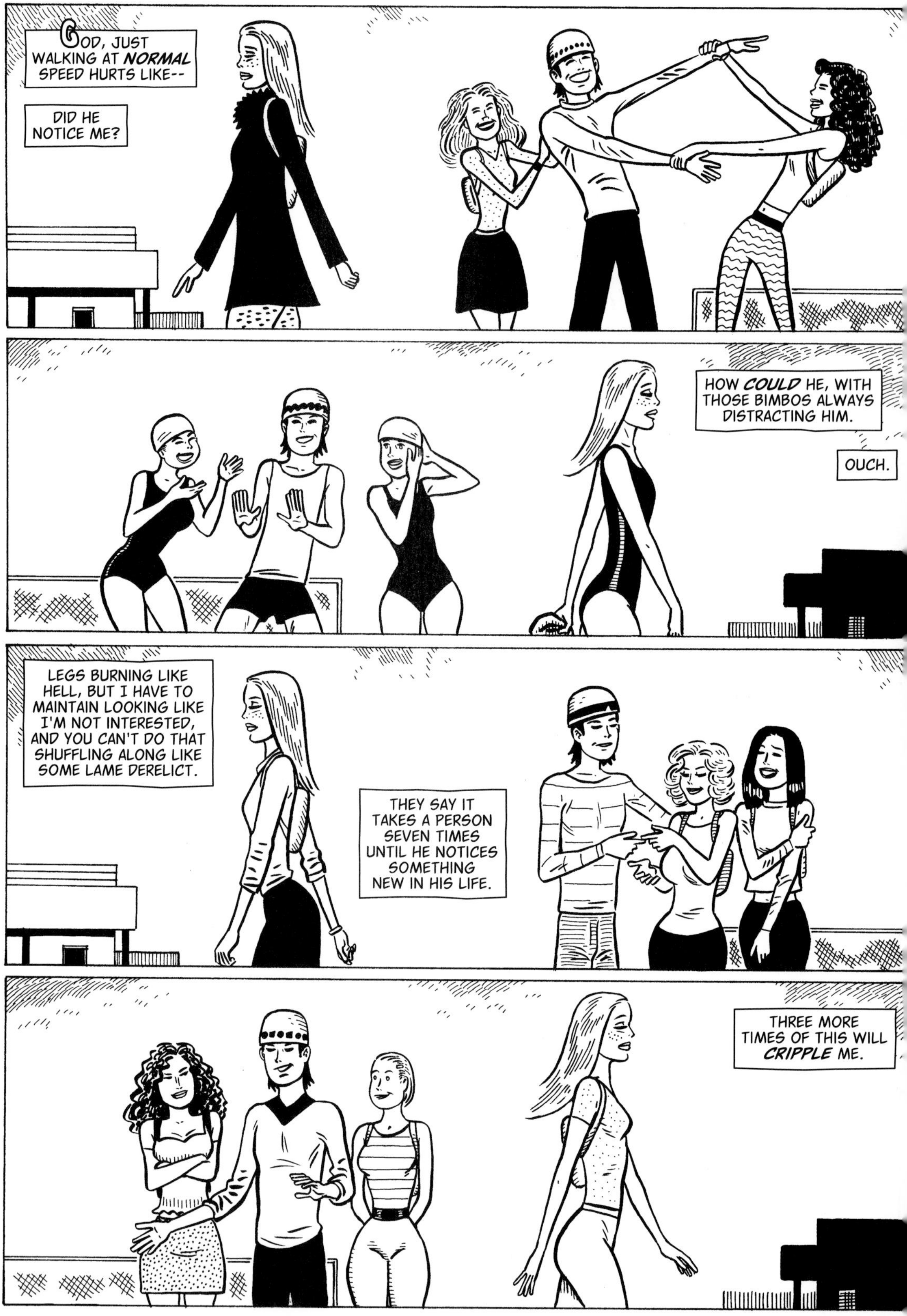
GOD, JUST WALKING AT *NORMAL* SPEED HURTS LIKE--
DID HE NOTICE ME?
HOW *COULD* HE, WITH THOSE BIMBOS ALWAYS DISTRACTING HIM.
OUCH.
LEGS BURNING LIKE HELL, BUT I HAVE TO MAINTAIN LOOKING LIKE I'M NOT INTERESTED, AND YOU CAN'T DO THAT SHUFFLING ALONG LIKE SOME LAME DERELICT.
THEY SAY IT TAKES A PERSON SEVEN TIMES UNTIL HE NOTICES SOMETHING NEW IN HIS LIFE.
THREE MORE TIMES OF THIS WILL *CRIPPLE* ME.

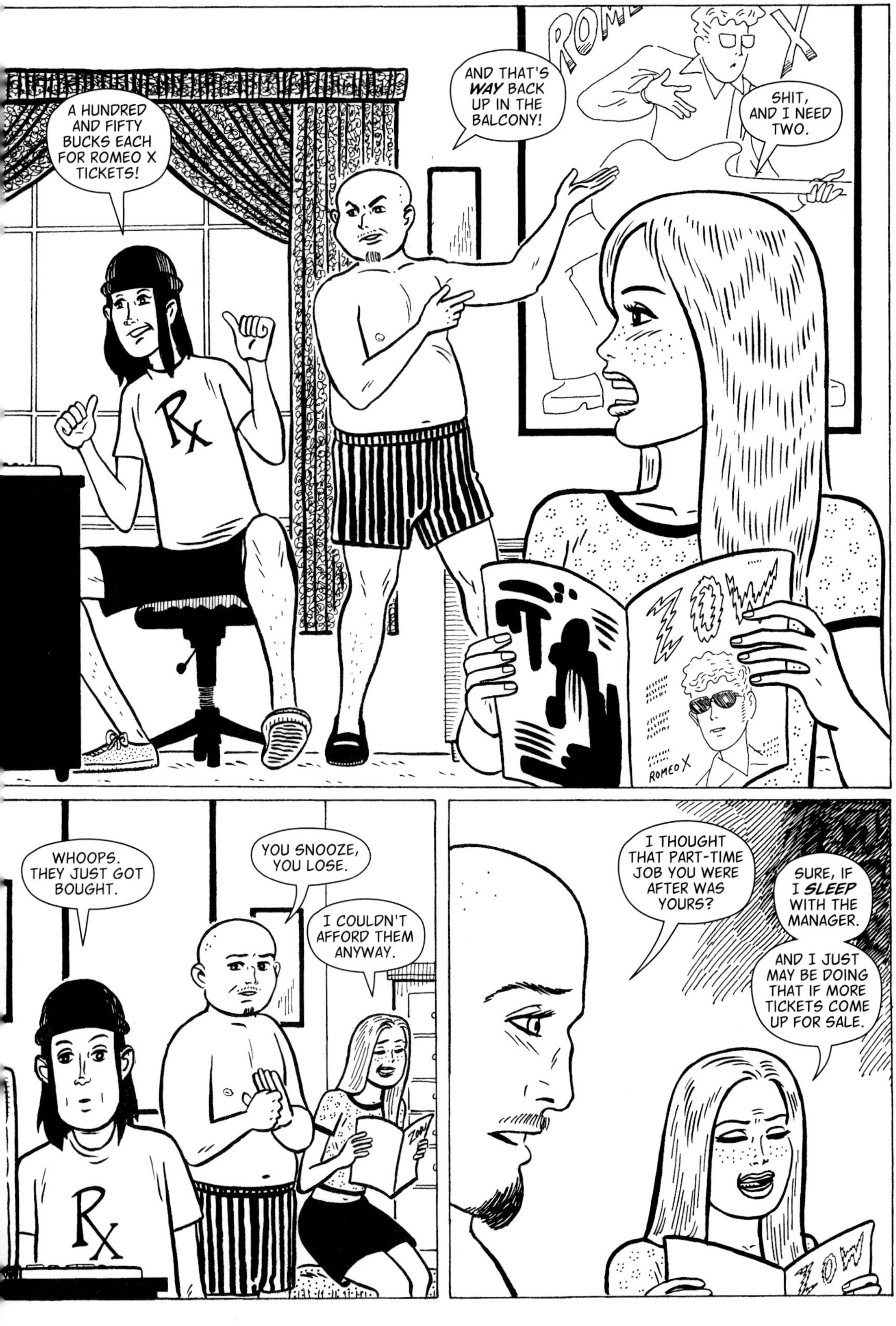
A HUNDRED AND FIFTY BUCKS EACH FOR ROMEO X TICKETS!
AND THAT'S WAY BACK UP IN THE BALCONY!
SHIT, AND I NEED TWO.
ROMEO X
WHOOPS. THEY JUST GOT BOUGHT.
YOU SNOOZE, YOU LOSE.
I COULDN'T AFFORD THEM ANYWAY.
I THOUGHT THAT PART-TIME JOB YOU WERE AFTER WAS YOURS?
SURE, IF I SLEEP WITH THE MANAGER.
AND I JUST MAY BE DOING THAT IF MORE TICKETS COME UP FOR SALE.

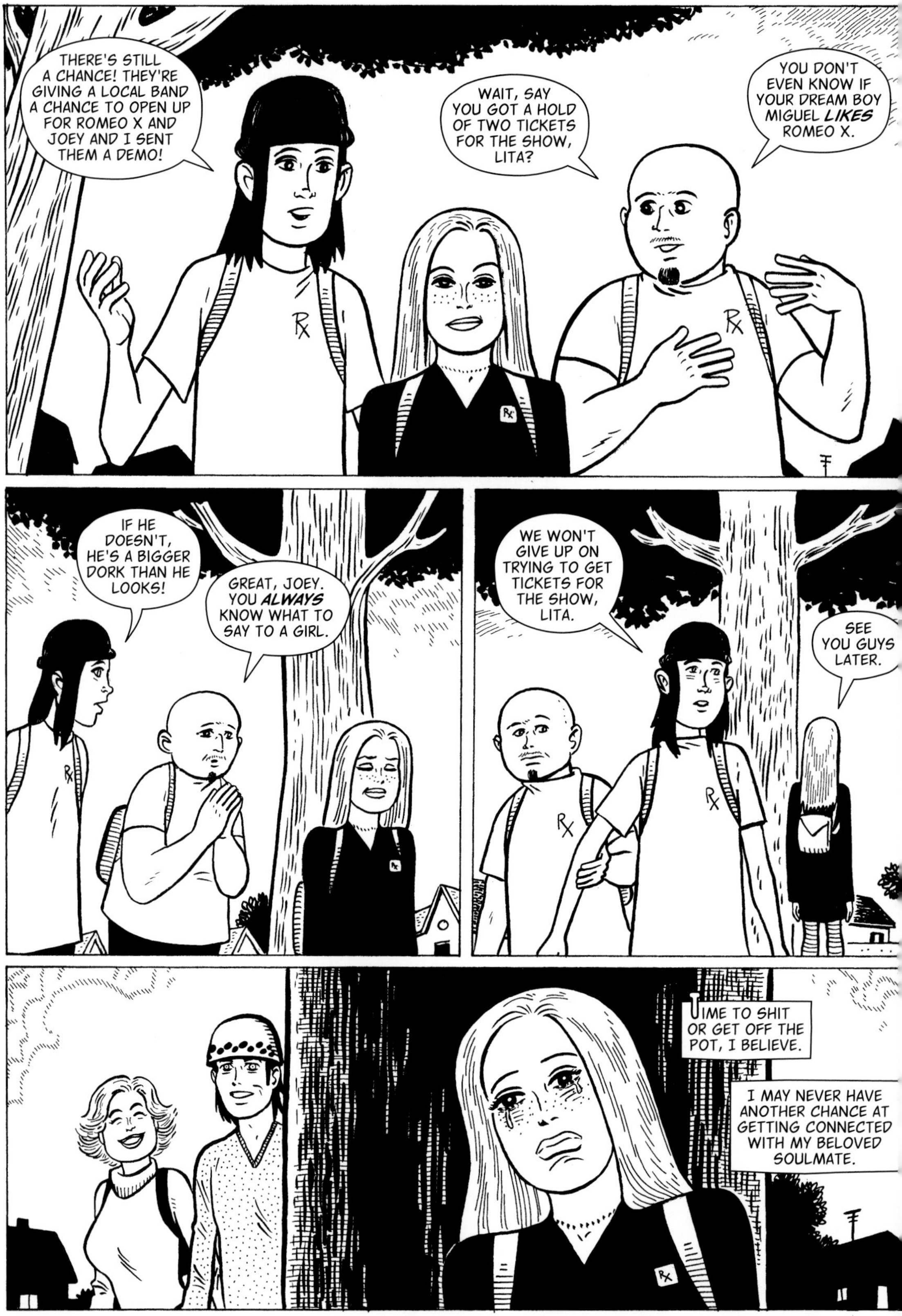

THERE'S STILL A CHANCE! THEY'RE GIVING A LOCAL BAND A CHANCE TO OPEN UP FOR ROMEO X AND JOEY AND I SENT THEM A DEMO!
WAIT, SAY YOU GOT A HOLD OF TWO TICKETS FOR THE SHOW, LITA?
YOU DON'T EVEN KNOW IF YOUR DREAM BOY MIGUEL LIKES ROMEO X.
IF HE DOESN'T, HE'S A BIGGER DORK THAN HE LOOKS!
GREAT, JOEY. YOU ALWAYS KNOW WHAT TO SAY TO A GIRL.
WE WON'T GIVE UP ON TRYING TO GET TICKETS FOR THE SHOW, LITA.
SEE YOU GUYS LATER.
TIME TO SHIT OR GET OFF THE POT, I BELIEVE.
I MAY NEVER HAVE ANOTHER CHANCE AT GETTING CONNECTED WITH MY BELOVED SOULMATE.

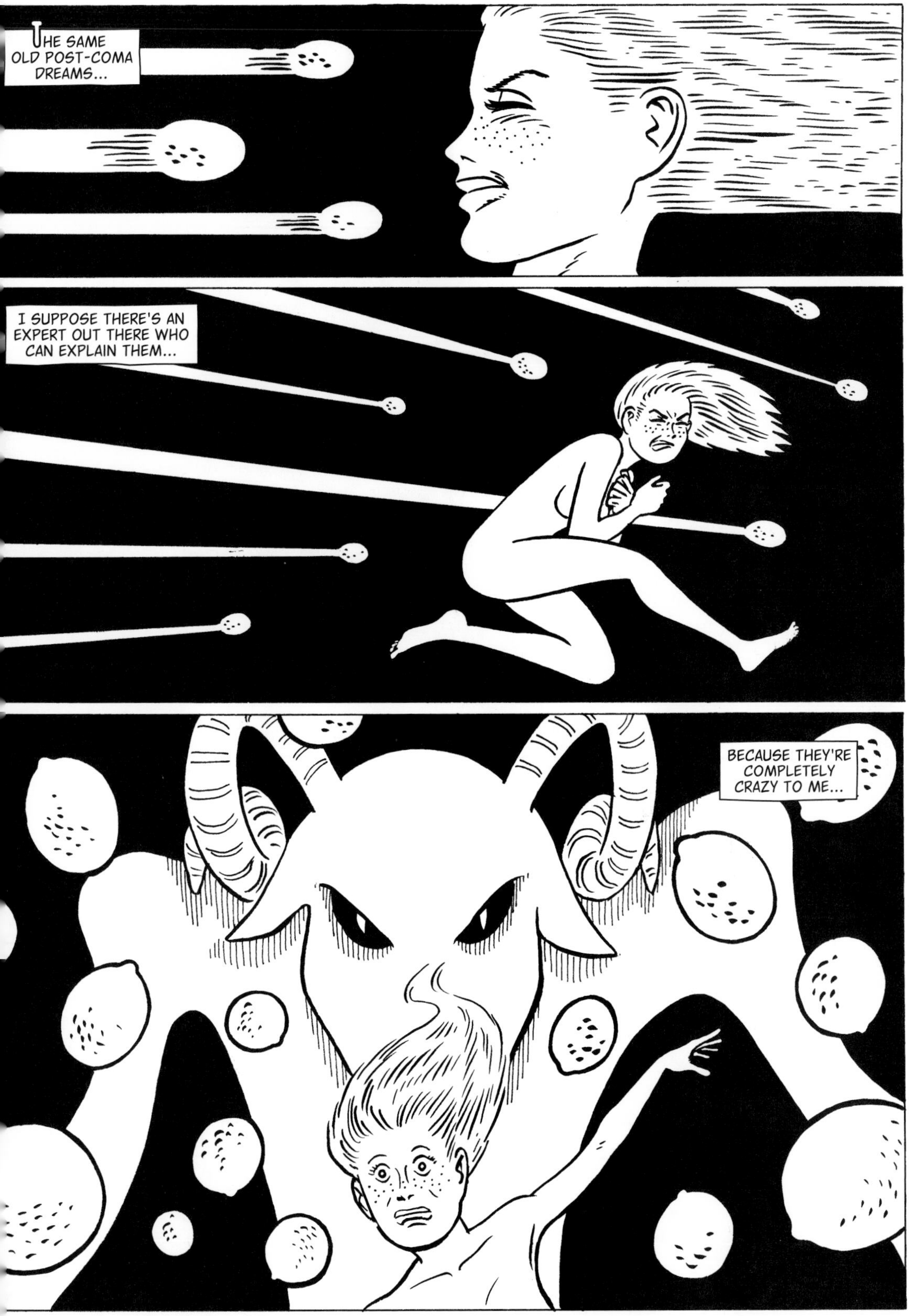
THE SAME OLD POST-COMA DREAMS...
I SUPPOSE THERE'S AN EXPERT OUT THERE WHO CAN EXPLAIN THEM...
BECAUSE THEY'RE COMPLETELY CRAZY TO ME...

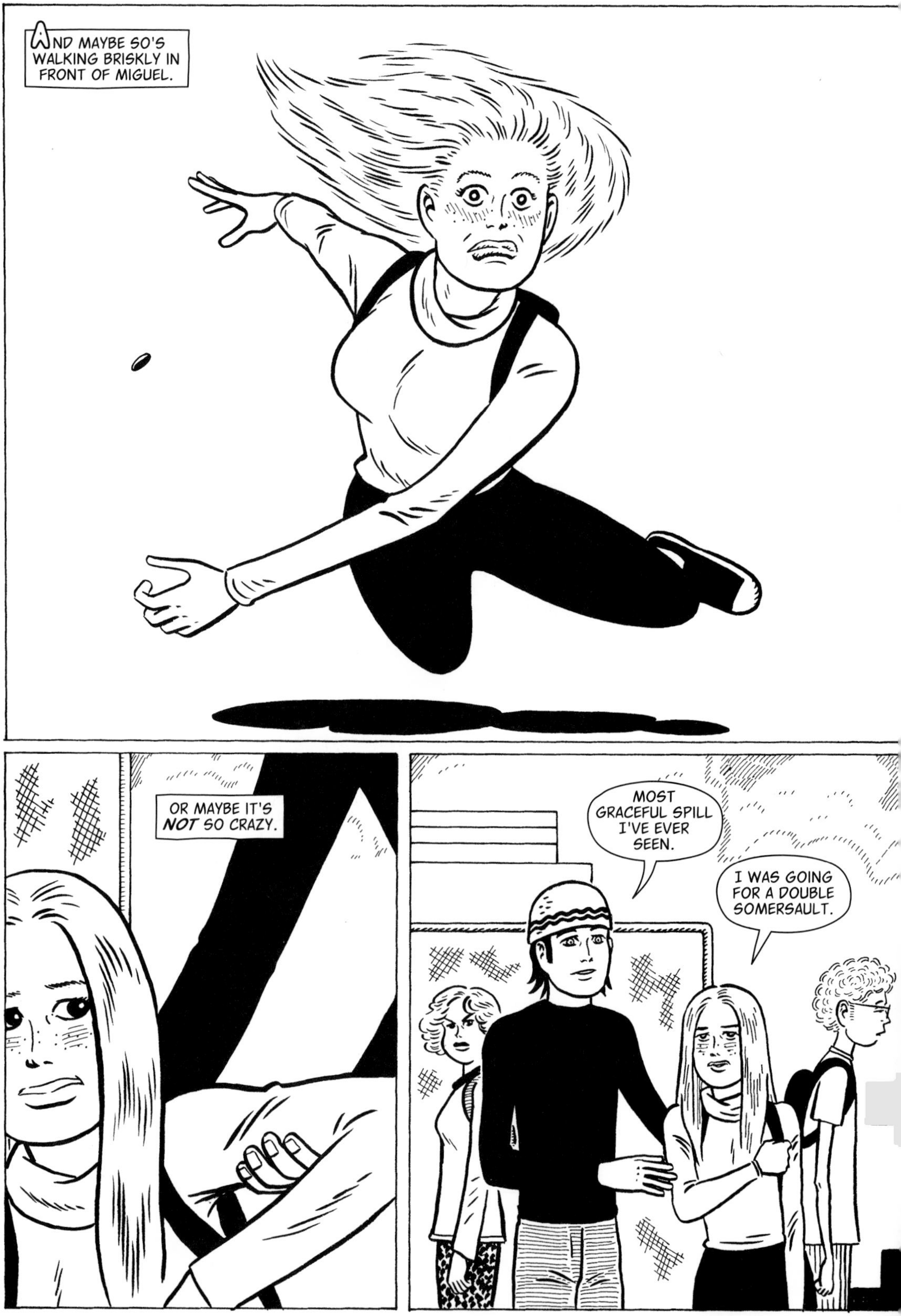
AND MAYBE SO'S WALKING BRISKLY IN FRONT OF MIGUEL.
OR MAYBE IT'S **NOT** SO CRAZY.
MOST GRACEFUL SPILL I'VE EVER SEEN.
I WAS GOING FOR A DOUBLE SOMERSAULT.

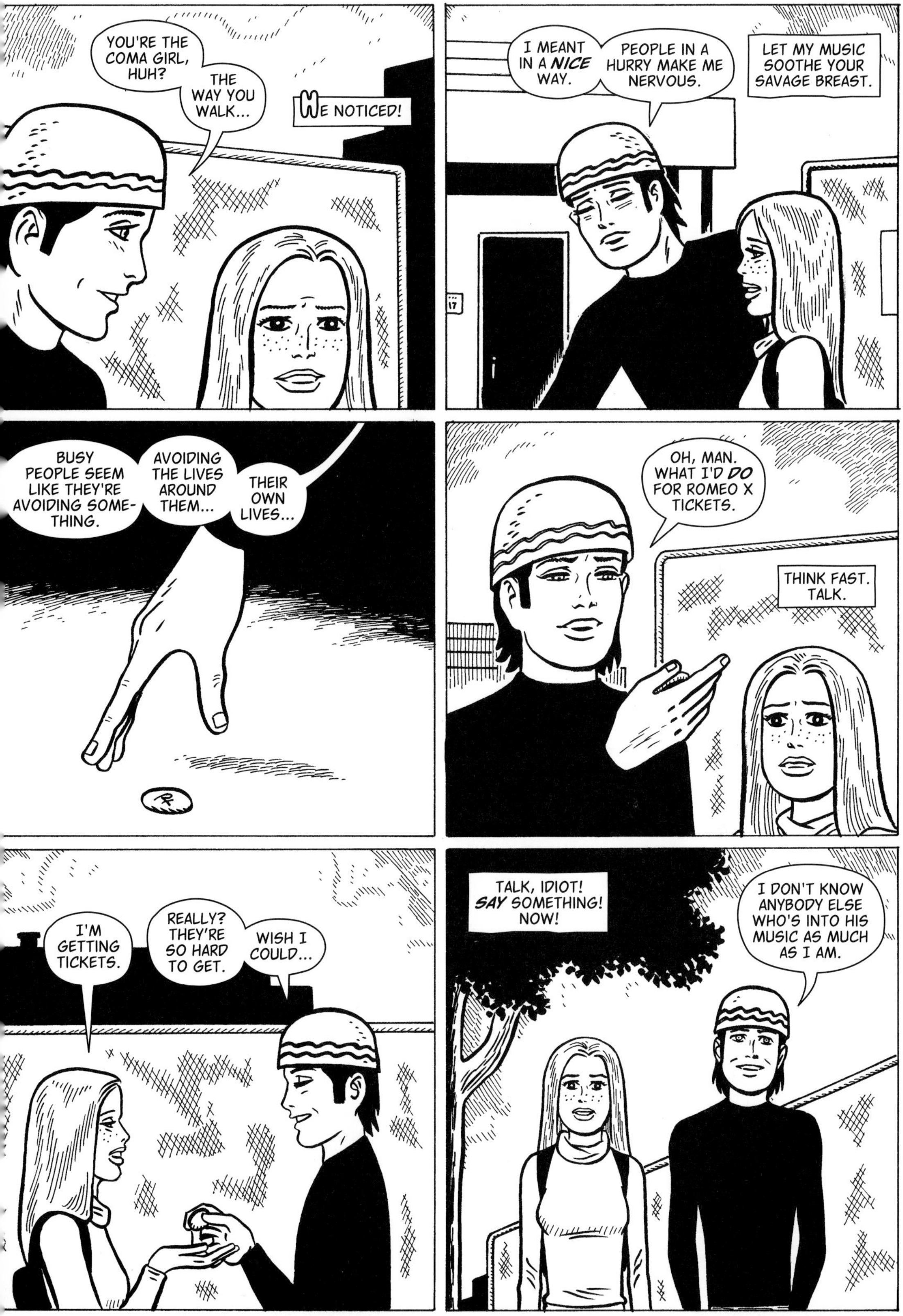
YOU'RE THE COMA GIRL, HUH?
THE WAY YOU WALK...
HE NOTICED!
I MEANT IN A NICE WAY.
PEOPLE IN A HURRY MAKE ME NERVOUS.
LET MY MUSIC SOOTHE YOUR SAVAGE BREAST.
BUSY PEOPLE SEEM LIKE THEY'RE AVOIDING SOME-THING.
AVOIDING THE LIVES AROUND THEM...
THEIR OWN LIVES...
OH, MAN. WHAT I'D DO FOR ROMEO X TICKETS.
THINK FAST. TALK.
I'M GETTING TICKETS.
REALLY? THEY'RE SO HARD TO GET.
WISH I COULD...
TALK, IDIOT! SAY SOMETHING! NOW!
I DON'T KNOW ANYBODY ELSE WHO'S INTO HIS MUSIC AS MUCH AS I AM.

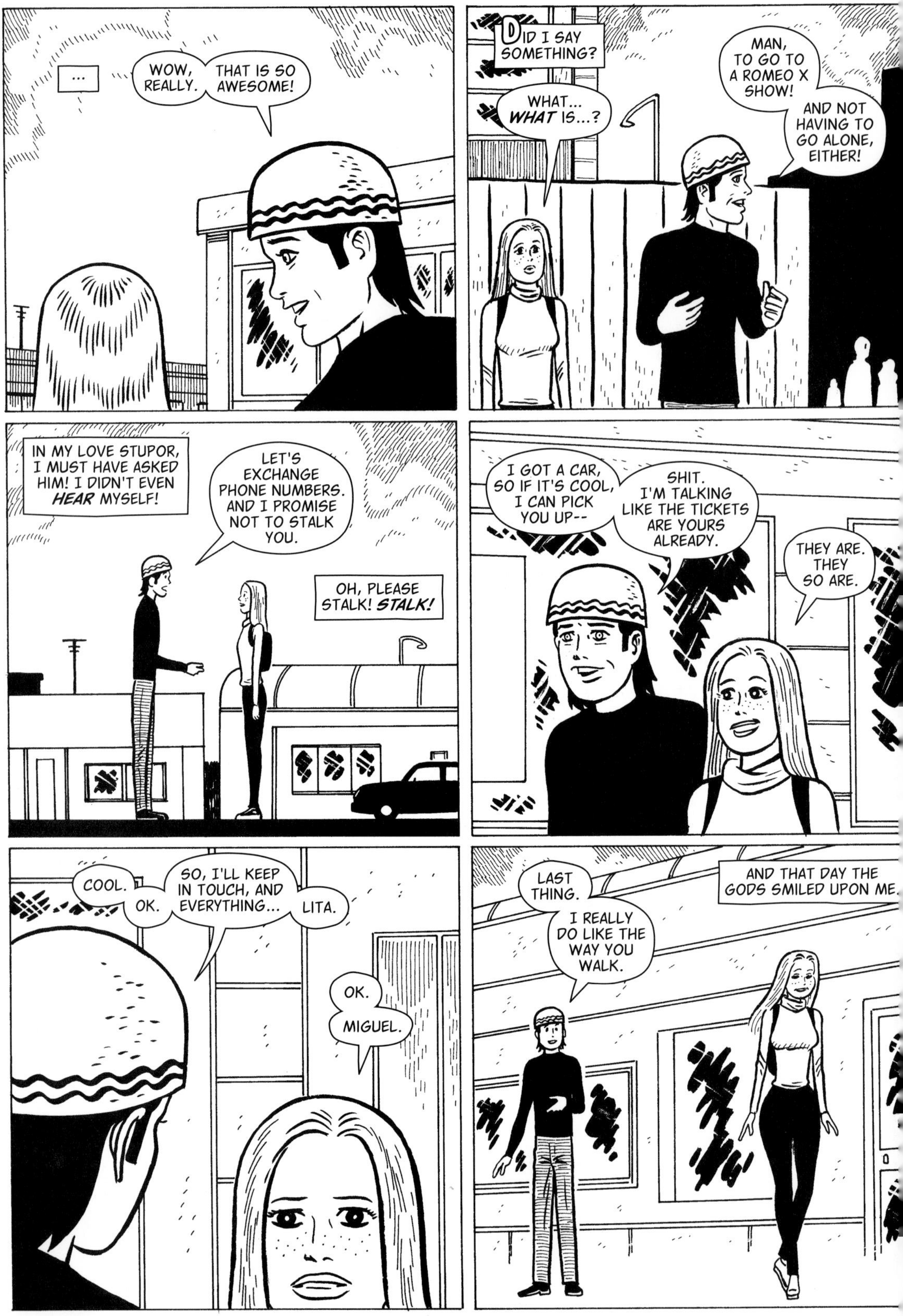
...
WOW, REALLY.
THAT IS SO AWESOME!
DID I SAY SOMETHING?
WHAT... WHAT IS...?
MAN, TO GO TO A ROMEO X SHOW!
AND NOT HAVING TO GO ALONE, EITHER!
IN MY LOVE STUPOR, I MUST HAVE ASKED HIM! I DIDN'T EVEN HEAR MYSELF!
LET'S EXCHANGE PHONE NUMBERS. AND I PROMISE NOT TO STALK YOU.
OH, PLEASE STALK! STALK!
I GOT A CAR, SO IF IT'S COOL, I CAN PICK YOU UP--
SHIT. I'M TALKING LIKE THE TICKETS ARE YOURS ALREADY.
THEY ARE. THEY SO ARE.
COOL.
OK.
SO, I'LL KEEP IN TOUCH, AND EVERYTHING...
LITA.
OK.
MIGUEL.
LAST THING.
I REALLY DO LIKE THE WAY YOU WALK.
AND THAT DAY THE GODS SMILED UPON ME.

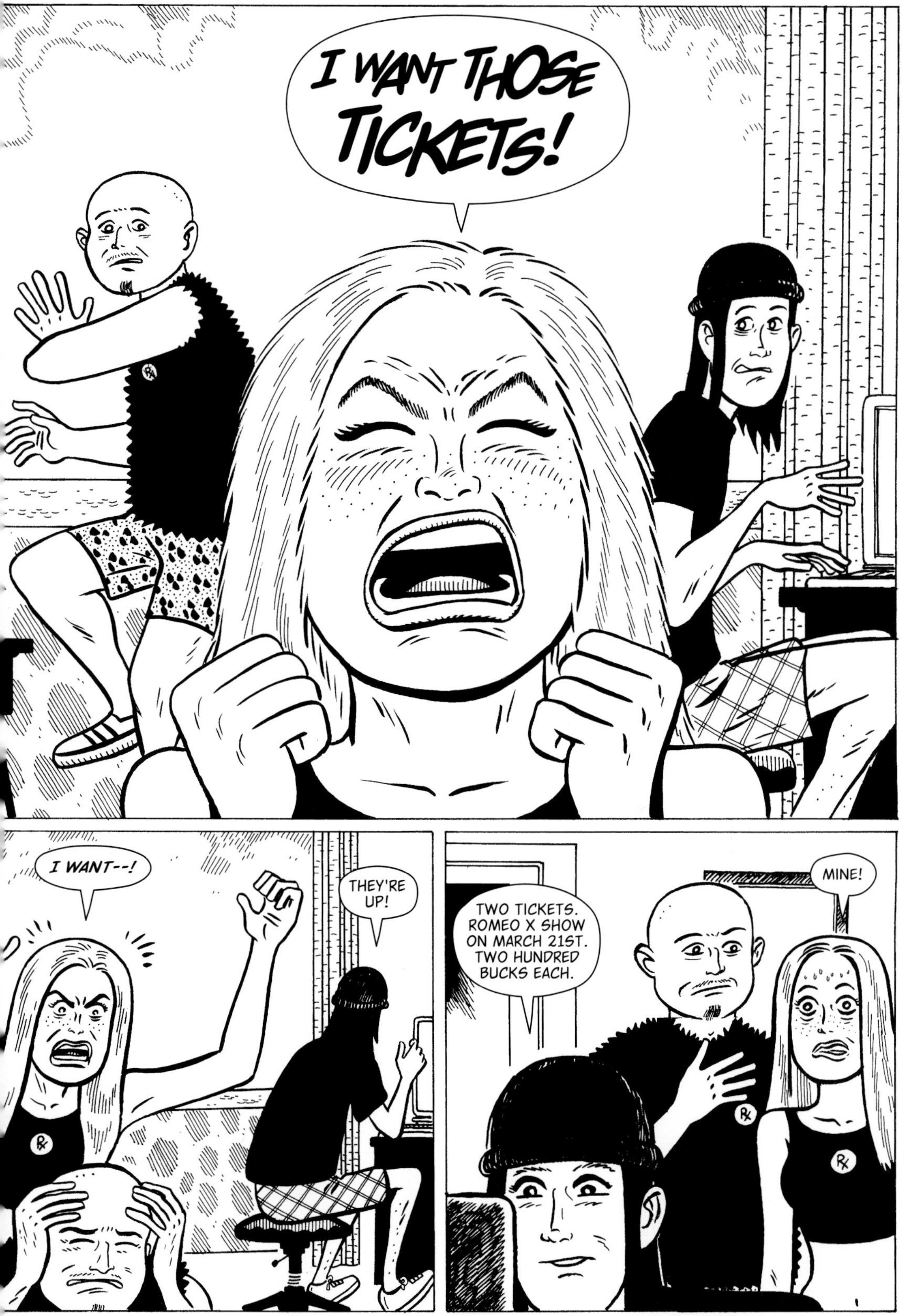
I WANT THOSE TICKETS!
I WANT--!
THEY'RE UP!
TWO TICKETS. ROMEO X SHOW ON MARCH 21ST. TWO HUNDRED BUCKS EACH.
MINE!

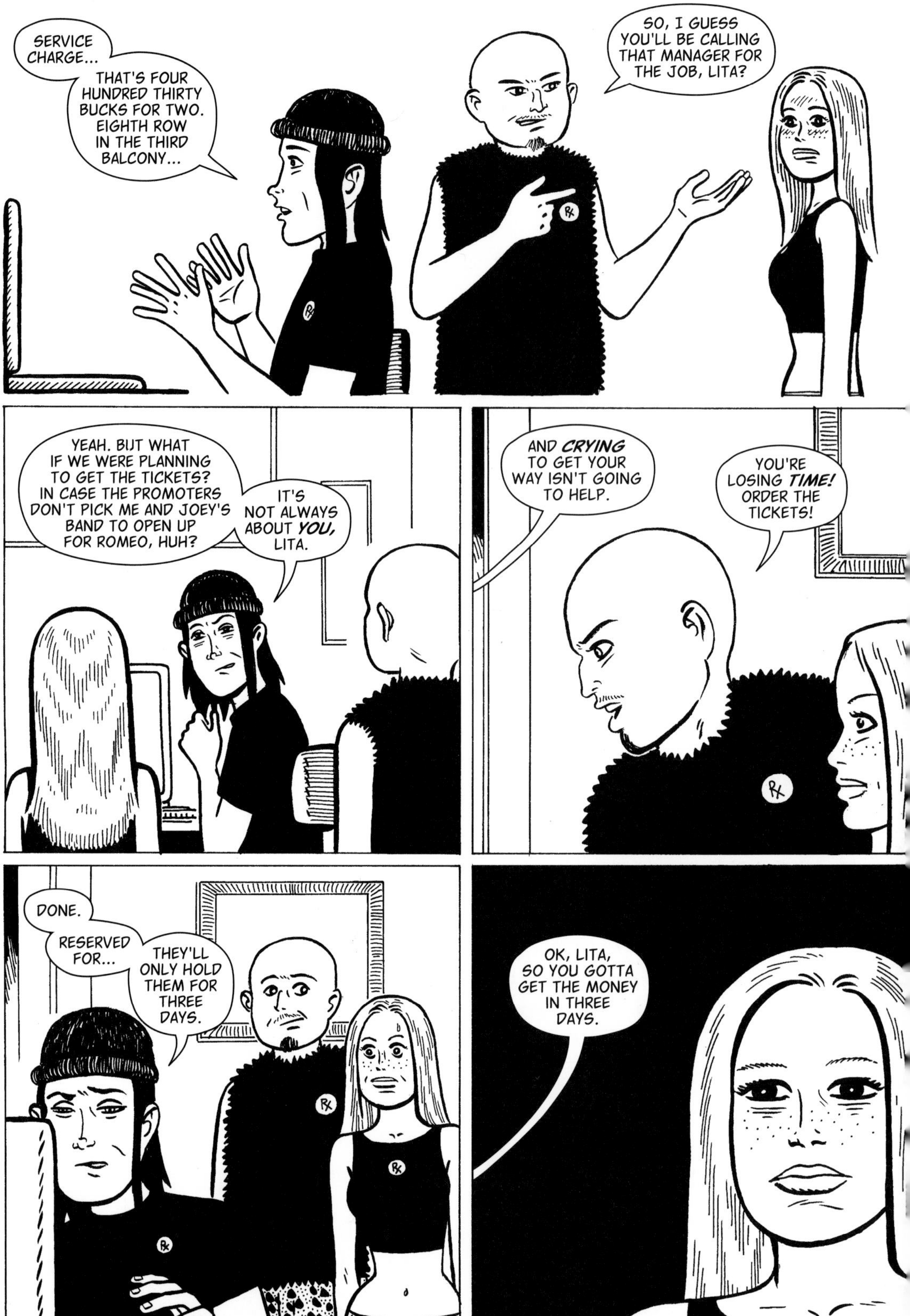
SERVICE CHARGE...
THAT'S FOUR HUNDRED THIRTY BUCKS FOR TWO. EIGHTH ROW IN THE THIRD BALCONY...
SO, I GUESS YOU'LL BE CALLING THAT MANAGER FOR THE JOB, LITA?
YEAH. BUT WHAT IF WE WERE PLANNING TO GET THE TICKETS? IN CASE THE PROMOTERS DON'T PICK ME AND JOEY'S BAND TO OPEN UP FOR ROMEO, HUH?
IT'S NOT ALWAYS ABOUT *YOU,* LITA.
AND *CRYING* TO GET YOUR WAY ISN'T GOING TO HELP.
YOU'RE LOSING *TIME!* ORDER THE TICKETS!
DONE.
RESERVED FOR...
THEY'LL ONLY HOLD THEM FOR THREE DAYS.
OK, LITA, SO YOU GOTTA GET THE MONEY IN THREE DAYS.

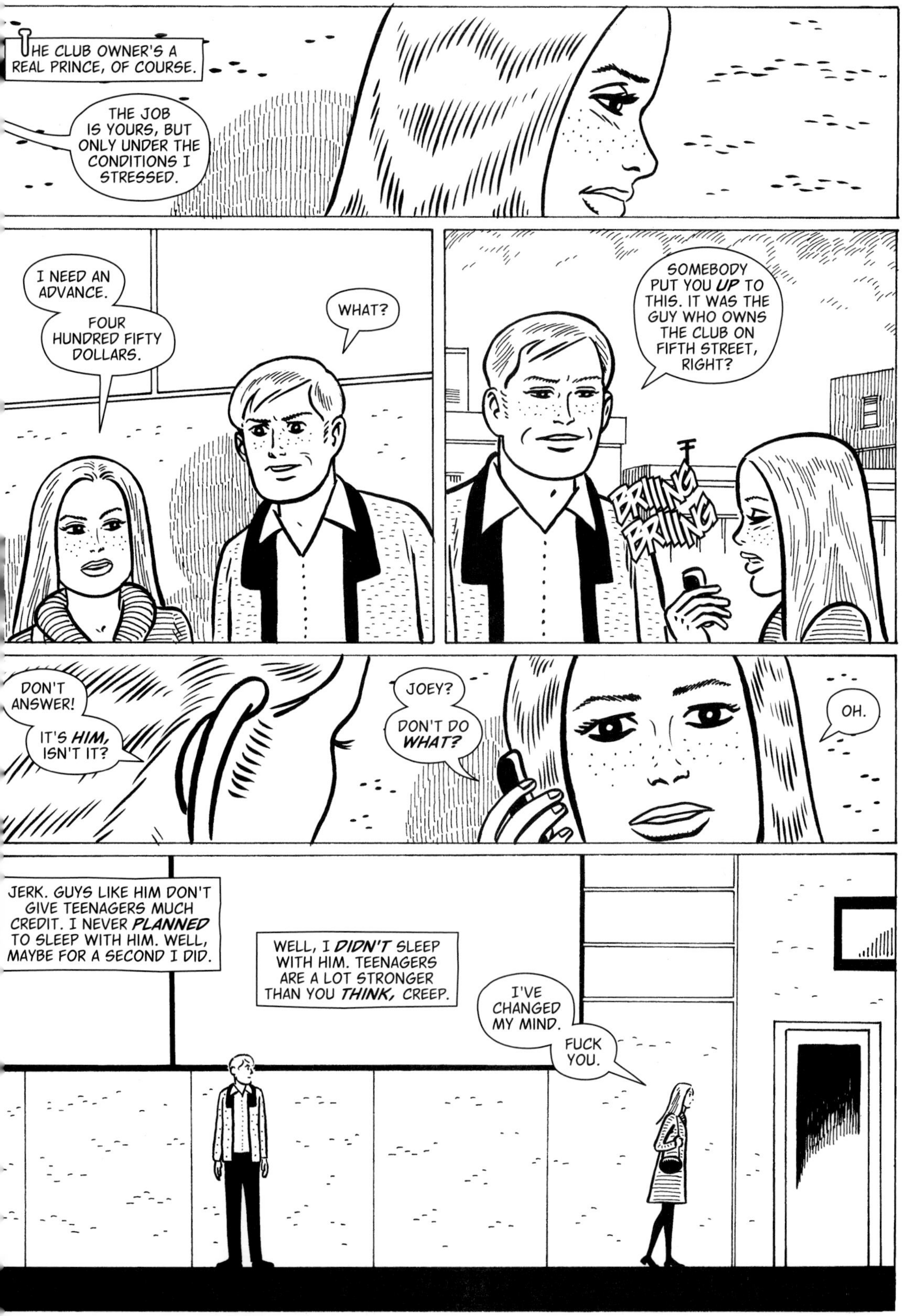
THE CLUB OWNER'S A REAL PRINCE, OF COURSE.
THE JOB IS YOURS, BUT ONLY UNDER THE CONDITIONS I STRESSED.
I NEED AN ADVANCE.
FOUR HUNDRED FIFTY DOLLARS.
WHAT?
SOMEBODY PUT YOU UP TO THIS. IT WAS THE GUY WHO OWNS THE CLUB ON FIFTH STREET, RIGHT?
BRIIING BRIIING
DON'T ANSWER!
IT'S HIM, ISN'T IT?
JOEY?
DON'T DO WHAT?
OH.
JERK. GUYS LIKE HIM DON'T GIVE TEENAGERS MUCH CREDIT. I NEVER PLANNED TO SLEEP WITH HIM. WELL, MAYBE FOR A SECOND I DID.
WELL, I DIDN'T SLEEP WITH HIM. TEENAGERS ARE A LOT STRONGER THAN YOU THINK, CREEP.
I'VE CHANGED MY MIND.
FUCK YOU.

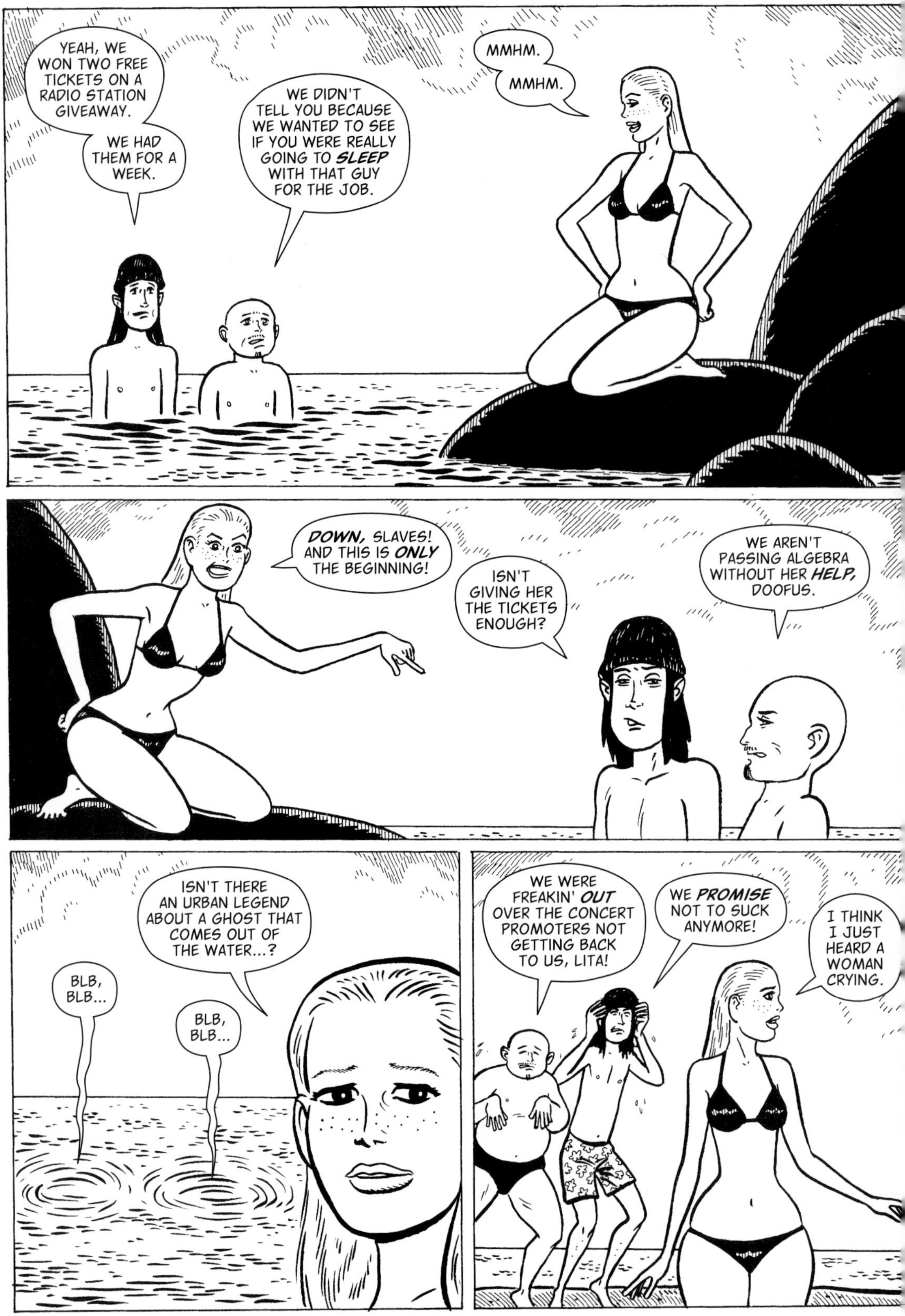
YEAH, WE WON TWO FREE TICKETS ON A RADIO STATION GIVEAWAY.
WE HAD THEM FOR A WEEK.
WE DIDN'T TELL YOU BECAUSE WE WANTED TO SEE IF YOU WERE REALLY GOING TO *SLEEP* WITH THAT GUY FOR THE JOB.
MMHM.
MMHM.
DOWN, SLAVES! AND THIS IS *ONLY* THE BEGINNING!
ISN'T GIVING HER THE TICKETS ENOUGH?
WE AREN'T PASSING ALGEBRA WITHOUT HER *HELP,* DOOFUS.
BLB, BLB...
BLB, BLB...
ISN'T THERE AN URBAN LEGEND ABOUT A GHOST THAT COMES OUT OF THE WATER...?
WE WERE FREAKIN' *OUT* OVER THE CONCERT PROMOTERS NOT GETTING BACK TO US, LITA!
WE *PROMISE* NOT TO SUCK ANYMORE!
I THINK I JUST HEARD A WOMAN CRYING.

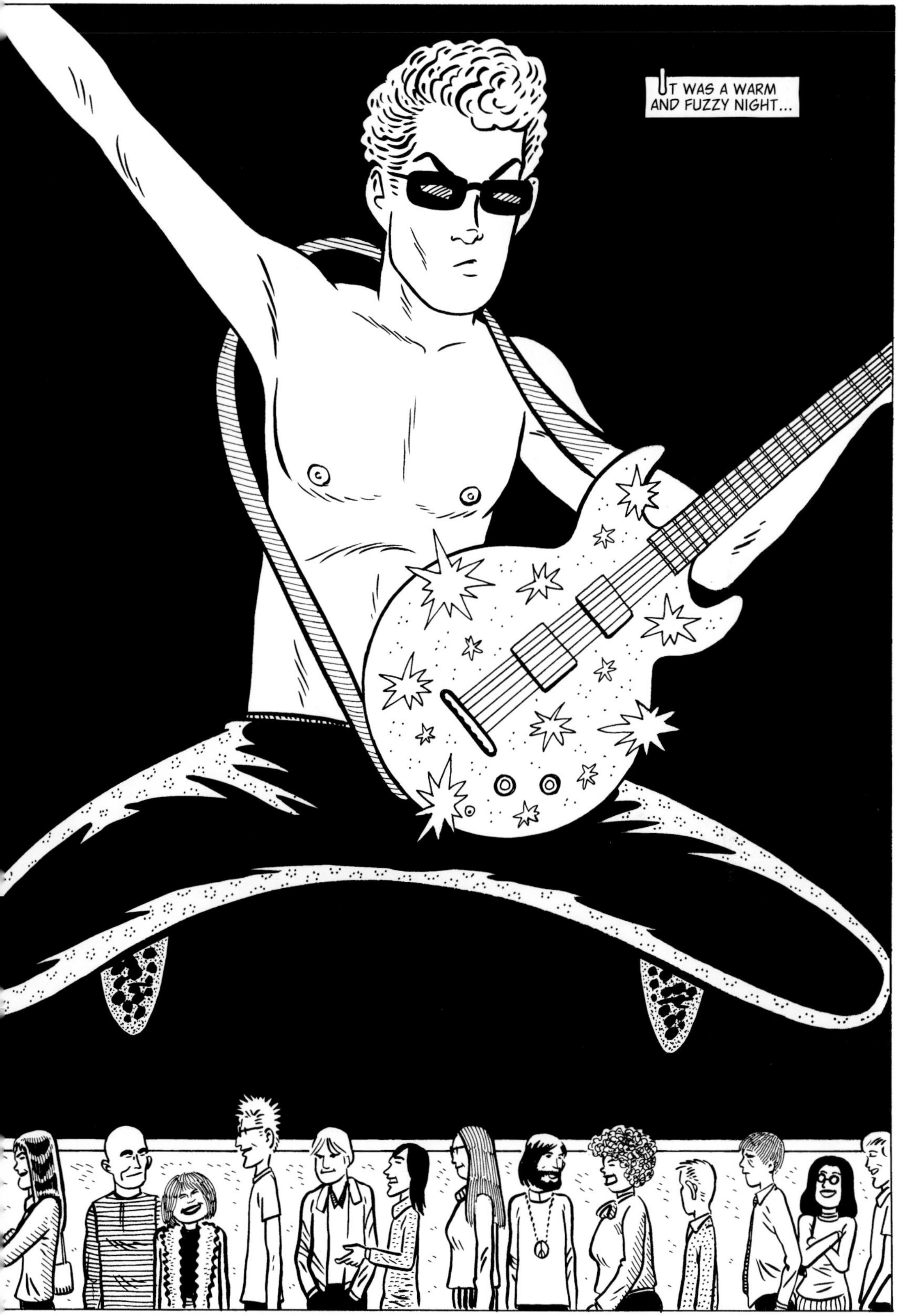
IT WAS A WARM AND FUZZY NIGHT...

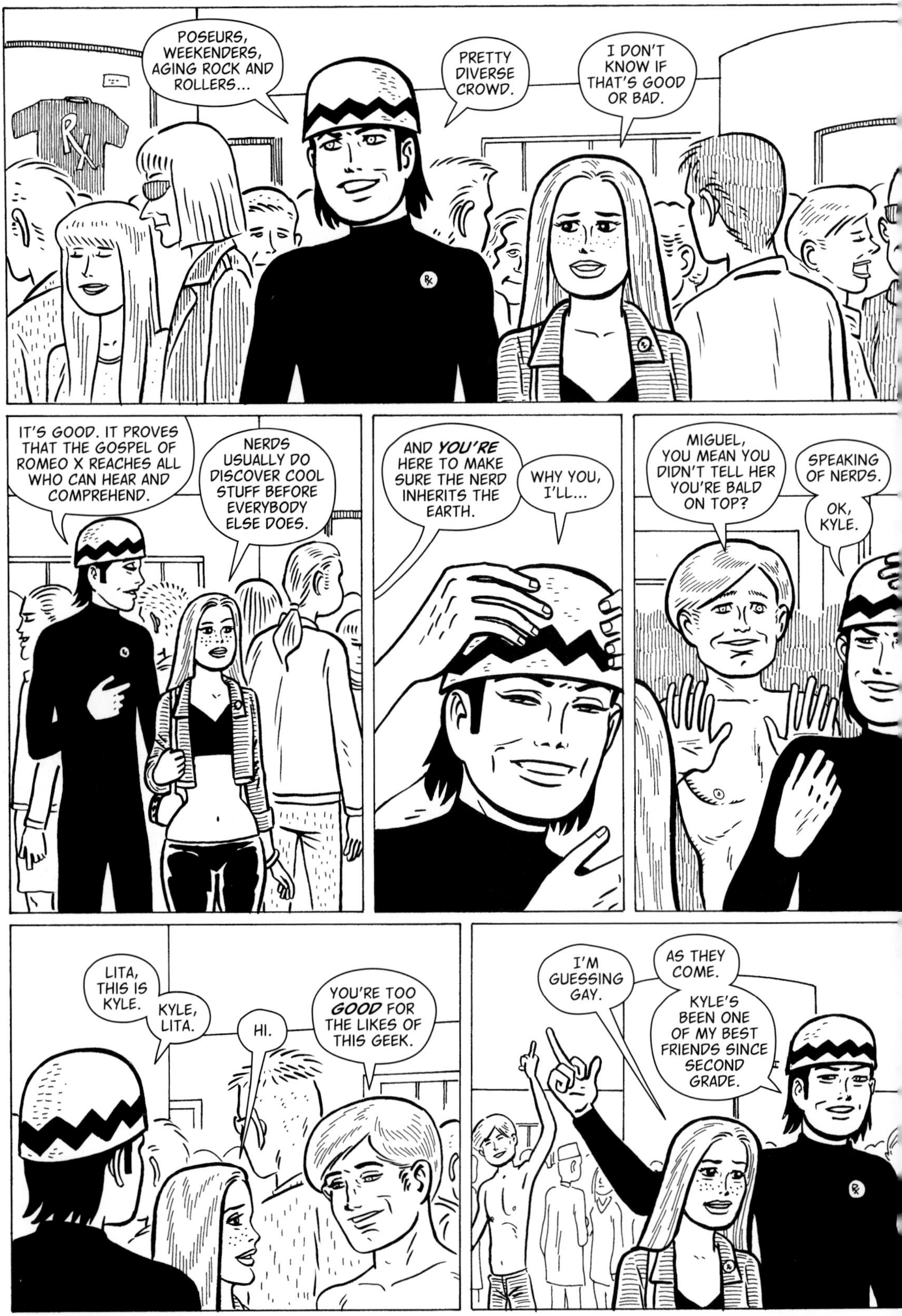
POSEURS, WEEKENDERS, AGING ROCK AND ROLLERS...
PRETTY DIVERSE CROWD.
I DON'T KNOW IF THAT'S GOOD OR BAD.
IT'S GOOD. IT PROVES THAT THE GOSPEL OF ROMEO X REACHES ALL WHO CAN HEAR AND COMPREHEND.
NERDS USUALLY DO DISCOVER COOL STUFF BEFORE EVERYBODY ELSE DOES.
AND YOU'RE HERE TO MAKE SURE THE NERD INHERITS THE EARTH.
WHY YOU, I'LL...
MIGUEL, YOU MEAN YOU DIDN'T TELL HER YOU'RE BALD ON TOP?
SPEAKING OF NERDS.
OK, KYLE.
LITA, THIS IS KYLE.
KYLE, LITA.
HI.
YOU'RE TOO GOOD FOR THE LIKES OF THIS GEEK.
I'M GUESSING GAY.
AS THEY COME.
KYLE'S BEEN ONE OF MY BEST FRIENDS SINCE SECOND GRADE.

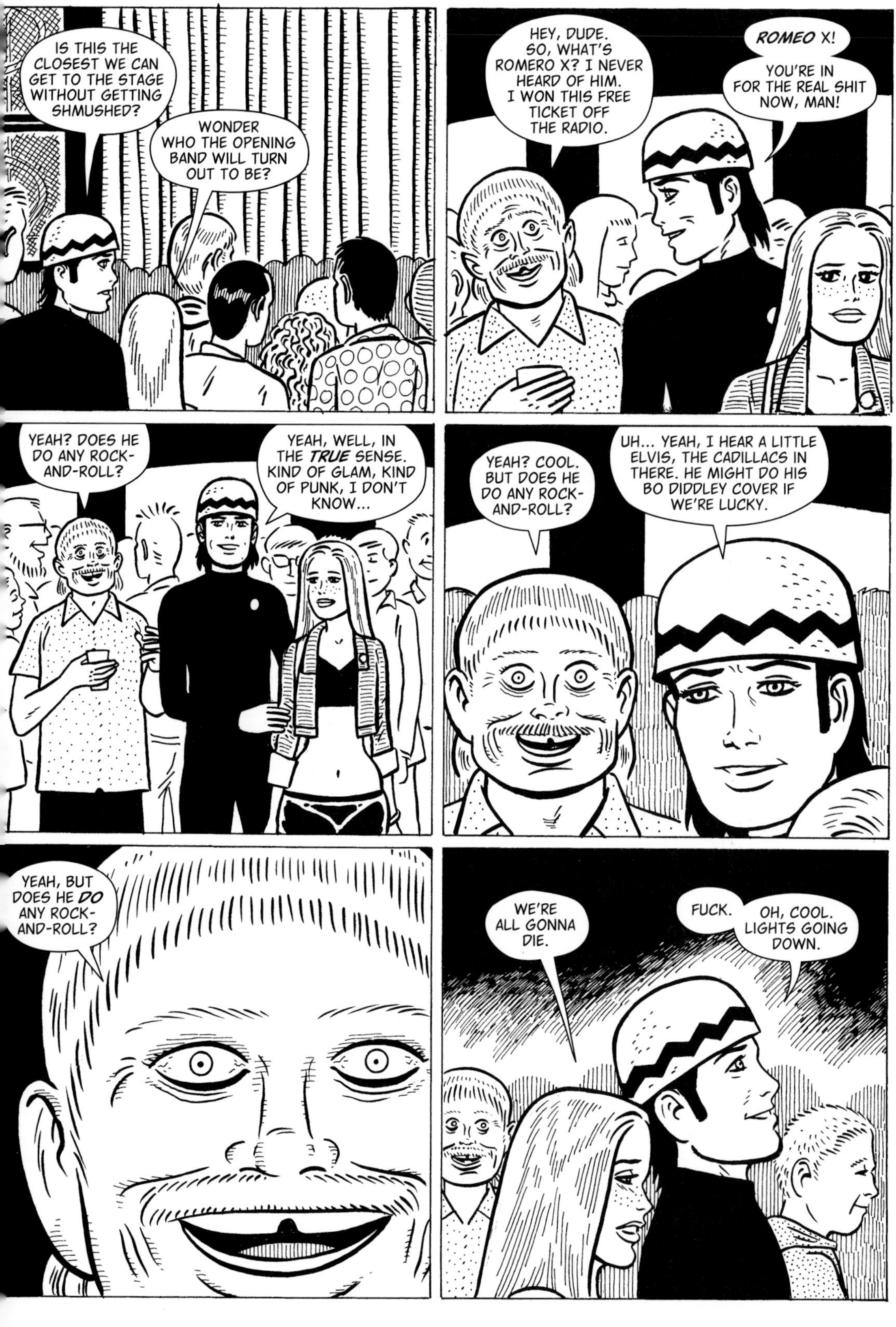
IS THIS THE CLOSEST WE CAN GET TO THE STAGE WITHOUT GETTING SHMUSHED?
WONDER WHO THE OPENING BAND WILL TURN OUT TO BE?
HEY, DUDE. SO, WHAT'S ROMERO X? I NEVER HEARD OF HIM. I WON THIS FREE TICKET OFF THE RADIO.
ROMEO X!
YOU'RE IN FOR THE REAL SHIT NOW, MAN!
YEAH? DOES HE DO ANY ROCK-AND-ROLL?
YEAH, WELL, IN THE TRUE SENSE. KIND OF GLAM, KIND OF PUNK, I DON'T KNOW...
YEAH? COOL. BUT DOES HE DO ANY ROCK-AND-ROLL?
UH... YEAH, I HEAR A LITTLE ELVIS, THE CADILLACS IN THERE. HE MIGHT DO HIS BO DIDDLEY COVER IF WE'RE LUCKY.
YEAH, BUT DOES HE DO ANY ROCK-AND-ROLL?
WE'RE ALL GONNA DIE.
FUCK.
OH, COOL. LIGHTS GOING DOWN.

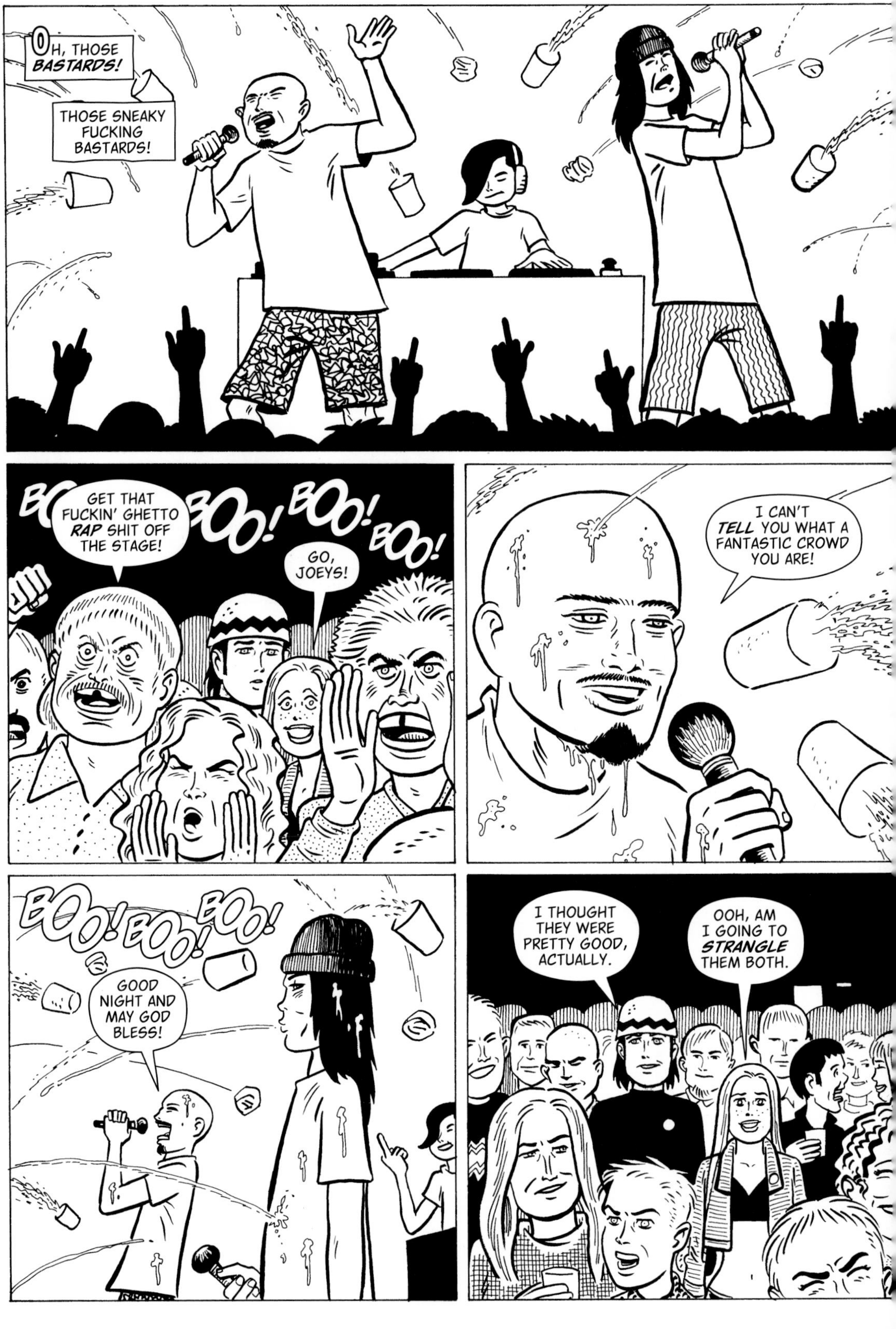
OH, THOSE BASTARDS!
THOSE SNEAKY FUCKING BASTARDS!
BOO! BOO! BOO! BOO!
GET THAT FUCKIN' GHETTO RAP SHIT OFF THE STAGE!
GO, JOEYS!
I CAN'T TELL YOU WHAT A FANTASTIC CROWD YOU ARE!
BOO! BOO! BOO!
GOOD NIGHT AND MAY GOD BLESS!
I THOUGHT THEY WERE PRETTY GOOD, ACTUALLY.
OOH, AM I GOING TO STRANGLE THEM BOTH.

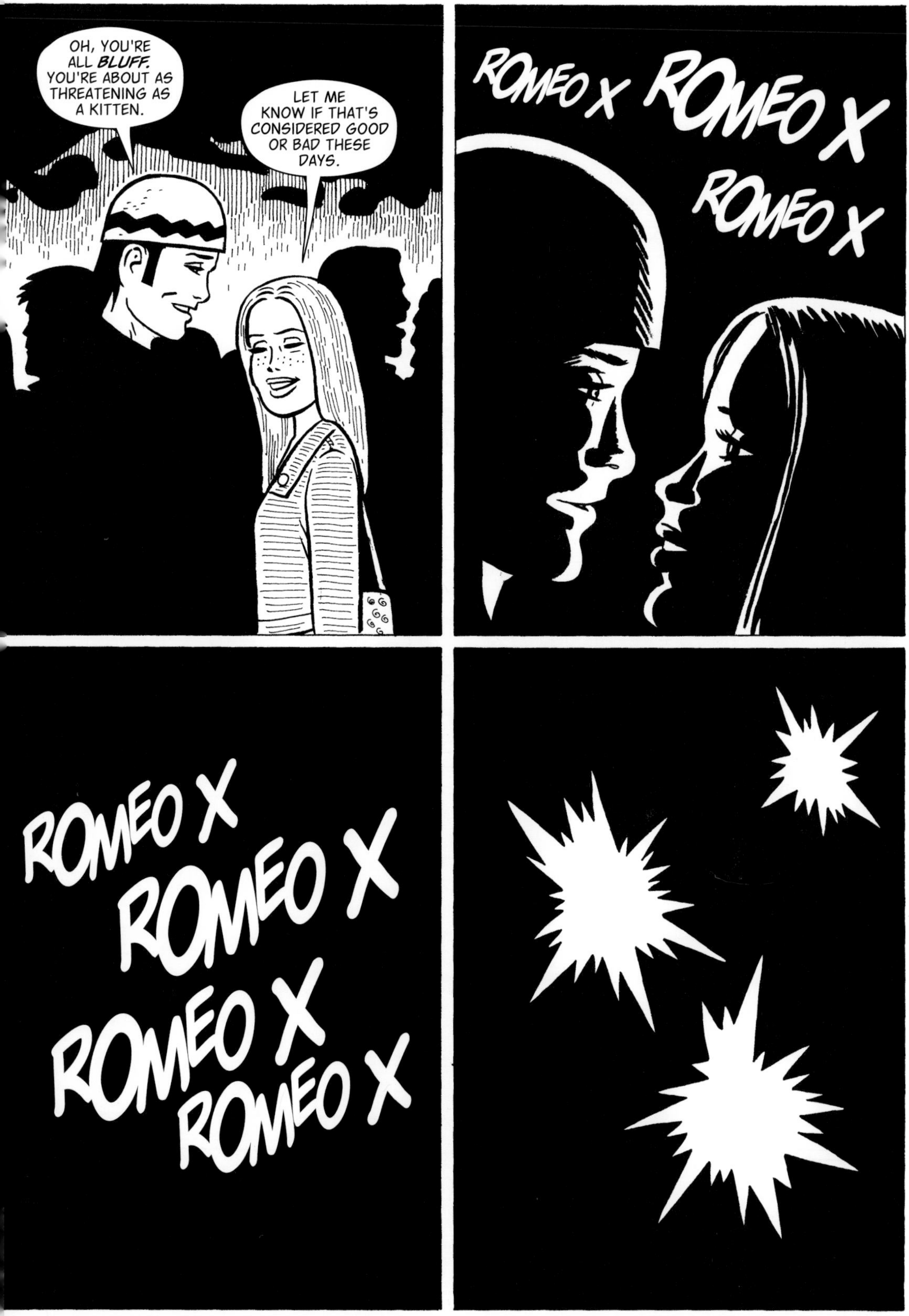

OH, YOU'RE ALL BLUFF. YOU'RE ABOUT AS THREATENING AS A KITTEN.
LET ME KNOW IF THAT'S CONSIDERED GOOD OR BAD THESE DAYS.
ROMEO X ROMEO X ROMEO X
ROMEO X ROMEO X ROMEO X ROMEO X

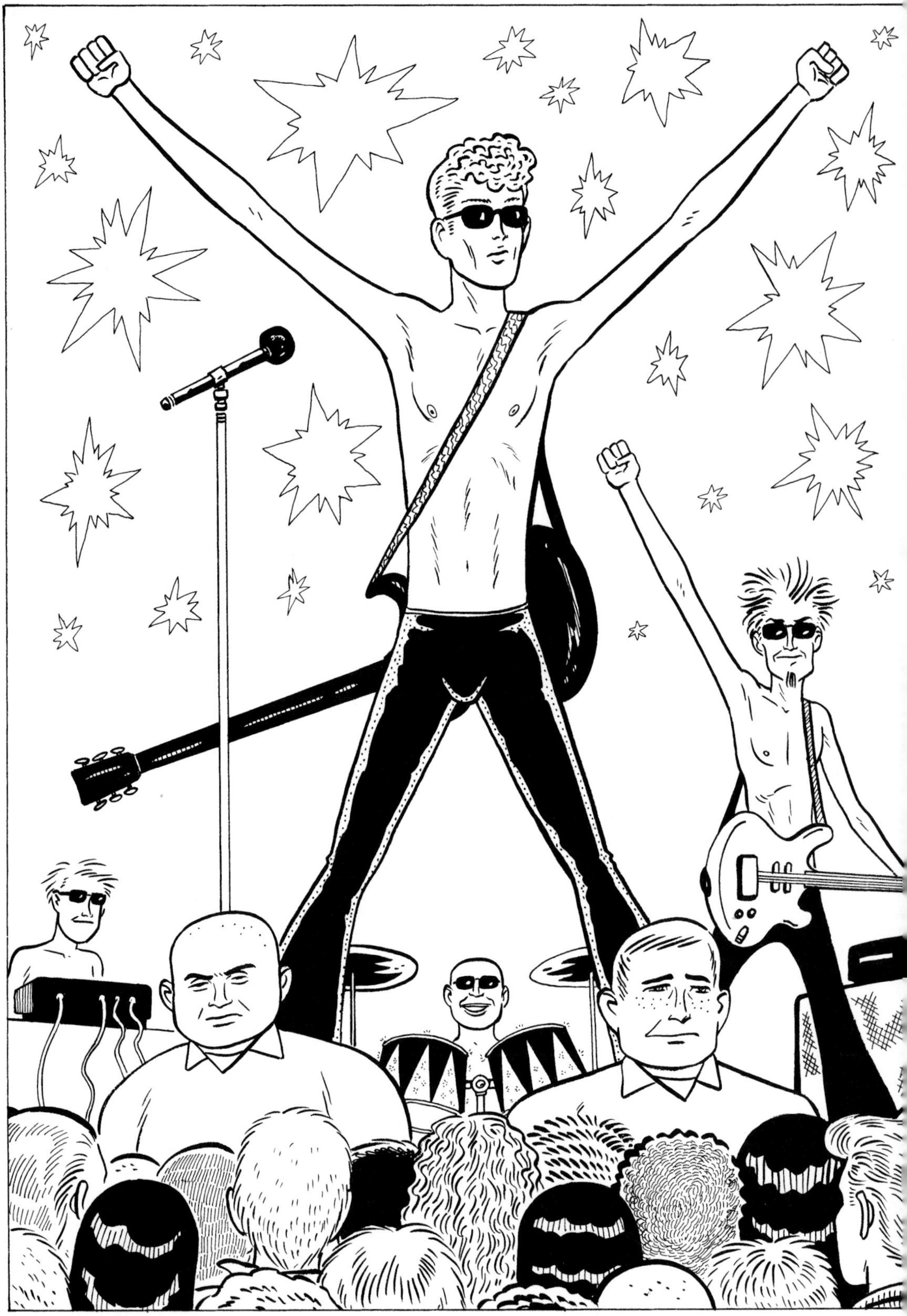

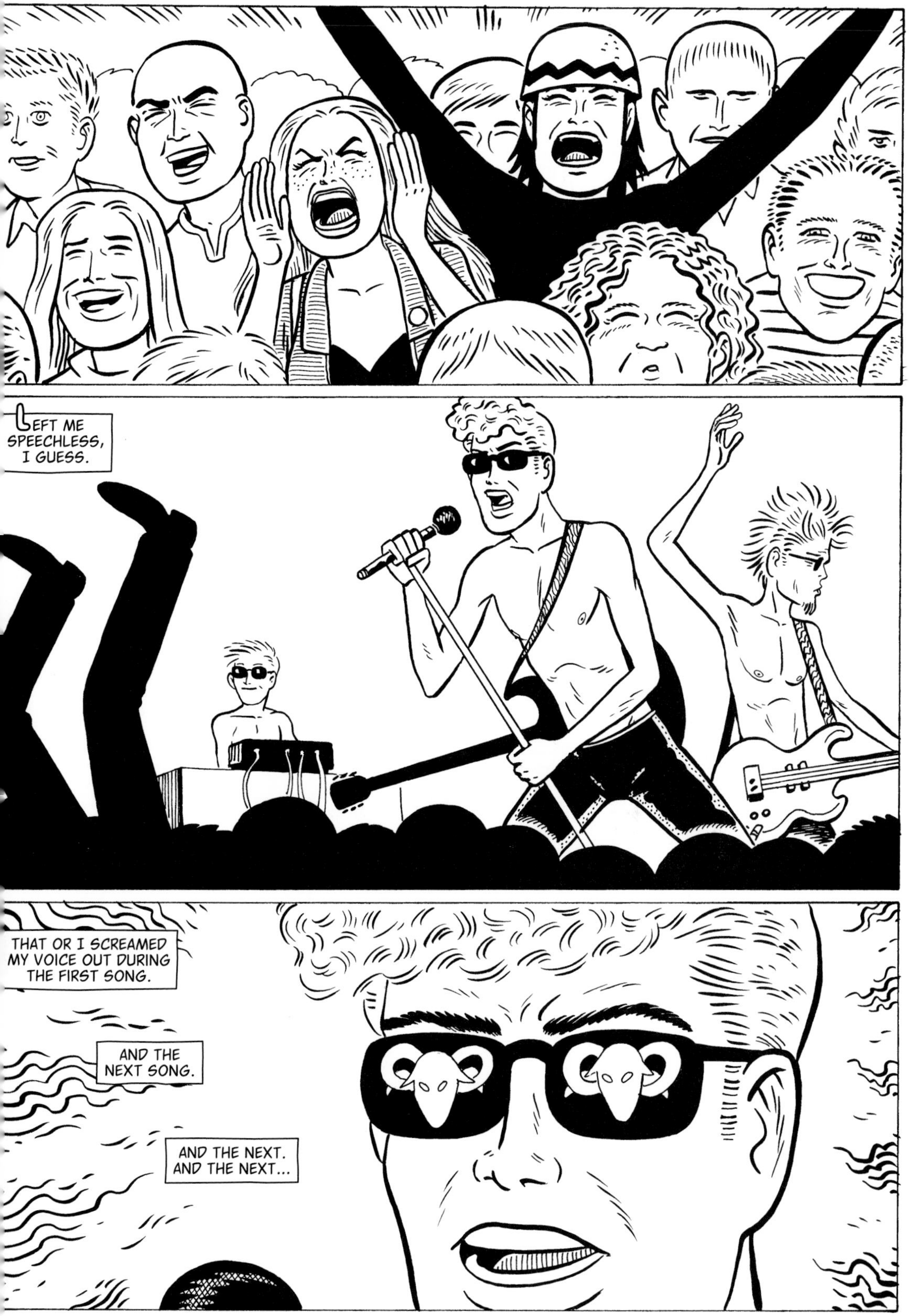
LEFT ME SPEECHLESS, I GUESS.
THAT OR I SCREAMED MY VOICE OUT DURING THE FIRST SONG.
AND THE NEXT SONG.
AND THE NEXT. AND THE NEXT...

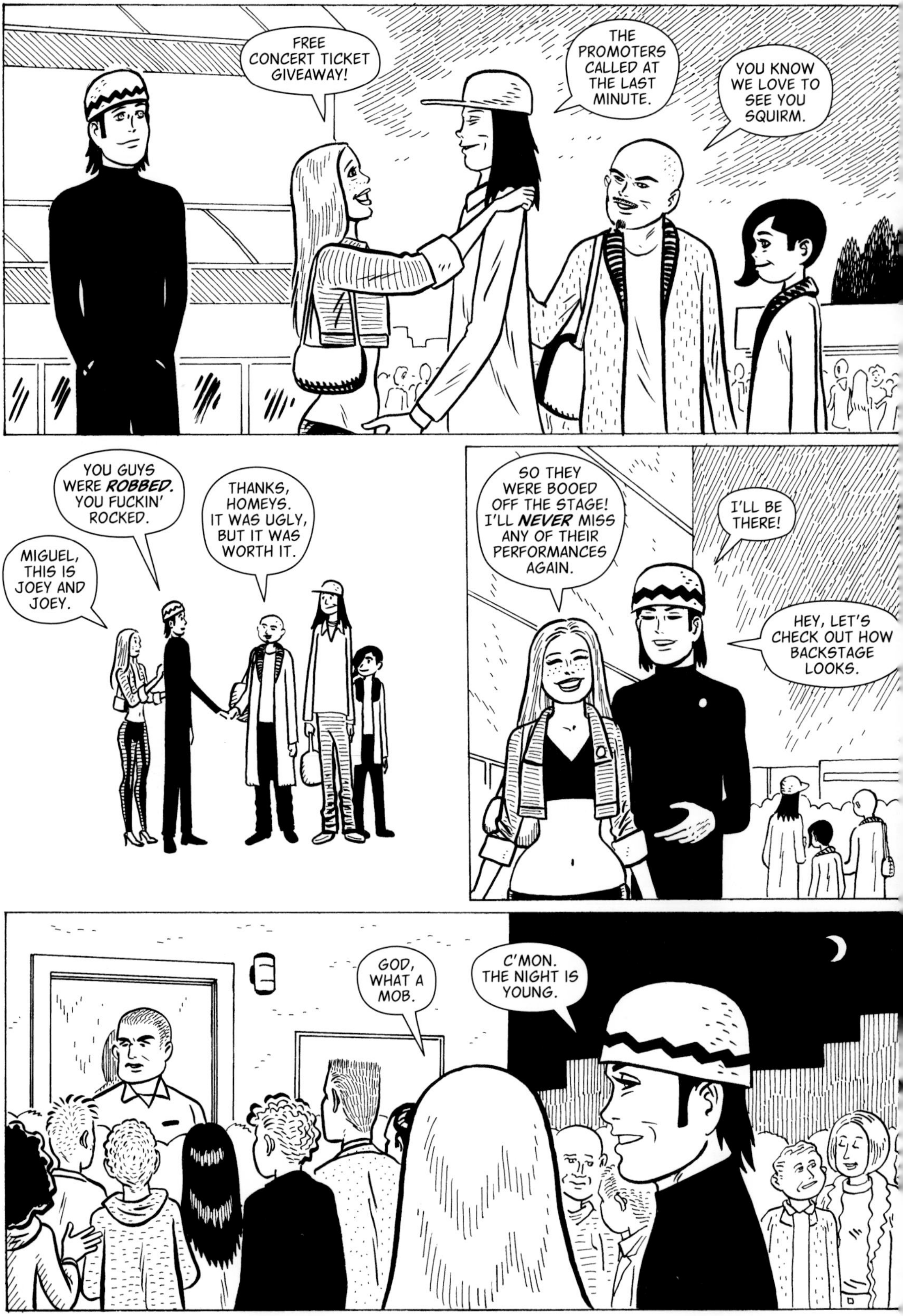
FREE CONCERT TICKET GIVEAWAY!
THE PROMOTERS CALLED AT THE LAST MINUTE.
YOU KNOW WE LOVE TO SEE YOU SQUIRM.
YOU GUYS WERE ROBBED. YOU FUCKIN' ROCKED.
THANKS, HOMEYS. IT WAS UGLY, BUT IT WAS WORTH IT.
MIGUEL, THIS IS JOEY AND JOEY.
SO THEY WERE BOOED OFF THE STAGE! I'LL NEVER MISS ANY OF THEIR PERFORMANCES AGAIN.
I'LL BE THERE!
HEY, LET'S CHECK OUT HOW BACKSTAGE LOOKS.
GOD, WHAT A MOB.
C'MON. THE NIGHT IS YOUNG.

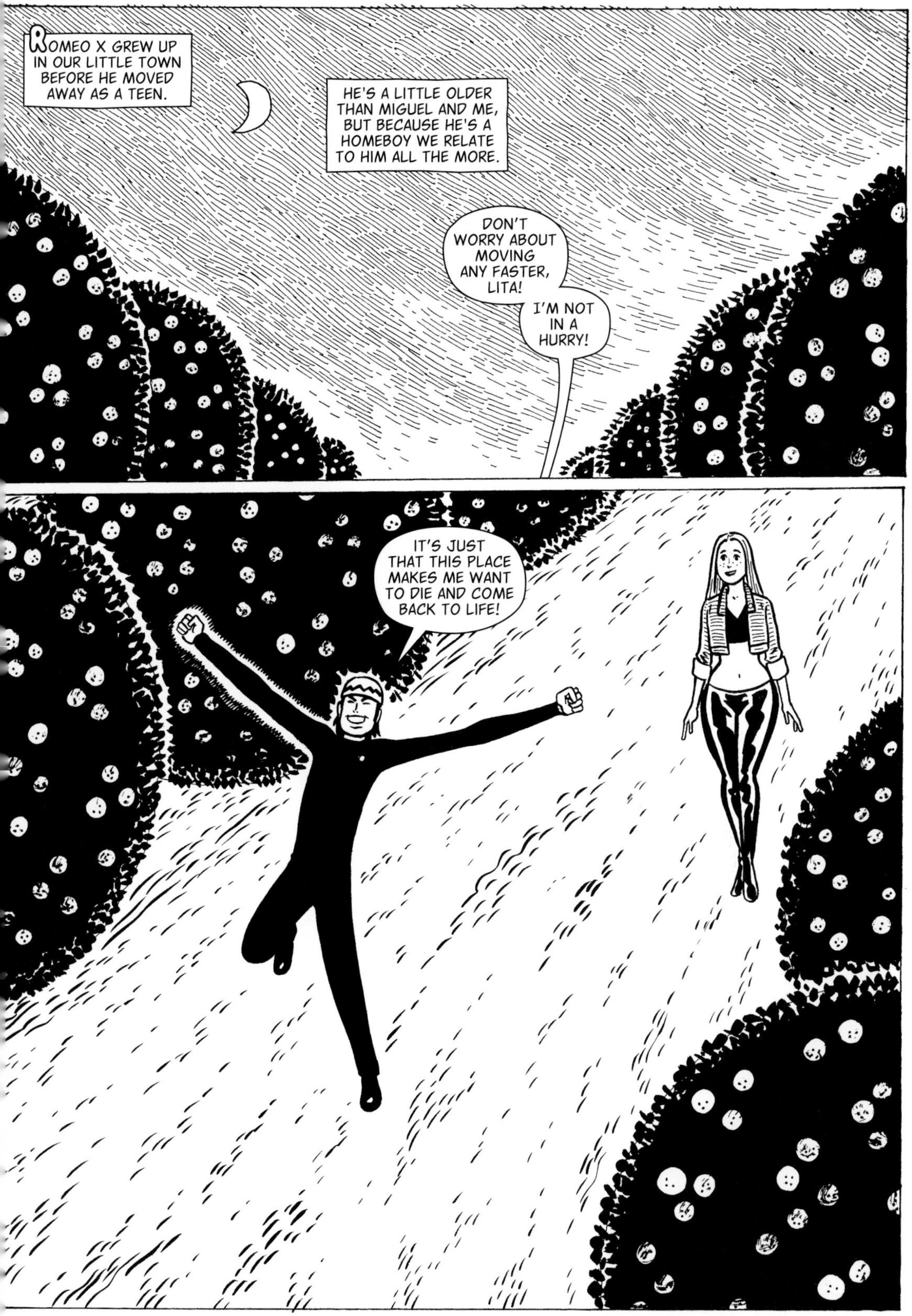
ROMEO X GREW UP IN OUR LITTLE TOWN BEFORE HE MOVED AWAY AS A TEEN.
HE'S A LITTLE OLDER THAN MIGUEL AND ME, BUT BECAUSE HE'S A HOMEBOY WE RELATE TO HIM ALL THE MORE.
DON'T WORRY ABOUT MOVING ANY FASTER, LITA!
I'M NOT IN A HURRY!
IT'S JUST THAT THIS PLACE MAKES ME WANT TO DIE AND COME BACK TO LIFE!

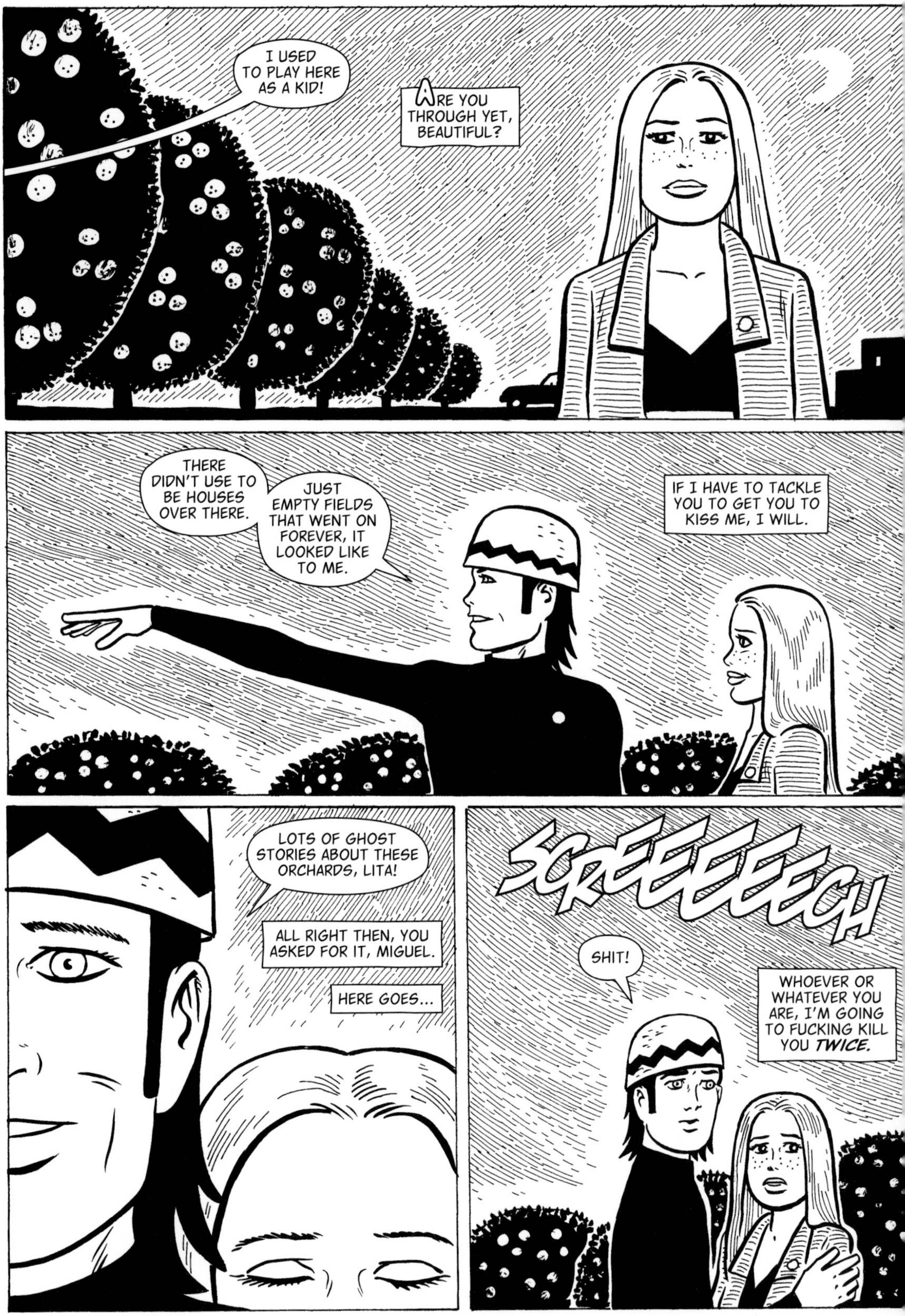

I USED TO PLAY HERE AS A KID!
ARE YOU THROUGH YET, BEAUTIFUL?
THERE DIDN'T USE TO BE HOUSES OVER THERE.
JUST EMPTY FIELDS THAT WENT ON FOREVER, IT LOOKED LIKE TO ME.
IF I HAVE TO TACKLE YOU TO GET YOU TO KISS ME, I WILL.
LOTS OF GHOST STORIES ABOUT THESE ORCHARDS, LITA!
ALL RIGHT THEN, YOU ASKED FOR IT, MIGUEL.
HERE GOES...
SCREEEEEECH
SHIT!
WHOEVER OR WHATEVER YOU ARE, I'M GOING TO FUCKING KILL YOU *TWICE.*

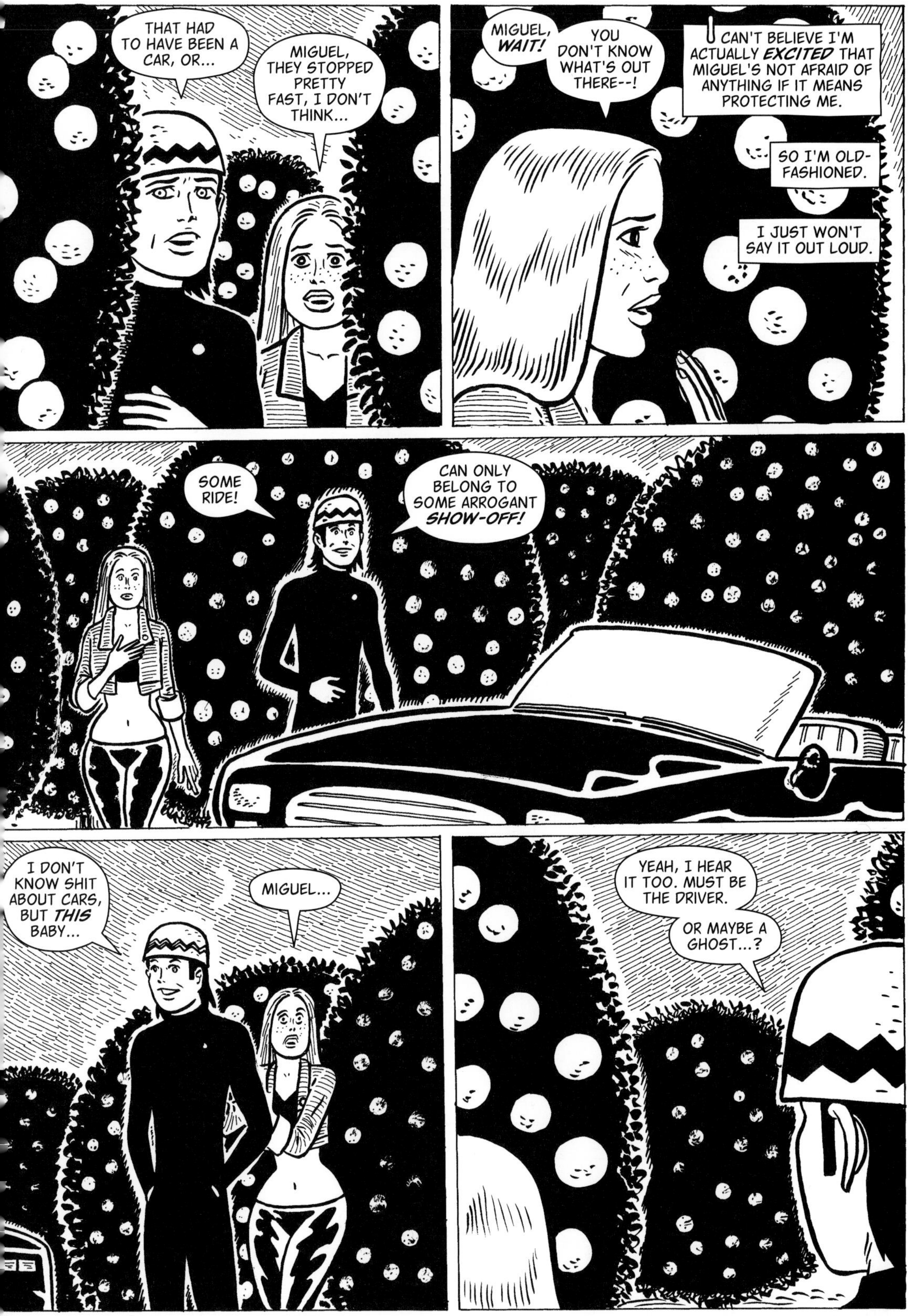
THAT HAD TO HAVE BEEN A CAR, OR...
MIGUEL, THEY STOPPED PRETTY FAST, I DON'T THINK...
MIGUEL, *WAIT!*
YOU DON'T KNOW WHAT'S OUT THERE--!
I CAN'T BELIEVE I'M ACTUALLY ***EXCITED*** THAT MIGUEL'S NOT AFRAID OF ANYTHING IF IT MEANS PROTECTING ME.
SO I'M OLD-FASHIONED.
I JUST WON'T SAY IT OUT LOUD.
SOME RIDE!
CAN ONLY BELONG TO SOME ARROGANT ***SHOW-OFF!***
I DON'T KNOW SHIT ABOUT CARS, BUT ***THIS*** BABY...
MIGUEL...
YEAH, I HEAR IT TOO. MUST BE THE DRIVER.
OR MAYBE A GHOST...?

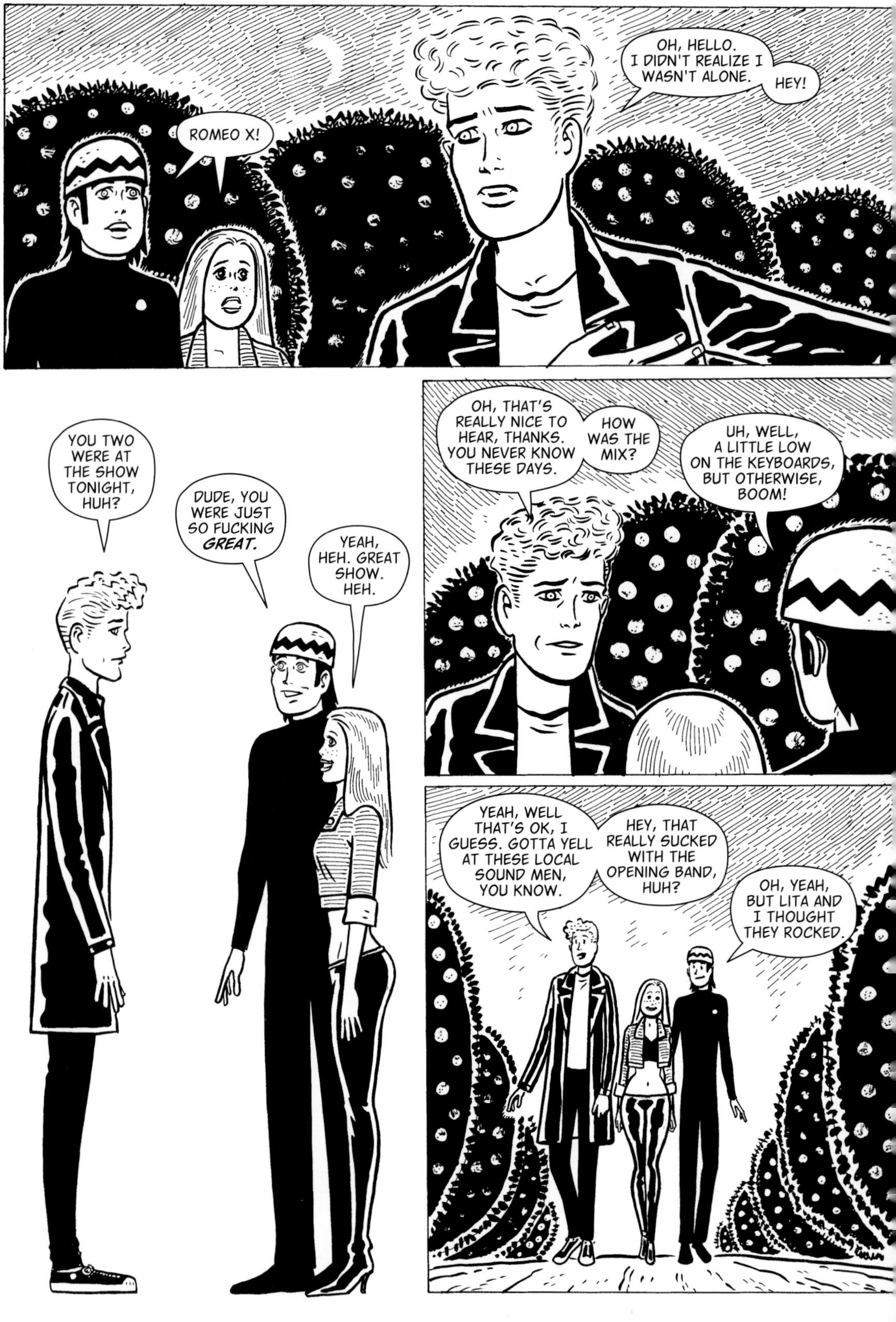
ROMEO X!
OH, HELLO. I DIDN'T REALIZE I WASN'T ALONE.
HEY!
YOU TWO WERE AT THE SHOW TONIGHT, HUH?
DUDE, YOU WERE JUST SO FUCKING *GREAT.*
YEAH, HEH. GREAT SHOW. HEH.
OH, THAT'S REALLY NICE TO HEAR, THANKS. YOU NEVER KNOW THESE DAYS.
HOW WAS THE MIX?
UH, WELL, A LITTLE LOW ON THE KEYBOARDS, BUT OTHERWISE, BOOM!
YEAH, WELL THAT'S OK, I GUESS. GOTTA YELL AT THESE LOCAL SOUND MEN, YOU KNOW.
HEY, THAT REALLY SUCKED WITH THE OPENING BAND, HUH?
OH, YEAH, BUT LITA AND I THOUGHT THEY ROCKED.

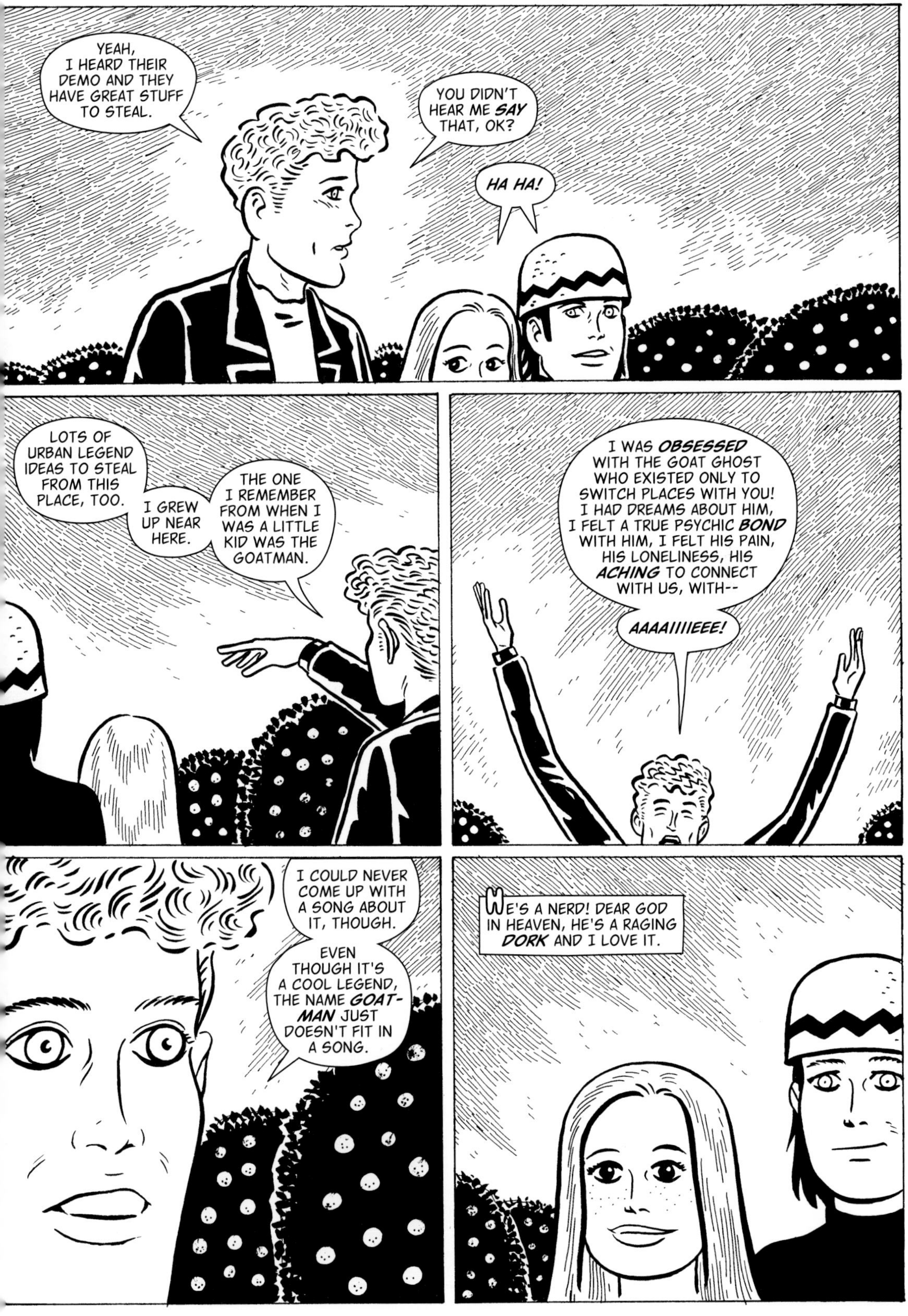
YEAH, I HEARD THEIR DEMO AND THEY HAVE GREAT STUFF TO STEAL.
YOU DIDN'T HEAR ME SAY THAT, OK?
HA HA!
LOTS OF URBAN LEGEND IDEAS TO STEAL FROM THIS PLACE, TOO.
I GREW UP NEAR HERE.
THE ONE I REMEMBER FROM WHEN I WAS A LITTLE KID WAS THE GOATMAN.
I WAS OBSESSED WITH THE GOAT GHOST WHO EXISTED ONLY TO SWITCH PLACES WITH YOU! I HAD DREAMS ABOUT HIM, I FELT A TRUE PSYCHIC BOND WITH HIM, I FELT HIS PAIN, HIS LONELINESS, HIS ACHING TO CONNECT WITH US, WITH--
AAAAIIIIEEE!
I COULD NEVER COME UP WITH A SONG ABOUT IT, THOUGH.
EVEN THOUGH IT'S A COOL LEGEND, THE NAME GOAT-MAN JUST DOESN'T FIT IN A SONG.
HE'S A NERD! DEAR GOD IN HEAVEN, HE'S A RAGING DORK AND I LOVE IT.

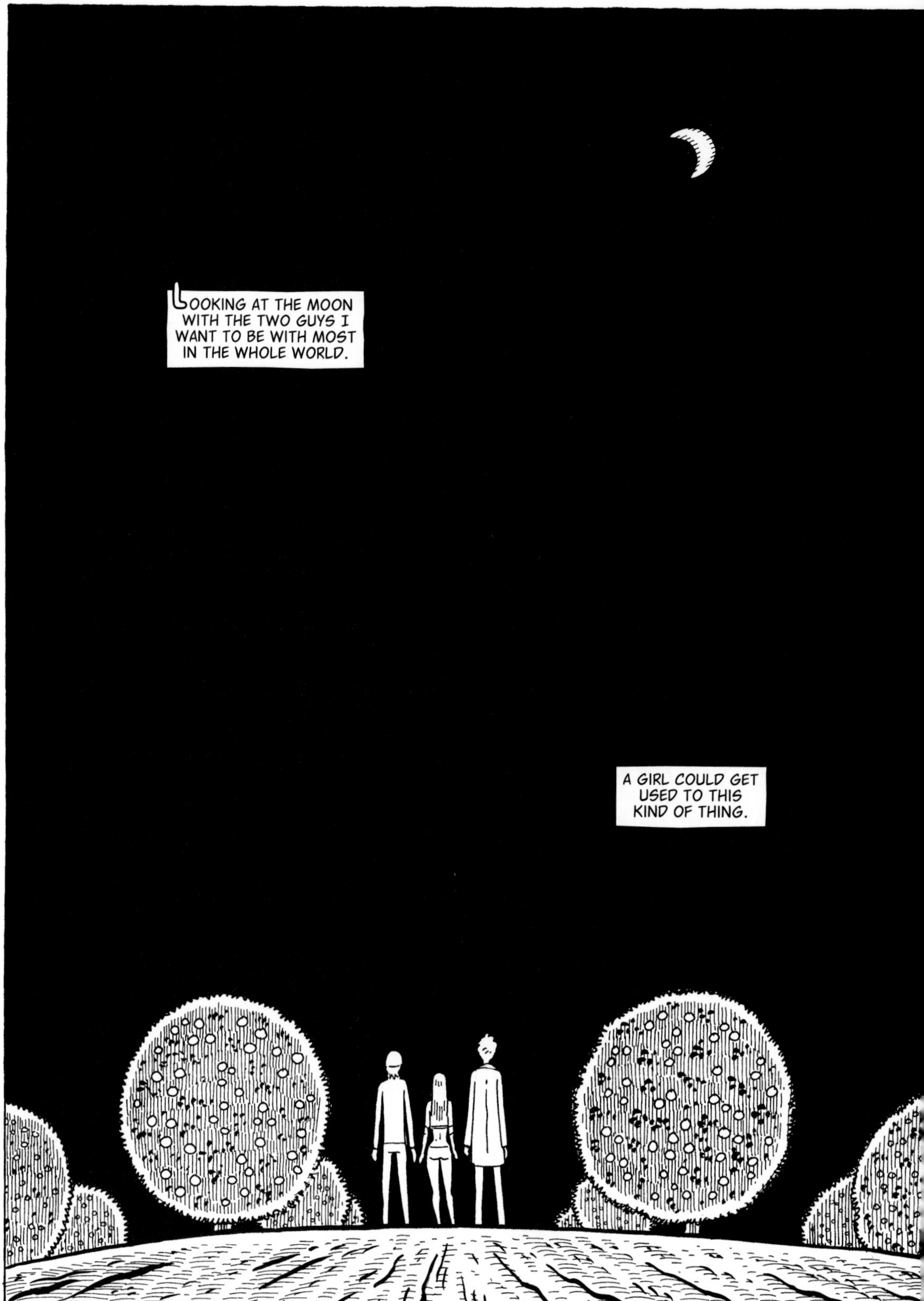
LOOKING AT THE MOON WITH THE TWO GUYS I WANT TO BE WITH MOST IN THE WHOLE WORLD.
A GIRL COULD GET USED TO THIS KIND OF THING.

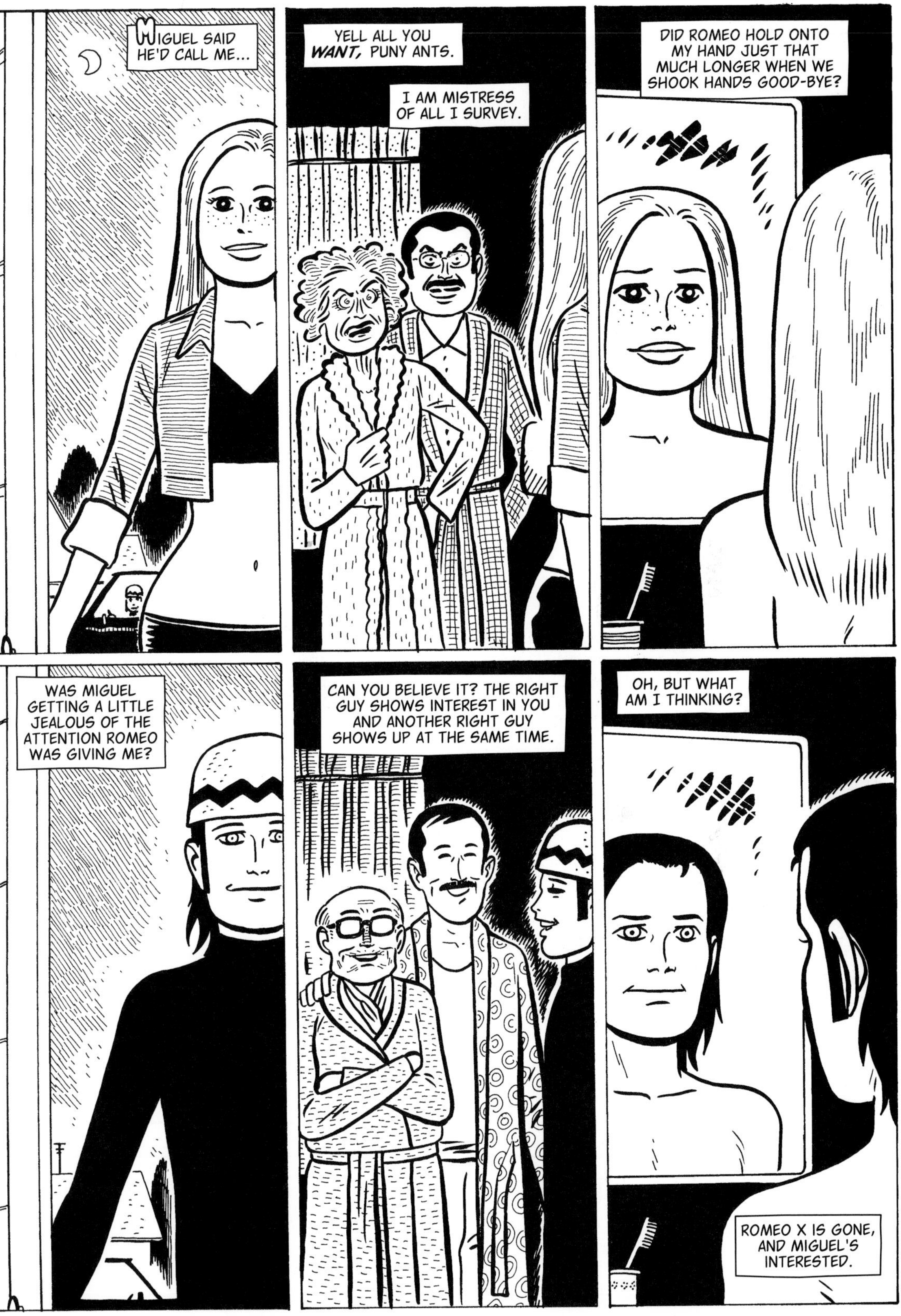
MIGUEL SAID HE'D CALL ME...
YELL ALL YOU WANT, PUNY ANTS.
I AM MISTRESS OF ALL I SURVEY.
DID ROMEO HOLD ONTO MY HAND JUST THAT MUCH LONGER WHEN WE SHOOK HANDS GOOD-BYE?
WAS MIGUEL GETTING A LITTLE JEALOUS OF THE ATTENTION ROMEO WAS GIVING ME?
CAN YOU BELIEVE IT? THE RIGHT GUY SHOWS INTEREST IN YOU AND ANOTHER RIGHT GUY SHOWS UP AT THE SAME TIME.
OH, BUT WHAT AM I THINKING?
ROMEO X IS GONE, AND MIGUEL'S INTERESTED.

LIFE IS GOOD.

LATEST CHECK-UP REVEALS I'M IN TIP-TOP SHAPE.

GRANDPARENTS IGNORING ME CAN ONLY BE A SIGN FROM HEAVEN.

MIGUEL NOT TOO PROUD TO FLIRT WITH ME IN FRONT OF HIS GIRLY GIRLS.

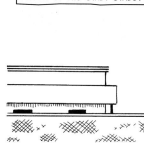

THE JOEYS MIGHT POSSIBLY OPEN FOR ROMEO AGAIN WHEN HE PLAYS UP NORTH.

IF I DON'T STRANGLE THEM FIRST.

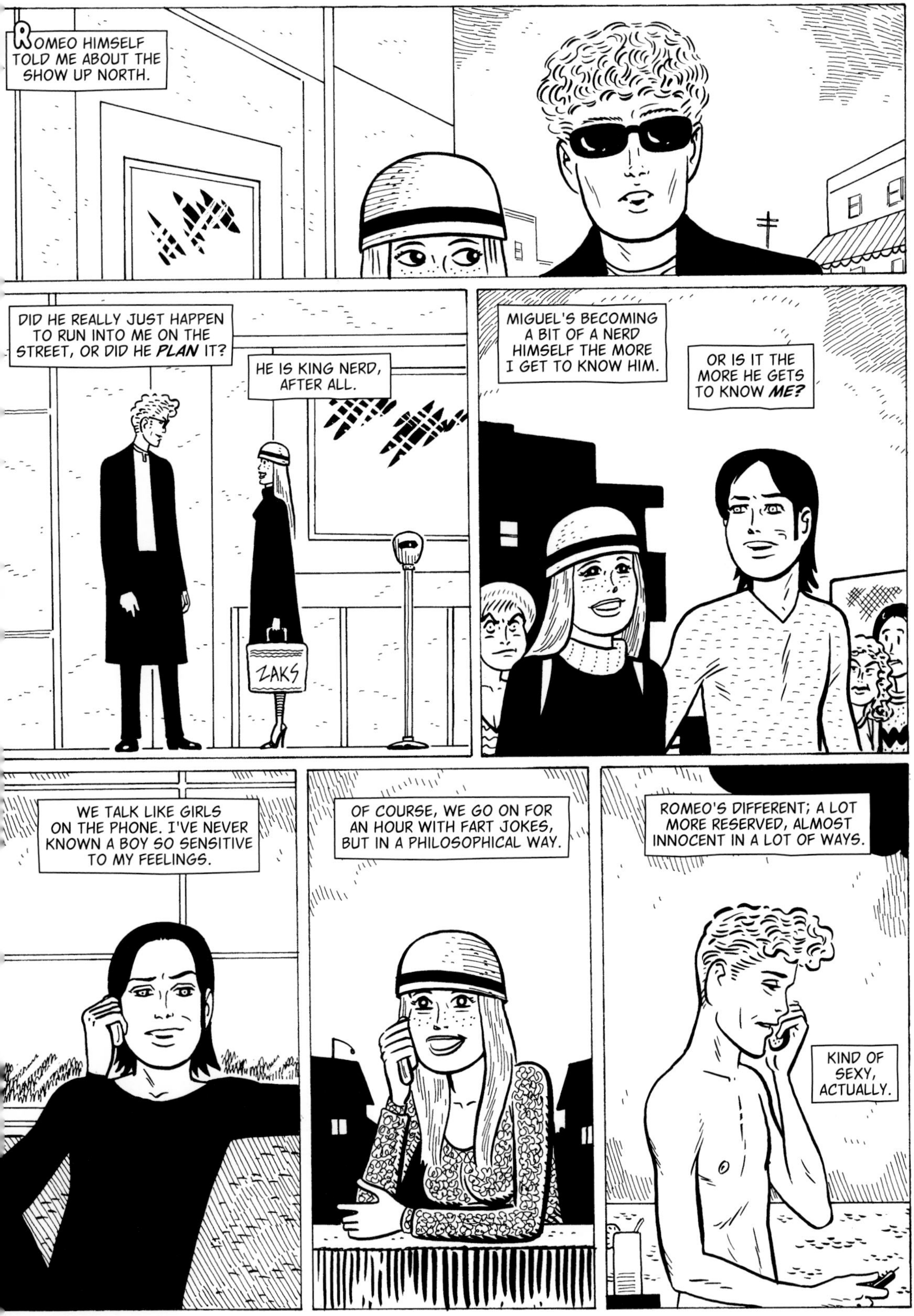
ROMEO HIMSELF TOLD ME ABOUT THE SHOW UP NORTH.
DID HE REALLY JUST HAPPEN TO RUN INTO ME ON THE STREET, OR DID HE PLAN IT?
HE IS KING NERD, AFTER ALL.
ZAKS
MIGUEL'S BECOMING A BIT OF A NERD HIMSELF THE MORE I GET TO KNOW HIM.
OR IS IT THE MORE HE GETS TO KNOW ME?
WE TALK LIKE GIRLS ON THE PHONE. I'VE NEVER KNOWN A BOY SO SENSITIVE TO MY FEELINGS.
OF COURSE, WE GO ON FOR AN HOUR WITH FART JOKES, BUT IN A PHILOSOPHICAL WAY.
ROMEO'S DIFFERENT; A LOT MORE RESERVED, ALMOST INNOCENT IN A LOT OF WAYS.
KIND OF SEXY, ACTUALLY.

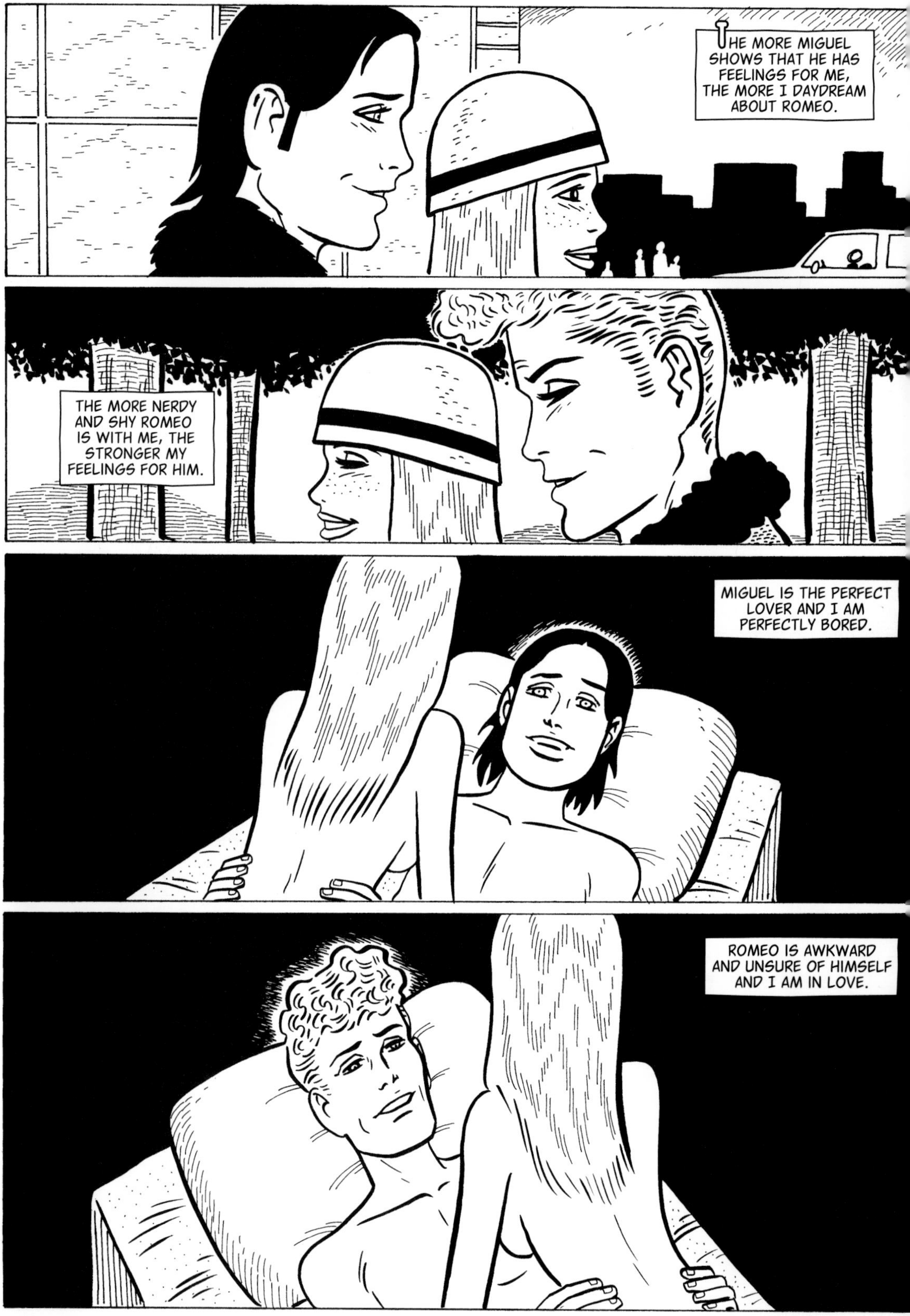
THE MORE MIGUEL SHOWS THAT HE HAS FEELINGS FOR ME, THE MORE I DAYDREAM ABOUT ROMEO.
THE MORE NERDY AND SHY ROMEO IS WITH ME, THE STRONGER MY FEELINGS FOR HIM.
MIGUEL IS THE PERFECT LOVER AND I AM PERFECTLY BORED.
ROMEO IS AWKWARD AND UNSURE OF HIMSELF AND I AM IN LOVE.

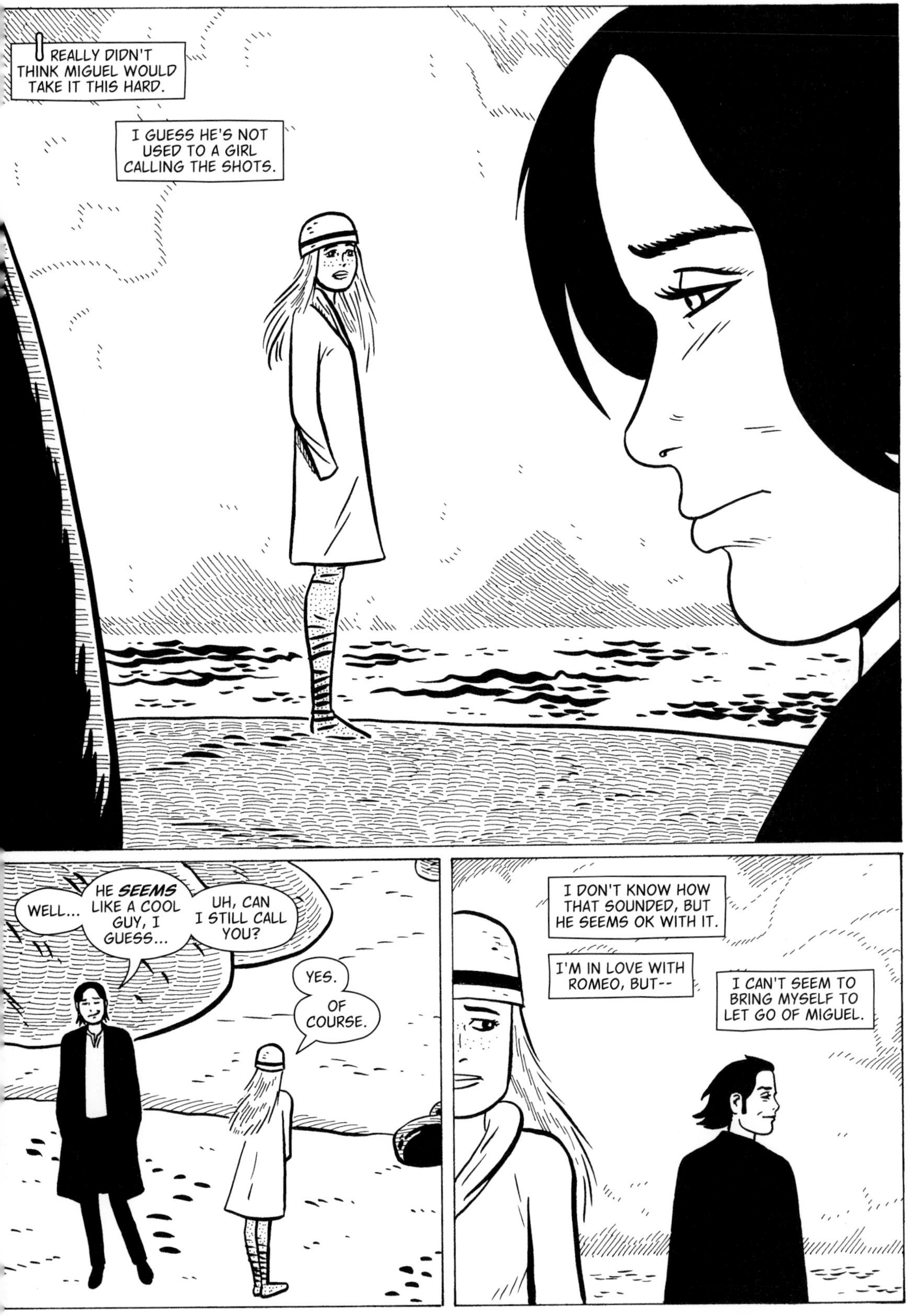
I REALLY DIDN'T THINK MIGUEL WOULD TAKE IT THIS HARD.
I GUESS HE'S NOT USED TO A GIRL CALLING THE SHOTS.
WELL...
HE SEEMS LIKE A COOL GUY, I GUESS...
UH, CAN I STILL CALL YOU?
YES.
OF COURSE.
I DON'T KNOW HOW THAT SOUNDED, BUT HE SEEMS OK WITH IT.
I'M IN LOVE WITH ROMEO, BUT--
I CAN'T SEEM TO BRING MYSELF TO LET GO OF MIGUEL.

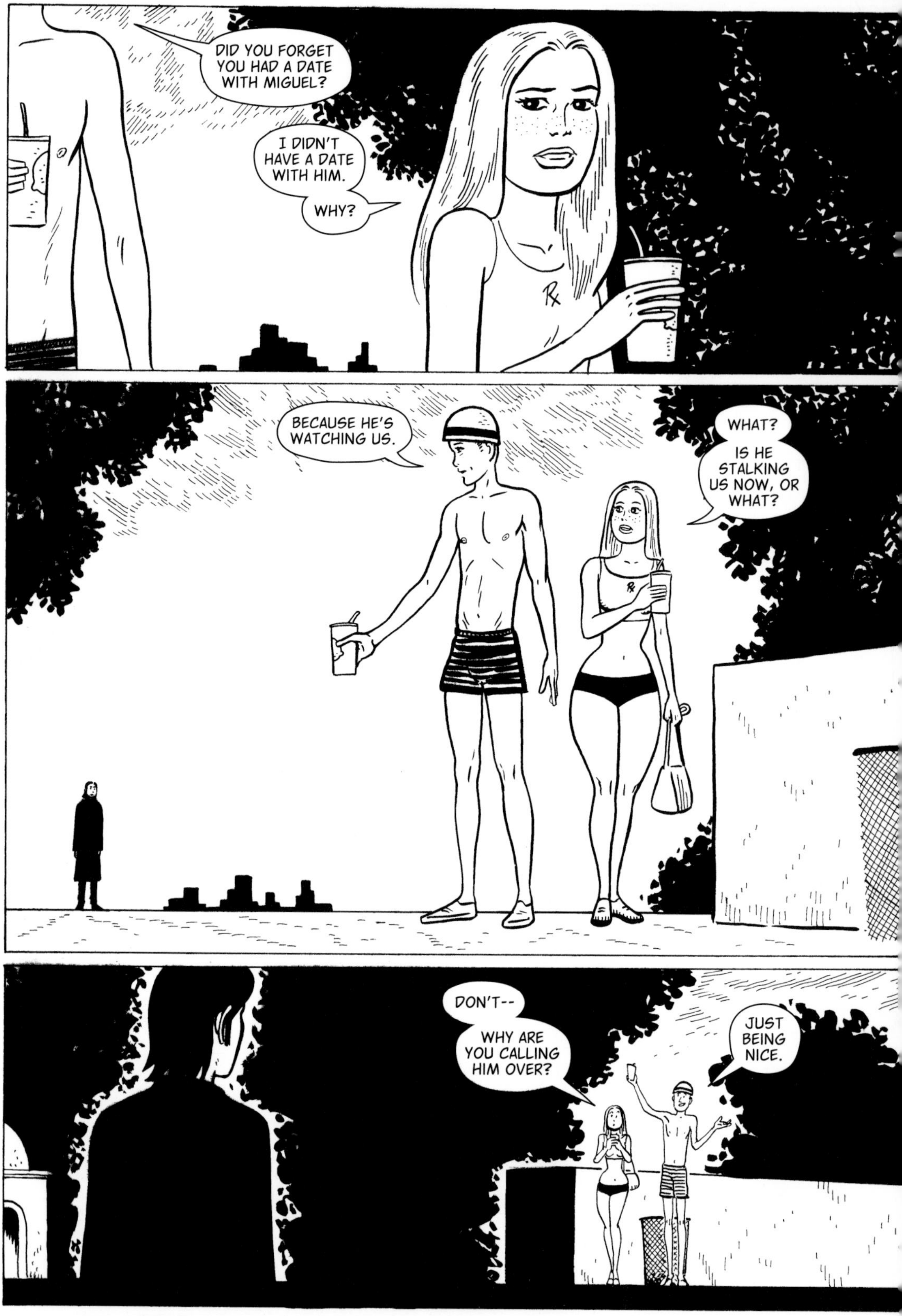
DID YOU FORGET YOU HAD A DATE WITH MIGUEL?
I DIDN'T HAVE A DATE WITH HIM.
WHY?
BECAUSE HE'S WATCHING US.
WHAT?
IS HE STALKING US NOW, OR WHAT?
DON'T--
WHY ARE YOU CALLING HIM OVER?
JUST BEING NICE.

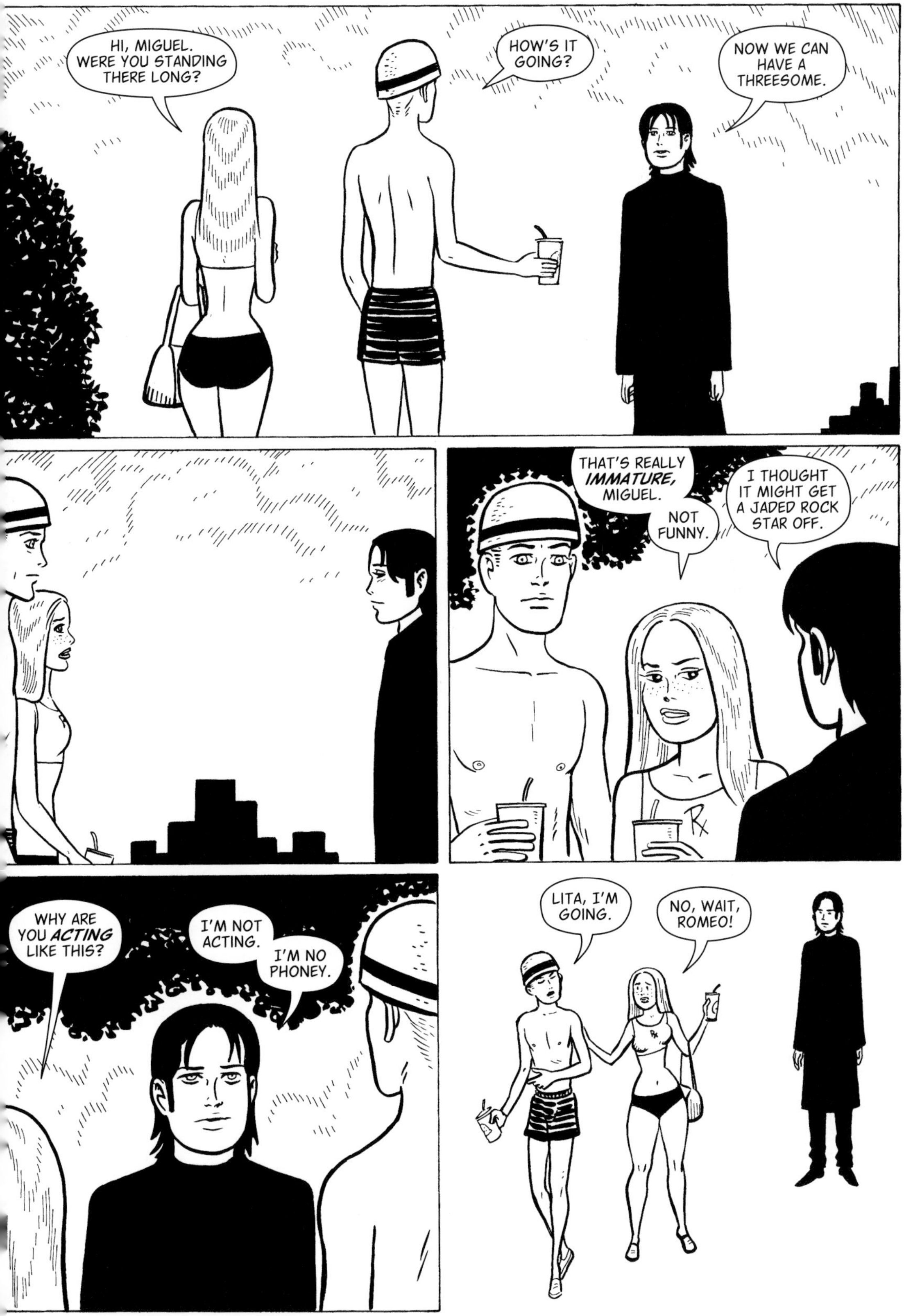
HI, MIGUEL. WERE YOU STANDING THERE LONG?
HOW'S IT GOING?
NOW WE CAN HAVE A THREESOME.
THAT'S REALLY IMMATURE, MIGUEL.
NOT FUNNY.
I THOUGHT IT MIGHT GET A JADED ROCK STAR OFF.
WHY ARE YOU ACTING LIKE THIS?
I'M NOT ACTING.
I'M NO PHONEY.
LITA, I'M GOING.
NO, WAIT, ROMEO!

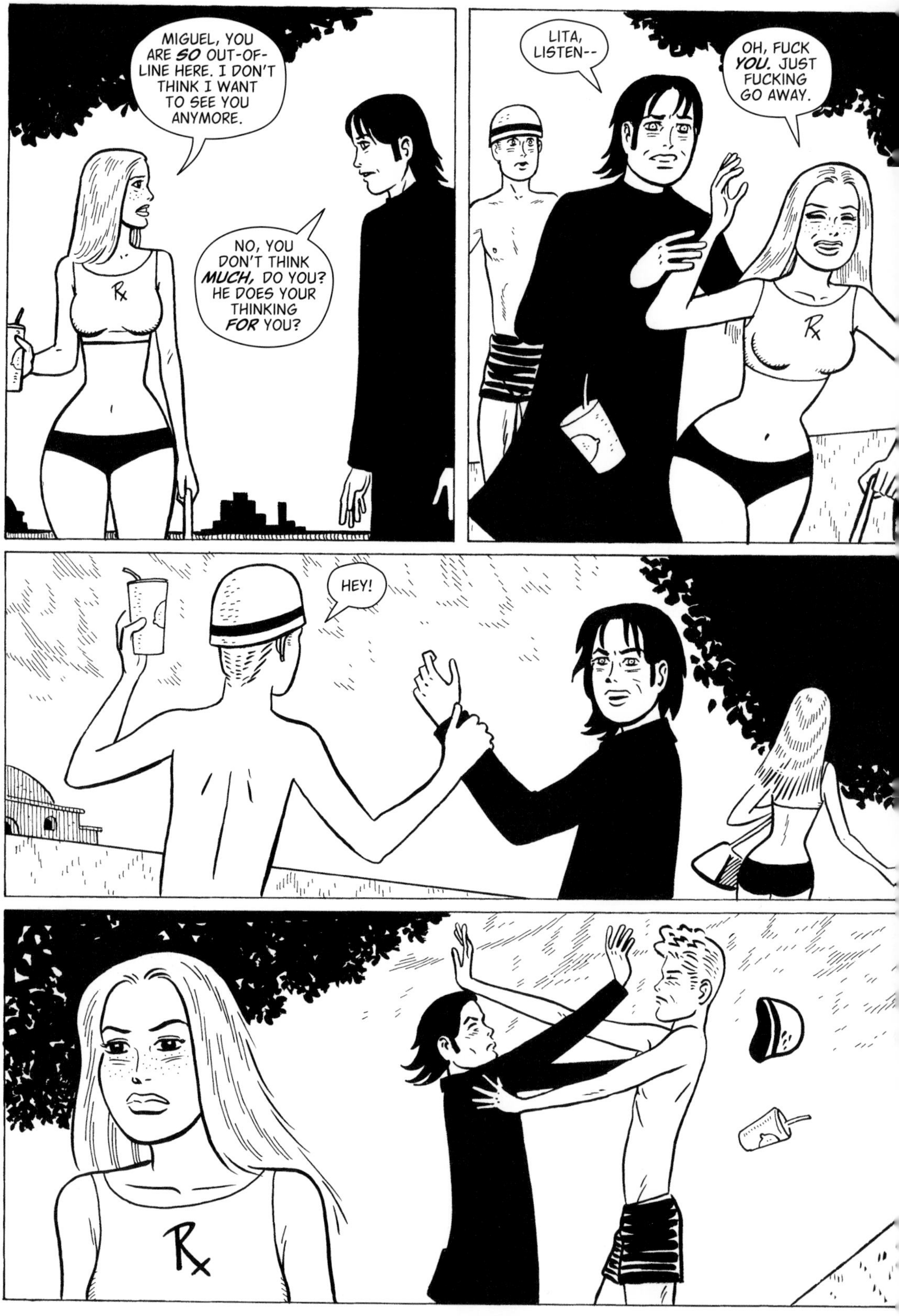
MIGUEL, YOU ARE SO OUT-OF-LINE HERE. I DON'T THINK I WANT TO SEE YOU ANYMORE.
NO, YOU DON'T THINK MUCH, DO YOU? HE DOES YOUR THINKING FOR YOU?
LITA, LISTEN--
OH, FUCK YOU. JUST FUCKING GO AWAY.
HEY!

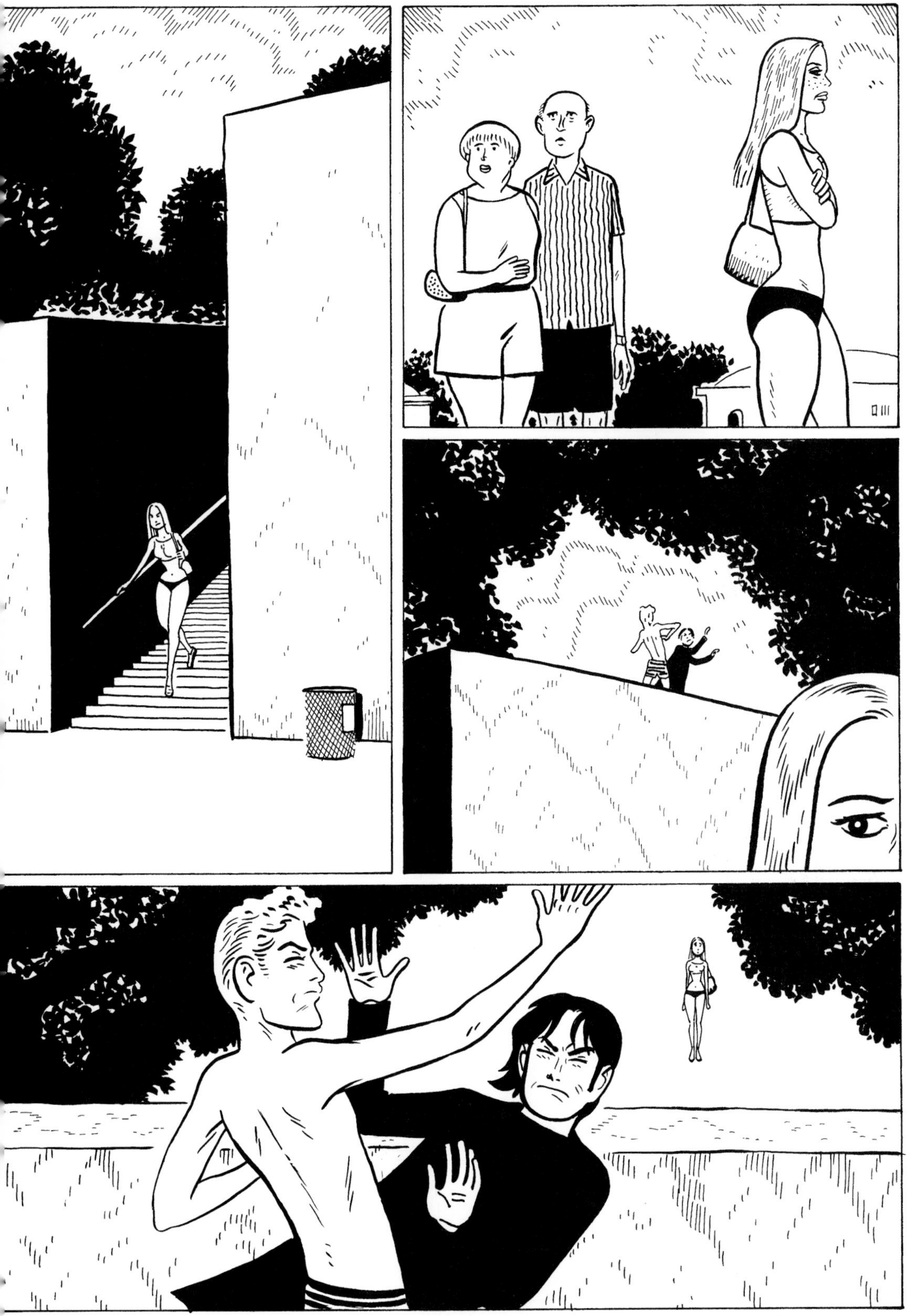

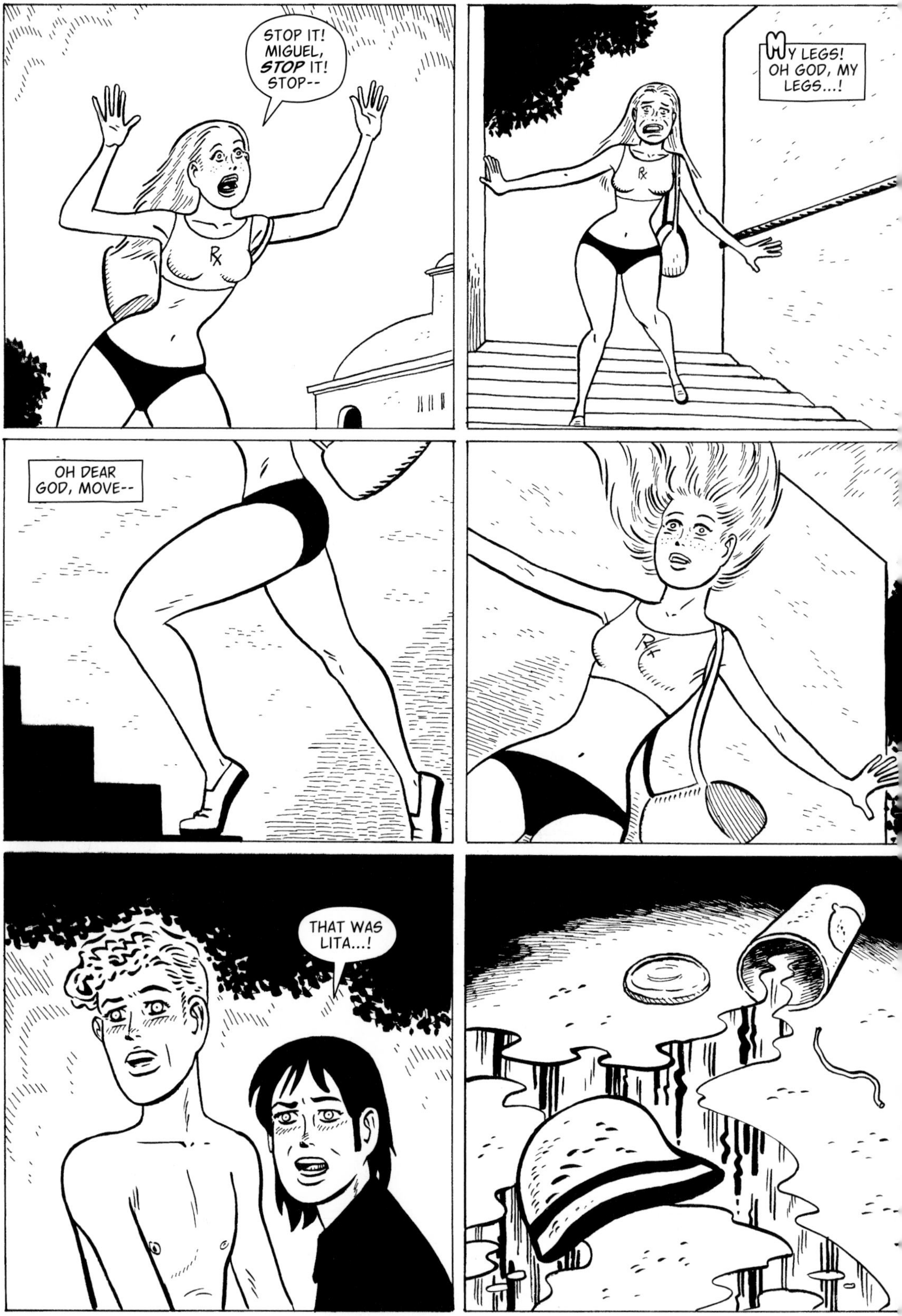
STOP IT! MIGUEL, STOP IT! STOP--
MY LEGS! OH GOD, MY LEGS...!
OH DEAR GOD, MOVE--
THAT WAS LITA...!

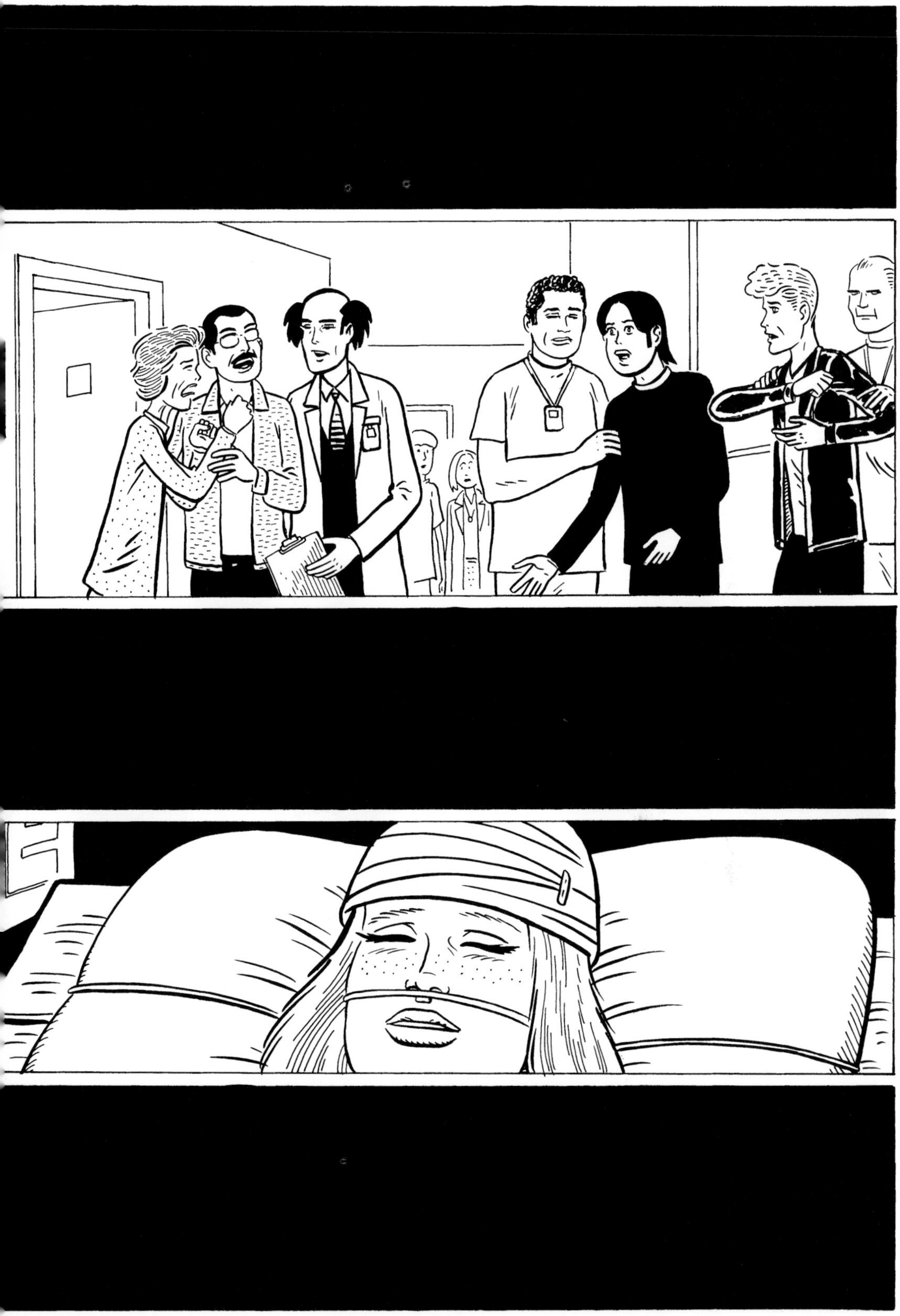

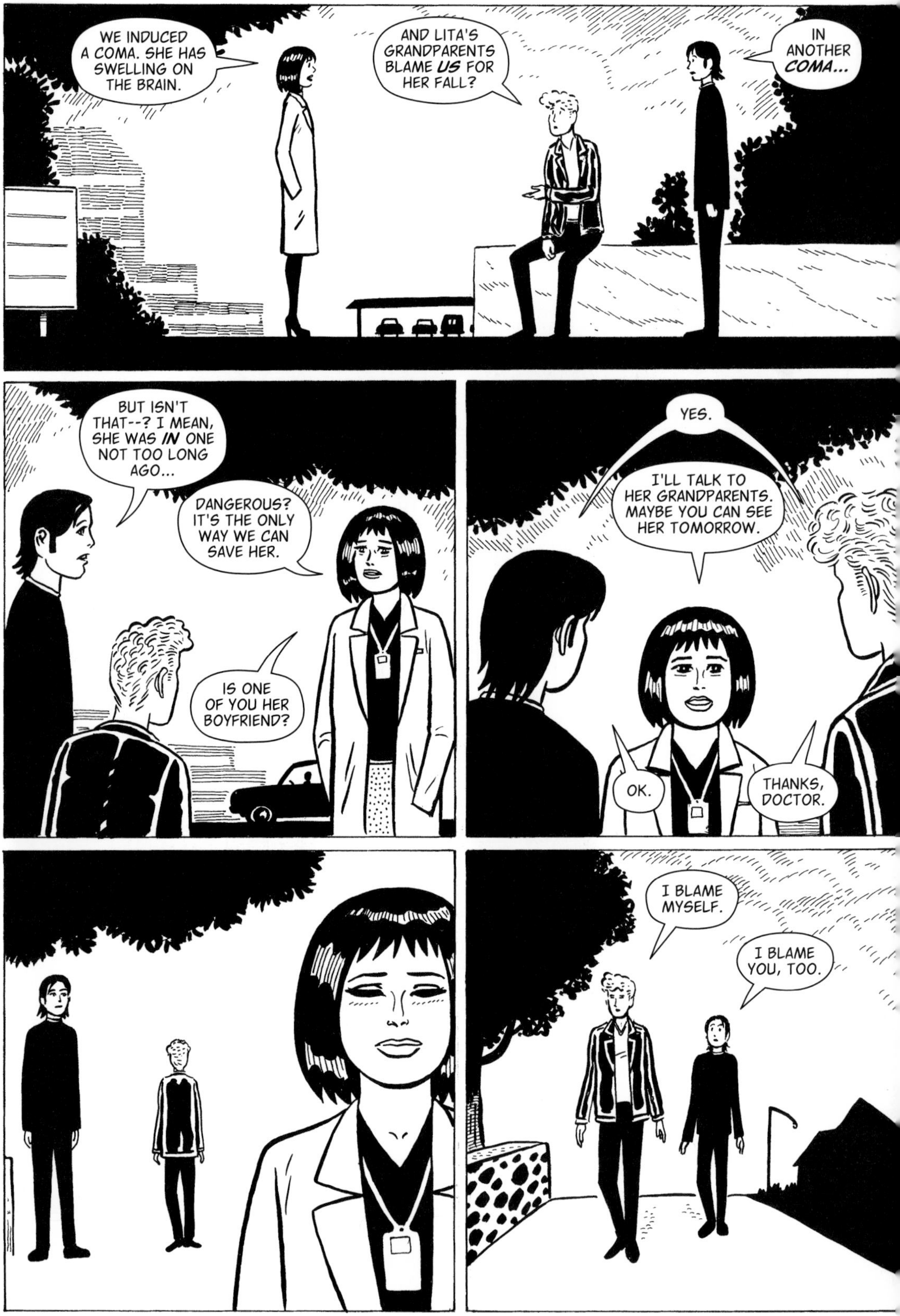

WE INDUCED A COMA. SHE HAS SWELLING ON THE BRAIN.
AND LITA'S GRANDPARENTS BLAME *US* FOR HER FALL?
IN ANOTHER *COMA...*
BUT ISN'T THAT--? I MEAN, SHE WAS *IN* ONE NOT TOO LONG AGO...
DANGEROUS? IT'S THE ONLY WAY WE CAN SAVE HER.
IS ONE OF YOU HER BOYFRIEND?
YES.
I'LL TALK TO HER GRANDPARENTS. MAYBE YOU CAN SEE HER TOMORROW.
OK.
THANKS, DOCTOR.
I BLAME MYSELF.
I BLAME YOU, TOO.

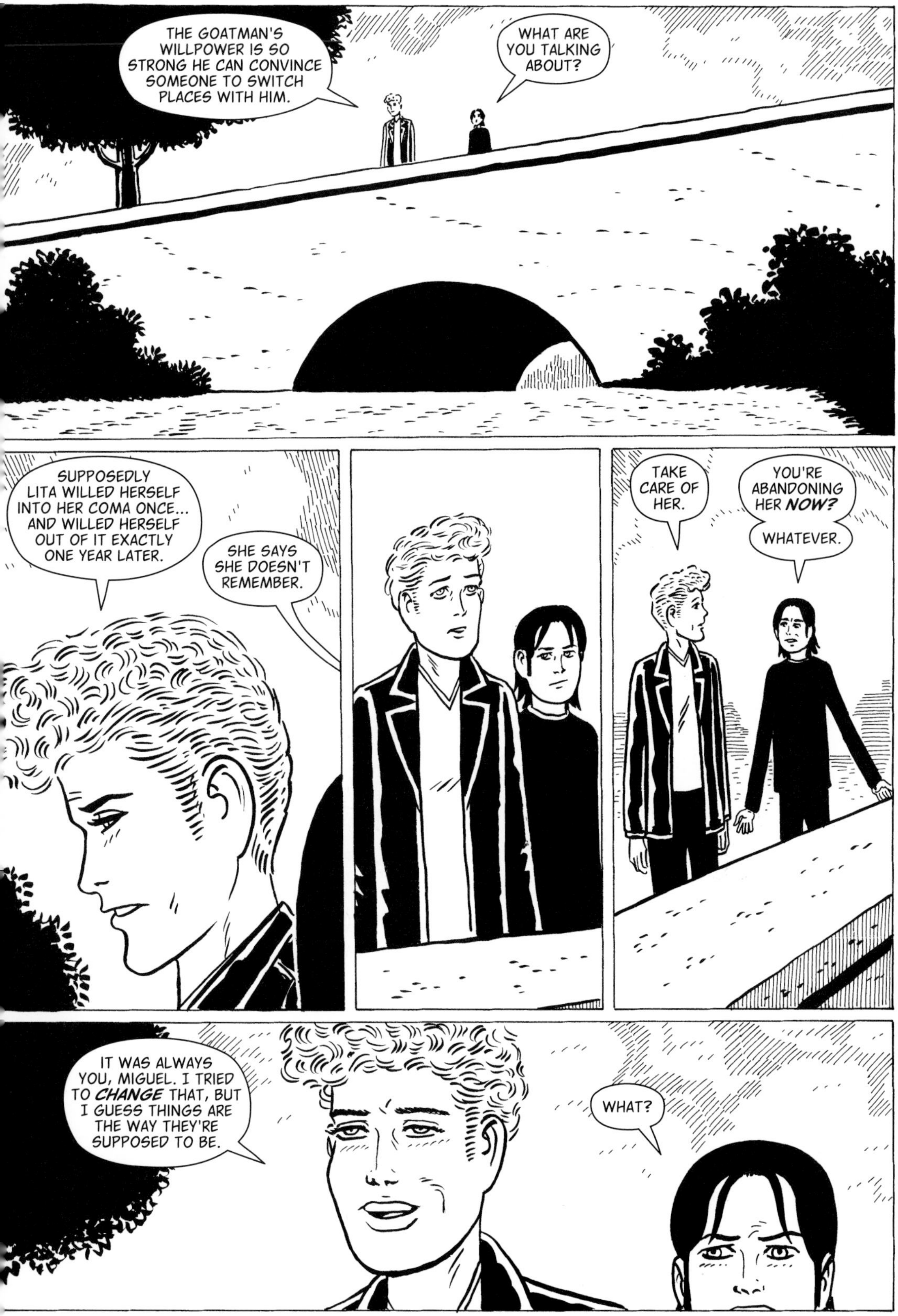
THE GOATMAN'S WILLPOWER IS SO STRONG HE CAN CONVINCE SOMEONE TO SWITCH PLACES WITH HIM.
WHAT ARE YOU TALKING ABOUT?
SUPPOSEDLY LITA WILLED HERSELF INTO HER COMA ONCE... AND WILLED HERSELF OUT OF IT EXACTLY ONE YEAR LATER.
SHE SAYS SHE DOESN'T REMEMBER.
TAKE CARE OF HER.
YOU'RE ABANDONING HER *NOW?*
WHATEVER.
IT WAS ALWAYS YOU, MIGUEL. I TRIED TO *CHANGE* THAT, BUT I GUESS THINGS ARE THE WAY THEY'RE SUPPOSED TO BE.
WHAT?

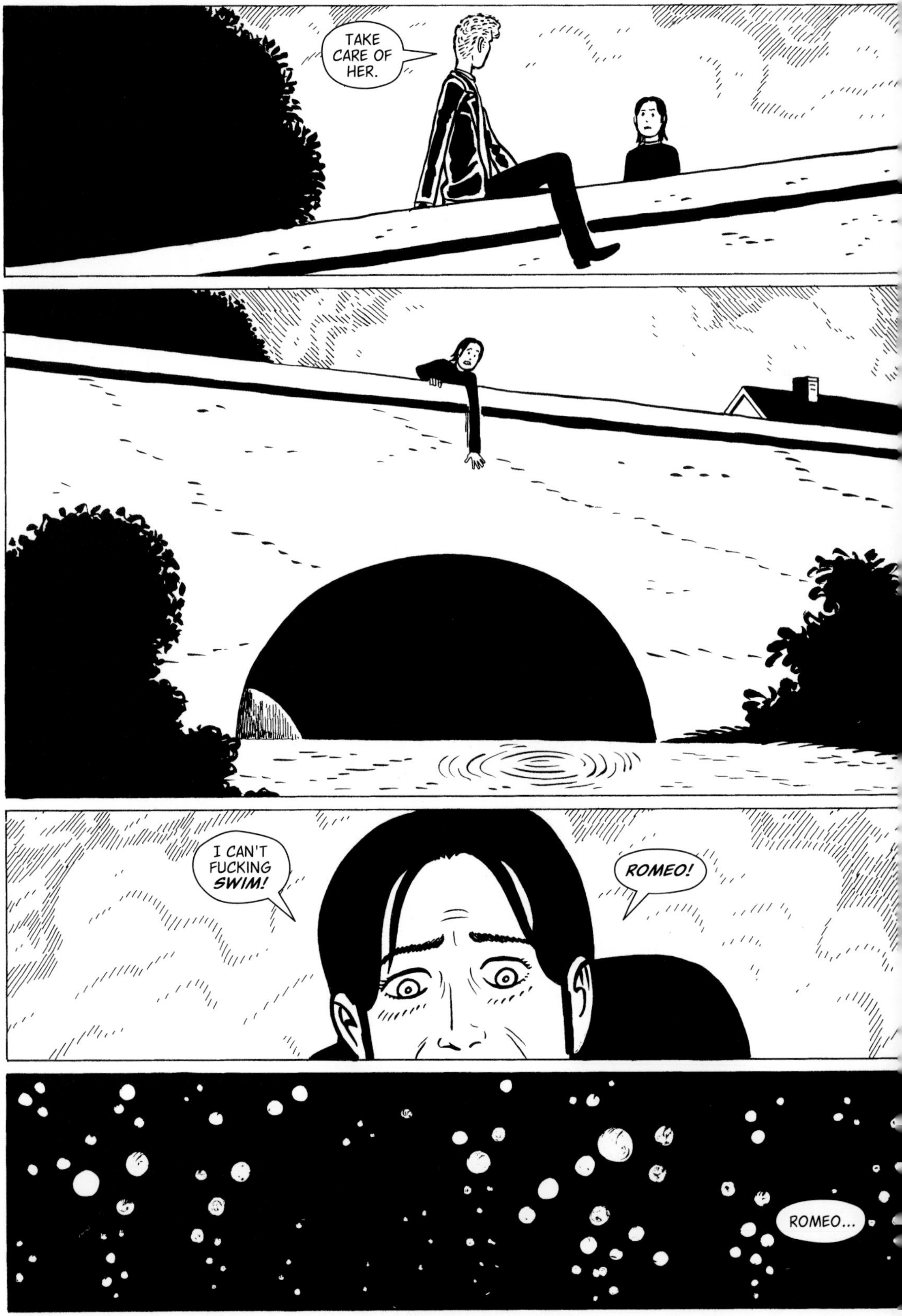
TAKE CARE OF HER.
I CAN'T FUCKING *SWIM!*
ROMEO!
ROMEO...

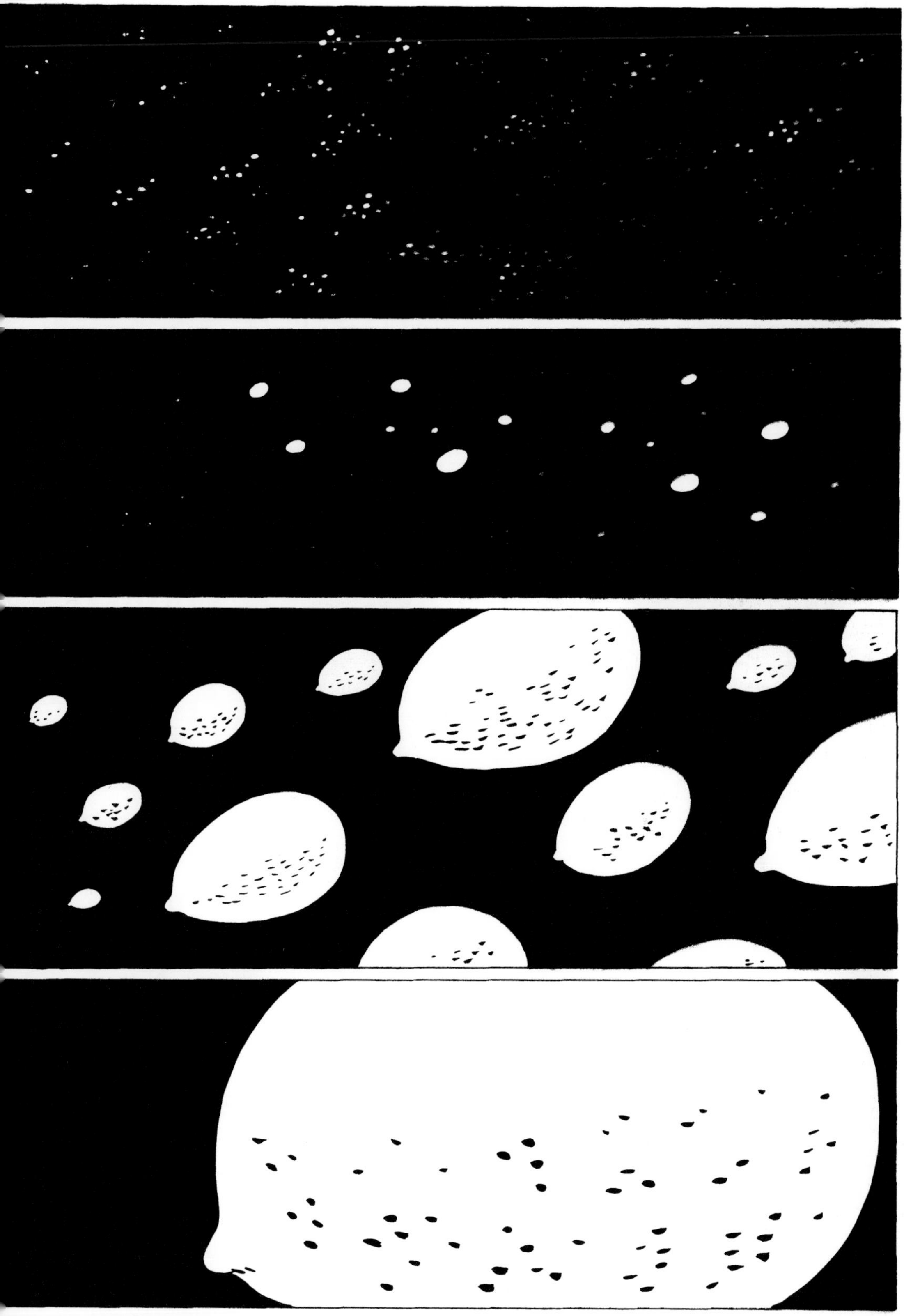

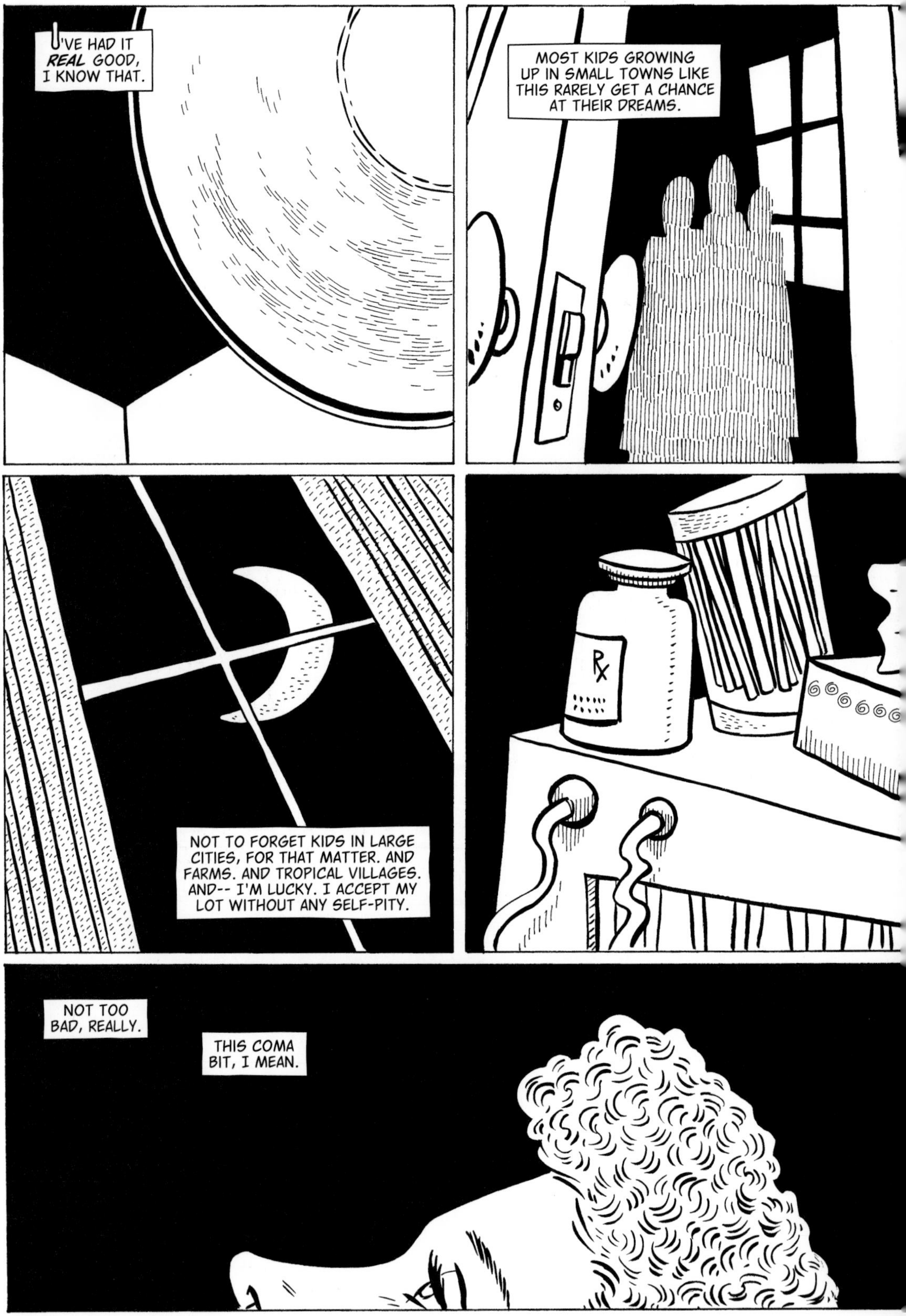
I'VE HAD IT *REAL* GOOD, I KNOW THAT.
MOST KIDS GROWING UP IN SMALL TOWNS LIKE THIS RARELY GET A CHANCE AT THEIR DREAMS.
NOT TO FORGET KIDS IN LARGE CITIES, FOR THAT MATTER. AND FARMS. AND TROPICAL VILLAGES. AND-- I'M LUCKY. I ACCEPT MY LOT WITHOUT ANY SELF-PITY.
NOT TOO BAD, REALLY.
THIS COMA BIT, I MEAN.

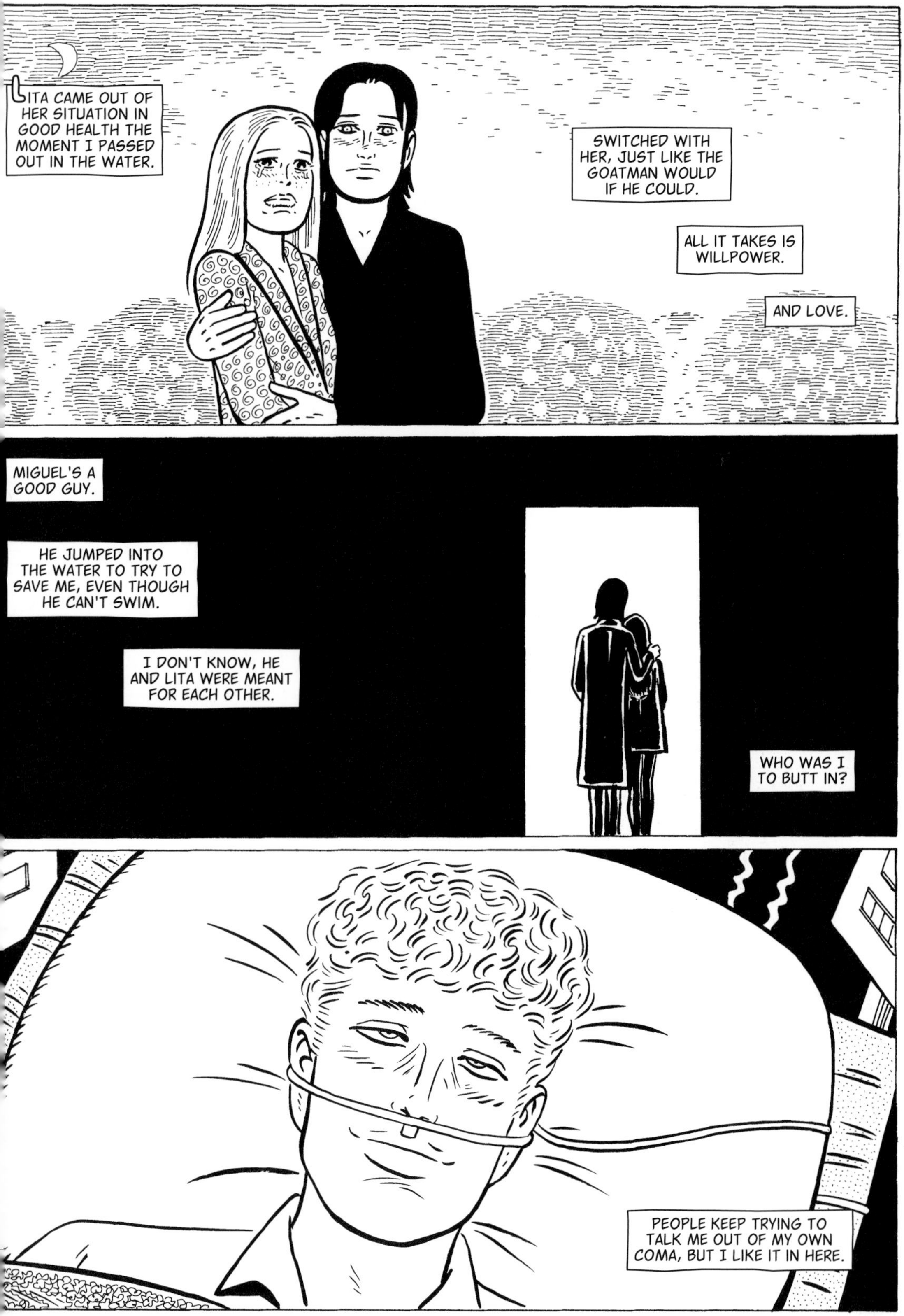
LITA CAME OUT OF HER SITUATION IN GOOD HEALTH THE MOMENT I PASSED OUT IN THE WATER.
SWITCHED WITH HER, JUST LIKE THE GOATMAN WOULD IF HE COULD.
ALL IT TAKES IS WILLPOWER.
AND LOVE.
MIGUEL'S A GOOD GUY.
HE JUMPED INTO THE WATER TO TRY TO SAVE ME, EVEN THOUGH HE CAN'T SWIM.
I DON'T KNOW, HE AND LITA WERE MEANT FOR EACH OTHER.
WHO WAS I TO BUTT IN?
PEOPLE KEEP TRYING TO TALK ME OUT OF MY OWN COMA, BUT I LIKE IT IN HERE.

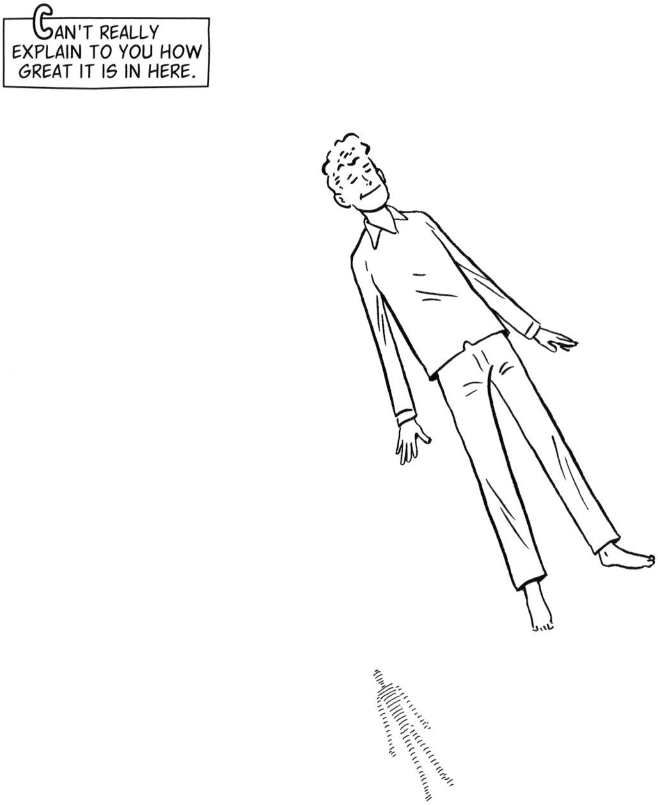
CAN'T REALLY EXPLAIN TO YOU HOW GREAT IT IS IN HERE.

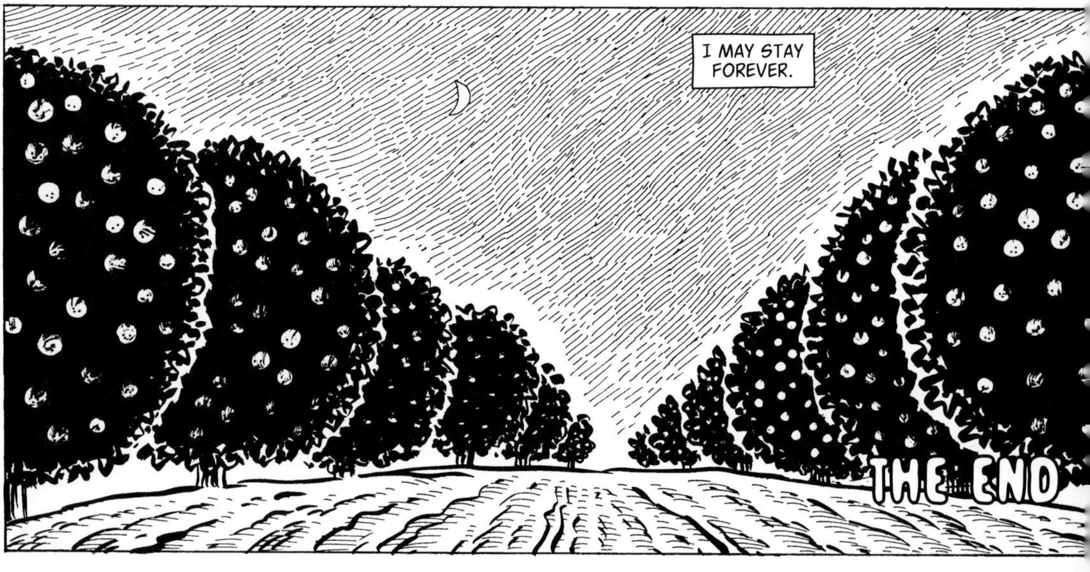
I MAY STAY FOREVER.
THE END

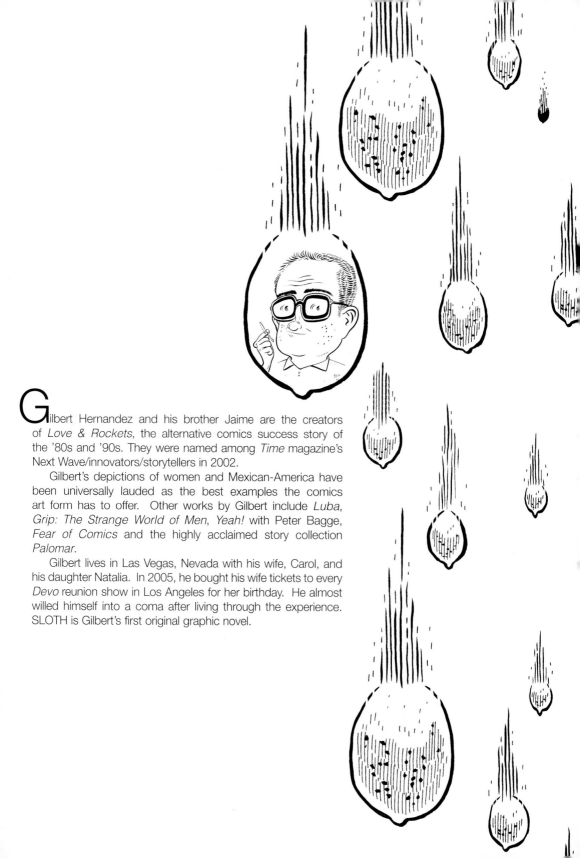

Gilbert Hernandez and his brother Jaime are the creators of *Love & Rockets*, the alternative comics success story of the '80s and '90s. They were named among *Time* magazine's Next Wave/innovators/storytellers in 2002.

Gilbert's depictions of women and Mexican-America have been universally lauded as the best examples the comics art form has to offer. Other works by Gilbert include *Luba*, *Grip: The Strange World of Men*, *Yeah!* with Peter Bagge, *Fear of Comics* and the highly acclaimed story collection *Palomar*.

Gilbert lives in Las Vegas, Nevada with his wife, Carol, and his daughter Natalia. In 2005, he bought his wife tickets to every *Devo* reunion show in Los Angeles for her birthday. He almost willed himself into a coma after living through the experience. SLOTH is Gilbert's first original graphic novel.

Look for these other VERTIGO books:
All titles are suggested for mature readers

100 BULLETS
Brian Azzarello/Eduardo Risso

With one special briefcase, Agent Graves gives you the chance to kill without retribution. But what is the real price for this chance — and who is setting it?

DOOM PATROL
Grant Morrison/Richard Case/
John Nyberg/Doug Braithwaite/various

The World's Strangest Heroes are reimagined as even stranger and more otherworldly in this groundbreaking series exploring the mysteries of identity and madness.

FABLES
Bill Willingham/Lan Medina/
Mark Buckingham/Steve Leialoha

The immortal characters of popular fairy tales have been driven from their homelands and now live hidden among us, trying to cope with life in 21st-century Manhattan.

LUCIFER
Mike Carey/Peter Gross/Scott Hampton/
Chris Weston/Dean Ormston/various

Walking out of Hell (and out of the pages of THE SANDMAN), an ambitious Lucifer Morningstar creates a new cosmos modelled after his own image.

PREACHER
Garth Ennis/Steve Dillon/various

This modern American epic of life, death, God, love, and redemption is loaded to the brim with sex, booze, and blood.

THE SANDMAN
Neil Gaiman/various

The New York Times best-selling author blends modern myth, historical legend and dark fantasy in one of the most acclaimed and celebrated comics titles ever published.

TRANSMETROPOLITAN
Warren Ellis/Darick Robertson/various

This exuberant trip into a frenetic future stars an outlaw journalist named Spider Jerusalem who battles hypocrisy, corruption, and sobriety.

Y: THE LAST MAN
Brian K. Vaughan/Pia Guerra/José Marzán, Jr.

An unexplained plague kills every male mammal on Earth — all except Yorick Brown and his pet monkey. Will he survive this new, emasculated world to discover what killed his fellow men?

HEAVY LIQUID
Paul Pope

A mysterious man known as "S" is on a quest for Heavy Liquid — which is at once a drug and an art form.

100%
Paul Pope

Four love-crossed strangers collide in futuristic Manhattan.

THE ORIGINALS
Dave Gibbons

For two childhood friends, there's nothing more important than belonging to the Originals. But being a part of the "in" crowd brings its own deadly consequences.

THE QUITTER
Harvey Pekar/Dean Haspiel

The creator of *American Splendor* reveals his troubled teen years as the neighborhood bully.

CAN'T GET NO
Rick Veitch

A daringly poetic exploration of one man's spiritual road trip across America in the wake of 9-11.

Search the Graphic Novels section of vertigocomics.com for art and info on every one of our hundreds of books.
To purchase any of our titles, call 1-888-COMIC BOOK for the comics shop nearest you or go to your local book store.

VERTIGOCOMICS.COM